THE
ORWELL
TOUR

THE
ORWELL
TOUR

TRAVELS THROUGH THE LIFE
AND WORK OF GEORGE ORWELL

OLIVER LEWIS

ICON

Published in the UK in 2023
by Icon Books Ltd, Omnibus Business Centre,
39–41 North Road, London N7 9DP
email: info@iconbooks.com
www.iconbooks.com

ISBN: 978-1-78578-961-8

Typeset in Cheltenham by Marie Doherty

Printed and bound in the UK

For my father

Contents

Introduction

The concept for this book came in the way any good idea should; not planned nor by design, but out of circumstance. I can't remember how I first came across George Orwell or his works. I have a hazy – very hazy – recollection of watching the film of *Nineteen Eighty-Four* aged five or six. George Orwell was my father's favourite author. He was introduced to Orwell by his father, my grandfather, who I knew until I was 26 when he died in his 109th year. He was born in 1903, the same year as Eric Blair.

I was fortunate as a budding historian to spend many hours with my grandfather towards the end of his life. He told me so much about the history of the 20th century, especially the first half, I feel almost as if I lived through it. My real enthusiasm for Orwell, which began properly in May 2015, post-dated my grandfather's death. It is a great regret to me that I never had the opportunity to broach Orwell with him, knowing that it probably would have led to a week's worth of discussion. In his library, much of which was acquired in the 1930s and 1940s when he read Economic History at the London School of Economics, were copies of *Animal Farm* and *The English People*.

The first Orwell work I read was *Animal Farm*, when I was around thirteen. After that I probably read most of the rest of his work over the course of the next ten years. I took a nice copy of *Burmese Days* with me on my year out in India after I left school, reading it on an enjoyably long sleeper train journey from Mumbai to Jaipur. I sent the copy back home, but unfortunately India Post did not deliver. The *Collected Essays* I read during a visit to California to stay with a friend from university, and I read one essay after another in between cycling trips across the Golden Gate Bridge and road trips to Yosemite National Park and Bodega Bay. Every time I re-read Orwell's work I am left with a re-energised perspective of it, with something new which I was not aware of on the first or second reading. Connecting with his work is to create a life-long partnership between reader and writer.

When I first set out on *The Orwell Tour* I had no plan for what I would do or write about. I had resigned from my monotonous job in London to commence a master's degree in History, and planned a summer of enjoyment free from the shackles of the daily commute. I had arranged to visit Myanmar with a friend in the September, and prior to that, in the July, a week-long visit to some friends who own a small Scottish island close to the isle of Jura, where Orwell had written *Nineteen Eighty-Four*. My best friend from university is from Suffolk, and his parents had invited me to stay in August, close to Southwold, where Orwell and his parents lived in the late 1920s. As I was considering the summer that was approaching, it suddenly dawned on me that each of these places had close association with George Orwell. What if I visited his house in each location, and wrote about it? A quick check revealed no one had done such a journey before. I rationalised that perhaps it was time that someone did.

I was fulfilling a need somewhere within me to experience the very many places which shaped Orwell and his writing. I wanted to present them to readers who may not have had the opportunity, may indeed never have the opportunity, to undertake the journeys themselves. Place, as numerous biographers have concluded, was incredibly important to a man who delayed 'settling down' for as long as he could. Even then, the place of his choosing was an island in the Hebrides where he would only spend half the year, a good 48-hour journey from London in 1946.

When one immerses oneself in a project for two and more years, it is amusing how alert the senses become to the subject in question. There can be no doubt that George Orwell and 'Orwelliana' are a literary focal point of our age, and that his works have appeal and reference across social groups and racial or linguistic divides. I noted down every so often the situations in which I would see or overhear references to Orwell: at work, I was once sitting across from two colleagues discussing communication to other departments, when one of them said: 'This will get the message across, without being Big Brother.' His phrases have entered modern lexicology, frequently used to market new ideas or concepts in the media. BBC Radio Four, I noticed mid-way through my research, were exploring the lives of commuting cyclists using the hashtag '#FourWheelsGoodTwoWheelsBetter', an adaptation of a slogan from *Animal Farm*. Best of all was one morning when I opened the *Financial Times* to spot each of the newspaper's articles on the comments page separately making one or more references to Orwell. The more alert I was, the clearer it became to me that people value and respect George Orwell in a way that does not seem to be replicated with other writers. It seems to me that he speaks so truthfully and honestly that generation after generation of readers are attracted to his integrity. He communicates complicated ideas so coherently that every generation that passes is introduced to, and recognises, his genius.

The meticulous recording of observation was Orwell's undoubted strength, putting him into a class of his own among all 20th-century writers and a close second to Dickens – whom he admired greatly – as Britain's pre-eminent author in industrialised times. My interest in Orwell only grew as I read more of his work: I am seldom able to find anything he wrote with which I can find serious disagreement. Indeed, much of the logic he applied to so vast an array of subjects or problems remains as valid today as it was 80 or 90 years ago, which I might suggest is why his writing remains so popular.

This book is not intended to be a biography of Orwell – there is no shortage of them – nor was it ever intended to be a book at all really, since each visit was made separately, and not even in chronological order. It is not meant to be academic; there are lots of academic books on Orwell if that is what a reader is after. Instead, it is a reflection on a series of visits to those places that inspired Orwell, how they may have shaped him, and how they appear to the 21st century almost 70 years after his premature death, from tuberculosis, at the age of 46. A list of his novels, essays and journalism referenced in the text appears in the frontispiece. I hope, if only in a small way, it opens up the canon of Orwell's work to a new generation of readers, and refreshes his life and times for those already familiar with his work.

Oliver Lewis
Montgomery, August 2022

Note to readers

Without wishing to confuse readers, there are two points of style that require explanation. The first is that George Orwell's real name was of course 'Eric Blair', and he did not adopt the former consistently until well into the 1930s. I debated whether to use one or the other, or to switch half-way through, but thought it best to adopt 'George Orwell' or 'Orwell' consistently. In the earlier chapters, exploring Orwell's childhood and teenage years, there may be occasional references to 'Eric' or 'Blair' where I thought this made sense. Where there are references to original texts – diaries, letters and such like – the original 'Eric' or 'George' has been retained.

Where possible, i.e. within Britain and Europe, I was accompanied on my travels by my springer spaniel. Confusingly, and named long before I began my three-year tryst with Orwell's life and his work, he is also called George. I hope it is clear where I am referencing George the dog, rather than Orwell, the writer, but for the avoidance of doubt, any 'present tense' references to a 'George' will be about my springer and not George Orwell. Given the long and widespread range of travel, from among Scottish Islands to the plains of Spain, I am confident he enjoyed his participation in *The Orwell Tour* as much as I did.

List of Orwell's work referenced

I have tried to incorporate into each chapter an exploration of the works associated with each place; for instance, discussing *Burmese Days* in the context of my visit to Myanmar. This will inevitably involve a certain degree of 'book spoiling' for which readers are forewarned. The below is a list of Orwell's non-fiction books, novels, essays and journalism in the order in which they are referenced.

Animal Farm

'The English People'

Nineteen Eighty-Four

Burmese Days

'Shooting an Elephant'

'A Hanging'

'In Defence of English Cooking'

'Reflections on Gandhi'

'Such, Such Were the Joys'

Coming up for Air

'My Country, Right or Left'

'Why I Write'

A Clergyman's Daughter

Down and Out in Paris and London

Keep the Aspidistra Flying

The Road to Wigan Pier

'Books v. Cigarettes'

'England Your England'

'Boys' Weeklies'

'How the Poor Die'

'Bookshop Memories'

'Inside the Whale'

'Charles Dickens'

'Money and Guns'

Homage to Catalonia

'The Moon Under Water'

'Looking Back on the Spanish Civil War'

'Marrakech'

'A Nice Cup of Tea'

Talking to India

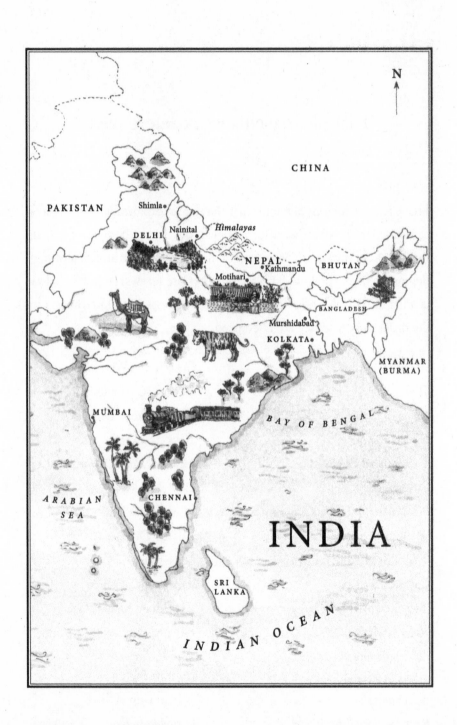

Motihari, State of Bihar, India

Birth (1903–4)

It comes as a surprise to many that George Orwell was born in India. For the most part, the general public's exposure to Orwell is strongly 'English' in cultural terms; *Animal Farm* an allegorical fairy tale of the Russian Revolution based on an English farm; *Nineteen Eighty-Four* a terrifying dystopia of a chillingly totalitarian England of the future. Both works feature in the UK school curriculum, and in the educational programmes of many other countries besides. They are two of the best-selling books in history. *Animal Farm* begins with the machinations of a working English farm and the full repertoire of farm animals found there – cows, sheep, pigs, horses, goats, dogs, geese. The livestock eventually rebel, overthrowing their farmer in a revolution to apparently seize control of the assets of the farm for the betterment of all animals. *Nineteen Eighty-Four* explores the experiences of a man – Winston Smith – who works in the dystopian government's censoring department. Beginning to question his purpose in this society of total control over thought and movement, he finds himself censored and ultimately erased.

India is a long way from both and thus, for many, this lanky, intelligent thinker is perhaps best linked by memory to London, Big Brother or the better-known characters of *Animal Farm*, such as Snowball.

1

Of course, for those better acquainted with his work, their knowledge will extend to exotic descriptions of the jungle or a bazaar from *Burmese Days*; or his essays 'Shooting an Elephant' and 'A Hanging'. Some might have a hazy memory that he was once a policeman in Burma, but the majority may be stumped when it comes to what took him there.

Orwell belonged to a now-vanished class of British society, generations of families that built their wealth and networks on the colonial relationship between Britain and India. India was obviously not the only possible destination for colonial service, but it was one in which a large cadre in British society came to specialise. The British population of India, at its greatest 160,000, was drawn largely from the upper-middle and upper classes – a group big enough to influence the English language with the introduction of words from Hindi including bungalow, pyjamas and hoity-toity.

Much of the Anglo-Indian tradition vanished when Britain withdrew from the subcontinent over a ten-year period, between India's independence as a dominion in 1947 and Pakistan becoming a republic in 1956. The families sold their assets, returned and pursued new opportunities at home. Gradually the economic and political importance of India for Britain declined. For anyone born after 1970 it is hard to imagine this 300-year association existed at all, although it could be inferred from Britain's well-established Indian communities.

Orwell coming from an 'Anglo-Indian' family, and having experienced the Raj at first hand as a police officer, had a formative effect. He resented the Blair family's relatively low status in the hierarchy of the administration of India, which was always mid-ranking in a social group obsessed with status, and he came to loathe the values of British India. Widespread snobbery and prejudice towards Indians, coupled with exposure to the iron rod of the Raj as seen from the perspective of the policeman's truncheon, turned him towards support for Indian independence.

Eric Arthur Blair was born in a remote region in the far north of British India on 25 June 1903. Motihari, where his father Richard was stationed as an agent in the Opium Department of the Government of India, was then in the 'Bengal Presidency', a huge swathe of the north-east administered from Calcutta. Close to the border with Nepal, Motihari's primary economic value was the opium crop.

The Blairs' involvement in this dark episode of British history might be another revelation for fans of Orwell. Reaching further back, to the late-18th and early-19th century, Orwell's paternal great-grandfathers derived immense prosperity from the slave trade, banking with Coutts Bank, although over the decades the wealth seems to have been frittered away as estates and assets were split between siblings. On his mother's side, the Limouzin family was Anglo-French, with very profitable business ventures in lower Burma. Orwell's mother Ida, like his father, was thus 'all-the-Raj' too, and it was in a hill station in British India where they met and were married.

‿

The closest international airport to Motihari is Kathmandu in Nepal, to which I flew to avoid a convoluted journey from an Indian city to the place of Orwell's birth. The descent to the border with India from Kathmandu was, however, a long overnight ordeal and not one I should ever wish to repeat. The 'deluxe', twelve-hour bus journey was anything but. As I boarded and found my seat, I noted my window was glassless. Instead a large, flattened cardboard box had been inserted to fill the void, a welcome which immediately flattened my enthusiasm. Once I had sat down, I quickly fiddled with the overhead light panel. Easily surpassing the wretchedness of my cardboard window, a cloud of granular dust descended onto my face, my squinting eyes and perplexed face uncertain of what to do next.

3

There was no sleep. It was as if the passengers were coins in a tin can being rattled, thrown up and down and side to side, over a very bumpy descent along the Kathmandu valley into India. The few times I did drop off were disrupted by some dramatic moment in the raucous Bollywood film screened for the benefit of my fellow passengers. With an abrupt jolt at 4am, about a kilometre from the Indian border, all of us disembarked. Half-conscious I stumbled onto a *tonga**, which wheeled slowly through the eerily un-busy streets of Birgunj, a dusty, unloved border town.

I was welcomed warmly at the Nepalese border post which, I noted after casting my eyes over the 'Foreigner Registration' book as I entered my details, receives three to four non-Nepalese/non-Indian nationals a month. The border itself is accessed via an enormous gate, the largest I have seen at a border anywhere. It resembles a blown-up version of the white picket fences at a British railway crossing, hung by two gigantic girders which are pulled up or down by a lever mechanism which requires two men to operate. It is the sort of quirky improvisation to be found all over the sub-continent, just one of the reasons travel there is so joyous.

In the 'no-man's land' crossing the border between India and Nepal, fires were smouldering on either side of a long, whitewashed bridge. Faint shades of purple in the sky suggested the sun was waking the day, as fruit bats with wingspans the length of my arms streaked between the silhouettes of a palm tree or two. On the Indian side, I entered the small border post, relieved to be at the mercy of the Government of India's vast bureaucracy. There is something comforting about its management of information, valued for its sake rather than as some means to another end.

The other benefit of being in India was access at long last to a railway, but I reached the station only to be told the next train to Motihari was not until 3pm and I would be better off taking a bus. The town

---

* A two-wheeled, cycle- or horse-pulled rickshaw.

on the Indian side of the border, Raxaul, is dusty and nondescript. As I clambered over the railway sleepers of the track leading in the direction of the bus station, I saw two dogs gnawing either end of the leg of another dog, whose now legless torso was strewn to one side of the line. I fast concluded this was a place I wanted to leave.

So I was back on a bus, but this time travelling over the Bihari plains; vast expanses of dry land, well-irrigated in part but demarcated by long stretches of sun-baked soil whose appearance had the effect of making my mouth feel parched. As the sun rose, I felt more and more uncomfortable, caked in dust from head to toe and perspiring so much as to feel sticky. I was queasy, longing for a shower and sustenance in somewhere with the bright lights of Delhi or Calcutta, wondering what on earth I was doing there as the engine ground down hard over the next mud-hole the bus had driven into. More dust cascaded into the chassis. A cloud obscured anything resembling a view.

On arrival in Motihari, I found it amusing to think that the Orwell of 1930s London – cold, grey, smoggy – first opened his eyes in this backwater-of-a-backwater in the outer extremities of India. I felt as if I was at the penultimate stop on a journey to the end of the world, a last chance saloon. The streets were chaotic in the way only provincial Indian towns can be; cows in the middle of the road; pigs scoffing here and there; dogs darting about. Cars and *tongas* skated around as if on ice, on either side framed by a discordant medley of shops, stalls and hawkers, all of which seem to be selling the same thing: fruit or plastic chairs in garish colours, marine blue to lipstick pink.

I searched hard for a hotel. Eventually I found what looked like something dropped from a tornado which had ripped through Las Vegas and picked up a concrete, lime-green-painted monstrosity, then landed it in the middle of Bihar. It was clearly selling its services to a domestic audience since, scanning down the list of guests, as I always do when I register in a hotel, I noticed all had paid as little as 100 rupees a night. The hotel owner had pre-inserted 600 rupees by my name, discrimination I had neither the will nor the inclination to challenge.

My room was at the end of a long, open-air walkway, onto which the lime-green doors of each room opened. After un-padlocking I gained the impression the room had not been let for some time. The shutters of the windows were closed tight, daylight filtering through and striking the floor-to-ceiling mirror ahead of me. Turning the light switch, which shot out sparks in the gloom, I saw thousands of mosquitos drifting effortlessly around the room, gliding like jumbo jets set down to land. I went straight to the nearest ironmonger, bought a fire-extinguisher-sized can of mosquito killer, and sprayed the room with the desperation of a ghostbuster.

The town is split into two halves by a large tank, the sort of water lily-smothered lake found all over the subcontinent. A bridge over the tank, and the parades of shops either side of it, is the centre of business activity. Little English is spoken here, and for those who do, 'Oorvell?' is a hard-to-pronounce word devoid of meaning. I jumped on a *tonga* which inched over the bridge to the other side of the town. It dawned on me that finding the Blairs' house would be an afternoon's work. As we reached the end of the bridge the clock tower in the middle of the junction displayed the wrong time and beneath it, nonchalantly surveying all before it, was a kneeling buffalo.

Set down here, I went more or less person to person before finding, after working my way through fifteen-or-so bewildered Indians, a man whose eyes lit up. He enthusiastically guided my *tonga-wallah**, his arms moving all over the place, in the direction of the Orwell bungalow, which he added was a kilometre distant, 'at Gyan Babu Chowk'. As we travelled in the right direction, past chaos-filled bazaars peddling Indian

* The owner/operator of a tonga, 'wallah' meaning someone employed or trading something.

sweets, spices and every shape of fruit and vegetable, I found it hard to think that Ida Blair might once have frequented them, pram-pushing, and haggling over the price of chicken.

The approach to the Blairs' bungalow is down a bumpy lane, along which is a medley of narrow, concrete, two-storey houses and street stalls-cum-homes where, during the day, a small selection of household goods will be sold and, by night, the stalls dismantled to create beds. Appropriately for the author of *Animal Farm*, various corners where the road bends seem to be impromptu pig sties with pink and black pigs snuffling through the piles of filth which constitute their homes. Along the lane, which would be difficult but not impossible to drive down, goats, cows, dogs and chickens drift listlessly.

On the right, the houses disappear, and a scruffy, enclosed scrap of land comes into view. Entry to this compound is via a disproportion-ately grand, red-tiled gate, which, when opened, leads to the birthplace of George Orwell. This area, no more than half an acre, resembles an unkempt English railway siding: rusting bits of ancient machinery interspersed with clumps of nettles, the odd unloved flowering shrub, a pile of old bricks or two. Ahead of the visitor, 100 yards distant, is a red-and-white-painted archway, the sort that recalls the chapterhouse of some ancient abbey. Beyond this is an even bigger area of land, the main feature of which is a derelict red-brick warehouse.

This more extensive area, enclosed on all sides and about the same size as a cricket ground, is scrappier still: clumps of nettles become a forest; scraps of metal now abandoned tractors; and small build-ings half fallen, vines and creepers engulfing them. The dilapidated warehouse is presumably a former storage facility for the opium crop, the entire plot having been owned by the East India Company – ownership quite possibly still residing with its successor, the Government of India. Three bungalows, two on the left and one on the right of the chapterhouse archway, provided residences for the managers of

7

the Opium Department's operations, the middle one of which was the Blairs'.

⌇

The sorry tale of Britain's involvement in the opium trade is little remembered by the inheritors of the British story, but it is one that should be. Until comparatively recently – well within my grandparents' lifetimes – the British government of India received around a fifth of its tax revenue from shipments of opium to addicts in China. Britain's ownership of Hong Kong Island came as a result of the Opium Wars in the early 1840s, fought with China to open the country to imports of cheap, Indian-grown opium. Much of the wealth of Calcutta, 'the city of palaces', came from the crop.

It would not be hard to conceive that Britain's gradual withdrawal from India, which began in 1919, was sparked by the end of the trade, which came as a result of a ban on opium by China's first nationalist government formed in 1912. Richard Blair left the Opium Department in 1911, shortly before the department began to be wound down and British commercial interests redirected elsewhere. He was very much around, however, during a London-based inquiry into the trade, among whose members were the great and good. When the inquiry reported to Parliament in 1896 it decided that the moral foundations of the trade were sound, opium being socially acceptable in China in the same way alcohol was in the West.

Richard Blair must have been well aware of the controversy the trade aroused. A campaign led by Henry Wilson, a Liberal MP, led to the launch of the inquiry in the first place. With him being recently married and with a young family to support, it is hard to believe Richard Blair would have done anything but continue to serve in the Opium Department and accept the few privileges of status or income that came from his participation. Orwell, similarly, makes no reference to it, but he was ashamed enough about his family's awkward involvement in Britain's imperial story to write a novel about his experiences at the coal-face – *Burmese Days* – and enough essays on the shames of empire to fill a short book.

The Blairs' bungalow, unlike those on either side, appeared in excellent condition. The Rotary Club of Motihari, appreciating its historical and literary significance, have paid not just for its entire restoration and maintenance, but for a large, concrete-hewn sign and even a bust, albeit one which only at a stretch resembles Orwell. The head, 'moon-shaped' as Orwell described it himself, is the wrong shape. Occupied for a long time by government employees and, until recently, a teacher, the house is presently empty and the interior walls whitewash-bare. What I found most surprising was its small size: four rooms in all, and another three in an outhouse resembling something like a mini stable.

As I walked towards the house, a cadre of adolescents, two of whom lived in the decrepit house next door, sulked in and around the Blairs' home. A noticeably old lady, easily an octogenarian, sat cross-legged by the front gate. I later saw her arranging a bed in one of the rooms in the stable-like annexe in the rear yard, her eyes squinting, appearing nonplussed through her Gandhian, steel-rimmed spectacles. I learnt from one of the students, as we communicated in pidgin English, that the Orwell birthplace sees around a single visitor every month or twelve a year; an astonishingly low number of admirers, but when I recalled the way I had rattled around in the buses which brought me here, I realised why.

Plans have floated around for some time to create a museum. There would seem little point to one. Even among educated crowds in India's metropolises, only a small percentage of people have heard of Orwell, still fewer read his work. There would not be crowds of people queuing up to visit. For visitors from outside India, the journey is so arduous as to put most people off. What is important is that the house is well-preserved, and the site looked after. I could envisage the plot becoming a public park, an 'Orwell Park' perhaps.

Walking back along the lane I reflected further on the contrast between the generally austere work of Orwell – Room 101 from *Nineteen Eighty-Four*; his essay 'In Defence of English Cooking', each commenting on the conditions of wartime and wartime economy – and the chaotic surrounds of his place of birth. Approaching the end of the lane, I looked ahead to the hawker-filled *chowk* and glanced in either direction at the junction to make sure I wasn't moments from being mown down. In India, one develops a sort of sixth sense, discerning motion and risk-to-life at every juncture. In this trip alone my life must have flashed before my eyes twenty times or more.

From the far right, my brain told my feet to stop dead in their tracks, and my eyes blinked twice in disbelief of what was before me. Indifferently at work, in that 'grandmotherly' way Orwell described so well in 'Shooting an Elephant', was a working elephant. Its master, rested high up on the ridge of the elephant's back, was guiding it to use its trunk to gather the stalks of sugar cane strewn over the pavement below. I observed every movement of them both intensely, fascinated by the grace of this beautiful creature as it nudged its trunk against a steel gate and, opening it, thudded off behind.

Motihari is not just famous for Orwell. On the road back to the hotel I passed a museum dedicated to Gandhi. He visited Motihari in 1923 to champion the rights of poor farmers, chained by the greedy and uncaring British Raj to the production of cash crops. Orwell felt for Gandhi, as for many other complex figures, a fascination. As a leading British intellectual, supportive of India's independence, he had a natural interest in both Gandhi and the Indian National Congress. His essay 'Reflections on Gandhi', published in 1949, is an excellent overview of a man history will probably never forget.

Unusually, since most current observers place Gandhi in the saintly corner of historical public figures, Orwell was as much a critic as a fan, admitting he could never feel much of a liking for him. His best compliment was to write that Gandhi was 'an interesting and unusual man who enriched the world simply by being alive'. But Gandhi's strange suggestion that Europe's Jews should collectively commit suicide when confronted with the fascism of Germany lost him much of Orwell's sympathy.

Orwell also explores how, for most of Gandhi's time as a campaigner for independence, he was used by the British to deliver their aims. This is at odds with the popular historical narrative, promulgated by the likes of Richard Attenborough's film *Gandhi*, that Gandhi and the (British) government of India were sworn enemies. Orwell wrote: 'in every crisis he would exert himself to prevent violence – which, from the British point of view, meant preventing any effective action whatever – he could be regarded as "our man".' Orwell added that Gandhi's peaceful non-violence would not succeed in a country, such as Russia, where opponents 'disappear in the middle of the night', a not unreasonable defence of what British imperialism could tolerate. And yet, British India is not taught favourably in Indian schools. It is barely taught at all in British ones.

⌐

There is little to see at the Gandhi Museum and its dusty compound. I was its only visitor at the time, and do not think I would rush back. I remembered from previous miserable experiences during my year in the country that booking trains on Indian Railways could be complicated and time-consuming. So I determined to plan ahead and reserve tickets for my onward journey to Kathgodam, a nondescript town and railway junction from where I could begin my journey into the hills and up to Nainital, the hill station where Orwell's parents met.

Indian railway stations, especially their booking offices, might be an introvert's idea of hell. They are generally quite challenging to navigate, and at almost all times of day are rammed full of passengers of every size and character. Porters, in sweat-stained maroon turbans, rush around like wasps in a nest. Huge crates of cargo smother the platforms – usually wrapped in muslin, scrawled with something along the lines of 'INDIAN RAILWAYS NORTH-EASTERN RAILWAY (NER) DISEMBARK LUCKNOW'. Piles of human excrement on the track and a couple of foot-long rats scurrying around complete the scene.

For all this, rail travel in India is magnetising. I have a lust for it which is satisfied only by getting to India and booking the nearest sleeper to some exotic-sounding city. The system, if one can master its quirks, is a marvel. The fact it works at all is a testimony to humanity's ability to organise itself. Forty-thousand miles of track; 1.7 million employees and more passion than a thousand West End theatres combined.

The booking office was as usual filled with a mass of men and women, all slumbering along in something almost resembling a queue. Participation is only possible with a great deal of pushing and thrusting. This does not come naturally to me, complete as I am with the Englishman's sense of personal space. However, wherever I am in the world, I seem to miraculously shred all sensibilities, shamelessly synchronising myself to the habits of my hosts.

I quickly found myself in the midst of 30 or so baying people, and fought my way to the front in the same way I would lose all grace pursuing victory in the scrum of a game of rugby at school. Knees, elbows and a great deal of sweat came from every direction. The joy that one feels when the familiar brown-and-white-coloured Indian Railways ticket is presented to the palm evokes the similar sensation of scoring a try. Most Indian Railways officials, certainly in a ticket office, will speak functional English. The booking system – another marvel given the sheer volume of trains, tickets and opportunities there are for errors – plotted my route to Kathgodam via Muzaffarpur Junction. A four-hour 'day' train would take me to the main line, crossing northern India, connecting Calcutta to Delhi. A sleeper would take me the rest of the way in about a day's travel.

I don't think anywhere can beat the romance of Indian place names, a characteristic used to great effect by Rudyard Kipling. 'Muzaffarpur Junction' is a name that could have come out of the pen of this greatest of all Anglo-Indian writers, and from there to Kathgodam came a slew of equally alluring place names, the type one should enjoy tracing one's eyes over in a copy of *The Times Atlas of the World*: Dighwara; Gorakhpur Junction; Badshahnagar; Shahjahanpur; Rampur.

The other enjoyable aspect of sleeper travel in India is its processes. There are a myriad of classes on all long-distance trains, with 'Two Tier Sleeper AC' being the best value for money. A familiar envelope of clean sheets is provided by the attendant, and a bearer will quickly approach to request one's preference for a 'Veg' or 'Non-Veg' meal, always offered on a steel tray or in a small foil box. It is invariably cheap and delicious, eaten cross-legged and with the yells of hawkers echoing through the carriage: 'Chai Chai Chai; Coffee. Pani Pani Pani; Lamb Cutlet', pronounced 'Coutloot'. I have a bad habit of hanging from the doors of trains in India, dangling with one arm gripped to the handlebars of the carriage. Given the chance I would probably clamber onto the roof, but this has been illegal for decades.

Waking early, I was hanging from the exit as the sleeper arrived in the morning at Kathgodam. The air was noticeably cooler and fresher in the breaking of the day. For some reason no railway line was ever built to Nainital, unusually so since, as I was to learn, it was of immense importance during the British era: the summer capital of the enormous 'United Provinces', to where the colonial administrators would retreat. Shimla, the summer capital of the Raj (as 'Simla'), and Darjeeling, the tea capital of the east, both still have train connections where a locomotive creeps up sharp curves, their engines huffing and puffing from exhaustion at their progress into the clouds.

One-hundred-and-fifty years ago the only access to Nainital was by horse-pulled carriage, a slow elevation to the town possibly preferable to the taxis of today. These race up and climb around 5,000 feet in 45 minutes. This presents not only a distinct safety risk on the road's twists and turns (two cars having driven off the road, down into the valley, over the course of my passing) but I saw at least a dozen passengers, including one in my shared taxi, yank the window of their cars down to spray vomit in the passing breeze. I have scarcely been on a hairier car journey than that on the road to Nainital, which has enough 'Hair Pin Bend' signs to match the curviest roads in mountainous Switzerland. My body swayed from left to right, and regularly jerked forward as the driver slammed on the brakes to avoid yet another head-on collision. I am the first to admit I am not the best driver in the world, but I still gasped in disbelief as cars *accelerated* as they approached a blind corner.

The vegetation on the surrounding valley sides was alpine, the air becoming cooler the higher one climbed. Lush green trees, Christmas-tree shaped, lined either side of the road, their pine and fir needles resembling the same mellow green in the fine-feathered plume of a peacock. The valley sides became steeper, a glance from the rear window revealing a departure from the smoky plains of India behind us.

The road eventually stopped winding, flattened out and with greater frequency houses passed on each side. Clothing flapped on washing lines tied between the balconies on squat, two-storey, galleried apartment blocks. People began filling the road in the way they seem to do in any Indian town, large or small. The entry to Nainital on this side of the town is unimpressive, cars slowing down through a street market that surrounds the town's bus station, but the view soon opens up to reveal the *tal*, or lake.

Nainital's location was first recorded by a Mr P. Barron in 1839. He described it as: 'by far the best I have witnessed in the course of a 1,500 miles trek in the Himalayas'. It is still hard not to be charmed by the location, a deep, turquoise-coloured, pearl-shaped lake, bounded on either side by steep, tree-clad hillsides. The town, like most in India, has sprawled in the years since independence, with the country's population growth but, for the time being at least, Nainital still possesses a sense of calm and a mostly intact heritage architecture. This combination produces the sensation of a time-warp, a place where the clocks seem to have stopped. Some Indians say Nainital and the other hill stations in India are an alien feature of their country. A novelty for many, these towns cling to the hills as living ghosts of the Raj, like a Dowager Duchess graces some vast country house: still elegant, straining to maintain dignity past prime, but the property of another age, and longing to be returned there.

The architecture of the Raj was a mixture of grandiose statements of power – Edwin Lutyens' Viceroy's Palace in New Delhi (in-fact New Delhi in its entirety), or Victoria Memorial in Calcutta and, more commonly, cheaply-constructed buildings erected hastily, usually single storey and roofed with corrugated iron. The latter are especially prevalent in the hill stations, possessing a fragility to match the tea-time dresses and gin-and-tonic-filled highball glasses which were once so familiar a presence in them.

These Alpine-style chalets pepper the hillsides but are now interspersed with concrete houses or other buildings. Nainital is popular with Delhiites – anything British in India usually claims status-value for wealthy Indians – and some have second homes there. In a world of supply and demand, the valley sides of Nainital supply the land and the demand creates itself. By and large, the newer buildings blend sympathetically with the old, and much better than in other hill stations, such as modern-day Shimla.

The lake, which of course cannot be built on, has not changed at all since the end of the Raj. Indian oarsmen scull their beige-painted rowing boats every hour of the waking day, and its shores are occupied by a handsome promenade enclosed by floral-patterned wrought-iron fencing. The Edwardians who developed Nainital at the beginning of the 20th century matched the designs of the town's benches with the railings, making it feel as if one has arrived in an English seaside town.

The road running along the lake on the town side (the other side of the valley is steeper and undeveloped) is lined by sizeable four-to-five-storey hotels, typically clinging precariously to the valley side with clumsy extensions to their rear. My hotel – The Elgin – was cavernous. My bedroom, 300 feet above the lake and thus reached only by an arduous stair climb, looked out across the lake and valley to provide a splendid perspective on the town, as if flying above it. Unfortunately for a hotel in the Himalayan foothills, there was no central heating, and hot water rarely. I thought that if I felt cold in its rooms, then Indian visitors must feel as if they have travelled to the North Pole.

The hillsides surrounding the town are so steep that they have a curious effect on light in the valley, making Nainital appear twilight-ish hours before the sun is due to set. The crests of the valley are straight and sharp, such that when the sun sets, the town, as one faces north, appears like the stage of a theatre. It is as if God were shining a torch down from on high, visitors awaiting an actor to appear 'stage left'. From the tops of the valley, reached via a hard vertical climb or, more conveniently, a cable car, the Himalayan peaks in all their ascendant glory can be viewed.

My objective in searching for the link to the Blairs was to explore the main Anglican church in the town. St John's in the Wilderness is as wonderful and evocative a name for a place of worship as one is likely to find anywhere. There are two in India and one in England, near Plymouth in Devon. Having read virtually every book and article about Orwell there is, I had realised there is confusion about this church, and I intended to clarify things for myself. It became apparent to me that some of Orwell's biographers have not always made the effort to visit significant places linked to his life, and confusion reigns. One expert on Orwell wrote that Eric Blair was christened at 'St John in the Wilderness, Motihari', and another that his parents met and were married at St John in the Wilderness 'in the north-west of India', which of course would today mean Pakistan. There is no Anglican church at Motihari – the town was too small to sustain one – and thus I wondered whether Orwell was taken by his parents to be christened at the place of their marriage.

St John in the Wilderness church was so named because it was, at the time of its founding in the 1840s, on the flat top of one of the lower hills that are a feature of the head of the valley. Then, the nearest buildings were a mile and more away, on the shore of the lake, but the town grew so much during the Raj that buildings gradually filled the space in between. Several Alpine-style chalet hotels form the 'in-fill', one of them wholly derelict and eerie in the sunset. Just across from the church, an enormous Victorian pile, resembling the sort of municipal building one might find in a market town in Derbyshire, now serves as the High Court of the state of Uttarakhand Pradesh.

I walked to the church from my hotel and noticed how the bustle of the waterfront – tourists bartering for a boat trip across the lake; the car drivers incessantly pressing their horns – soon died down. I saw troops of grey langurs, an almost uncannily human-looking species of monkey, jostling in the shrub-filled verges of the road. They move quickly but are carefree in the presence of humans. I think that they must see us being so characteristically similar to them in appearance that they co-exist happily. Mothers carry their young endearingly – the baby monkeys gripping their mothers' undercarriages like the heads of a thistle grip the fur coat of a dog. Their faces elevated to the sun, they seem not the least concerned by their carriers swinging nonchalantly from branch to branch.

St John's church is large and, from the outside, appears unloved. The brickwork in the tower is covered with epiphytes, and in every window, each half-boarded to protect it from intruders, panes of glass were missing. I was told by various Indians standing by that the church had been locked for some time, because the people who worship there only use it in the summer months, and no one knew where the key was. Only in India! After endless toing and froing, I pinned down the Anglo-Indian rector Mark Walsh who, in possession of a set of keys, agreed to give me a guided tour.

Reverend Walsh explained that there is no congregation at St John's and that the town's Anglican community, who worship at the church in the vicinity of the old Governor's Residence on the other side of the town, do their best to keep it well-maintained. On the inside the church is much better cared for – recently whitewashed, the floors swept clean and its mahogany chairs polished. Easily as big as a substantial English church, it is funny to think that a church of this scale was once necessary for a British community then numbering well over a thousand.

Likewise, it is strange to think that the George Orwell story began here, on a forested hilltop rise in a now forgotten hill station of British India. On 15 June 1897, Richard and Ida Blair walked down the spacious aisle at St John's, Ida's sister Blanche following as bridesmaid. I enquired whether there was a repository of records anywhere, the sort of thing that might end up being dumped in a rectory attic. I intended to search the baptismal and marriage records, but I was told there were none. Later I was able to confirm that Orwell was baptised at a missionary centre in Motihari, and not at St John's. Somewhere, I am confident, there will be piles of ledgers recording the church's marriages. India tends never to throw anything out.

It is surprising to see that many features of life in this Indian hill station have not changed since the end of British India. The churches are still open and hold services in English; there is a Freemason's Hall, and billiards rooms; a sailing association; and a Victorian lending library. Nainital remains famous for its schools – 'Sherwood College'; 'St Mary's Convent'; 'St Joseph's'. The billiards rooms are dimly lit, as they should be, and filled with green baize-topped billiards tables, which seem not to have been moved an inch since they were bought and installed by the British, who built the lakeside wooden structures that house them. In an adjacent building there was a room with rows of rickety little folding tables. I felt as if I was in an English village hall, waiting for a game of bridge to begin.

The lending library – Nainital Municipal Library – inhabits a quaint wooden structure that has been constructed on stilts extending out into the lake. It is no exaggeration to suggest that next-to-nothing has changed in the library since 1947, so it came as a surprise to find that it is still open – for an hour in the morning and three in the afternoon – every day. Inside the smell was musty, like a bookshop left to go to seed.

Every soft-cloth volume I took down from the library's dust-laden cabinets felt damp, as if at the last juncture before mould is set to grow. None of the books in English I cast my eyes over had been issued since the early 1950s. The titles were the usual sort of selection one might find in a Victorian gentleman's library: Thackeray, Hardy and Kipling. I reflected that there must be hundreds of libraries like this all over India. Extant, as real as everything else in today's India, but so very un-Indian.

I couldn't resist a visit to the town where the George Orwell story began without visiting a bookshop, to see whether it might stock some works written by him. Pradeep Tewari, the affable owner of R Narain and Co (Est. 1929), a bookshop a short stroll from the library, and also overlooking the lake, led me to a copy of *Nineteen Eighty-Four*. On clutching it, I asked: 'Did you know his parents met and were married here?' He answered with an inquisitive frown that he did not, followed quickly by: 'And so for all these years I have sold his books here, and did not know.'

Henley-on-Thames, Berkshire, England

A boy standing on his head (1904–17)

From northern India to Oxfordshire is a transition that would have been more remarkable in 1904 than in the 2010s, but it remains a feast of contrast nevertheless. I have concluded that the appeal of the subcontinent to Britons – visually, culinary or other – is to be found in their opposites in conduct and taste. Jawaharlal Nehru, India's first prime minister after independence, once described the English in India as 'rivers of ice', so divorced were they from the culture they had joined. The move from Indian summers to soggy England must have been a curiosity for the young Blair children. Aged just one, Orwell will not have remembered anything. Yet his family's Anglo-Indian heritage was a formative force in the development of his character.

Shiplake is a village on the west side of Henley, where the Blairs lived in one of four or more homes in the area over a fifteen-year period. Keeping track of the family's movements is not easy, but one house in Shiplake and two more on the 'Shiplake-side' of Henley were leased by them for certain. Debate surrounds the succession of homes they had just after Ida Blair returned from India soon after Orwell was born. It is a testimony to their shabby-chic 'poverty' that they moved around so much, a family unable to afford a permanent home but just about affluent enough to fund the rent for a succession of reasonably large and comfortable houses. Richard Blair remained in India until retirement in 1911. He returned to England just once, on leave, in 1907.

The Chilterns, Henley and Southwold, to where the Blairs would retire, are quintessentially English places. They each, during his first two formative decades, pressed upon Orwell's young mind the small 'c' conservatism which would later underpin his sense of patriotism. Melvyn Bragg has remarked that it would be hard to find two places in England more English than Henley and Southwold, 'if you were to spend a week looking'. They are key to cracking Orwell's psyche.

Henley has always been a wealthy town. In *Eric and Us*, the moving tribute to an old friend by Orwell's childhood sweetheart Jacintha Buddicom, reference is made to 'the river' being as popular for holidays then as the seaside. To signify the sense of exclusivity, Henley could be described as the Antibes or Martha's Vineyard of Orwell's time. Wealthy families had second homes at Henley. There is little of this tradition today – Henley as the hill station-type retreat for those escaping the heat and dust of London – but vestiges remain; holiday cottages, boat rentals and, of course, the famous annual rowing regatta.

It is difficult to resist being critical of Orwell at times. In the essay 'Such, such were the joys' he condemned his experience at St Cyprian's, a private preparatory school in Eastbourne, Sussex. He loathed the headmaster and his wife, and resented being surrounded by the sons of wealthier families. Of course, the inferiority complex Orwell took with him to Eton was arguably nothing compared to what he would have felt had he achieved his scholarship to the public school via instruction at an all-age elementary school. These were the woeful ill-funded state schools to which the overwhelming majority of British school-age children went, if they were lucky enough to access any schooling at all.

St Cyprian's was far from an all-age elementary state school. At the time of writing, approximately 4 per cent of all English children attend a prep school. Another 2 per cent might attend non-preparatory private school, with the other 94 per cent attending government-funded state schools of varying scale and standard. Even if eligible for reduced fees, the Blairs needed to be wealthy to consider paying any fees at all. Orwell originated from just below the top of the social tree, a descendant of a prosperous imperial family with all the connotations that this implied. India, Lower Burma or even France were not places with which the bulk of Britons were familiar in 1904.

The moment I realised the distance between the Blairs and the ordinariness of most Britons was during a tour of the Blair family houses. Each of them is an enormous villa with five or six bedrooms apiece, set in spacious, tree-laden grounds. The exclusivity of Henley or Shiplake today is helpful in reminding readers that not terribly much has changed with the passing of 100 years: towns no doubt filled still with wealthy families seeking entry to the best public schools, with offspring eagerly awaiting their results from Common Entrance. The gulf between this joyous, privileged lifestyle and 'the other' is not insignificant.

The roads in the area are poorly signposted. With the scattered pattern of settlement, it is difficult to tell where one village ends, and another begins. Shiplake is a non-nucleated village surrounded by interspersed hamlets. One of the hamlets seems to steal a bit of Shiplake's claim to fame with its own: 'Orwell Restaurant'. It was closed on the day I passed, but I was encouraged to see at least one business exploiting the Orwellian heritage to be found in the area.

Between the Orwell Restaurant and Shiplake proper are open fields, filled after harvest time by neat rows of wheat stubble. Even at 29, I find it hard to step directly on this without a pervasive sense of satisfaction in hearing the crunch. My elation was matched on this warm September day by my dog George who, surveying the nests of rodents laid bare by harvesting, danced in excitement. Back in the car, I drove south towards the river. At one junction, where traffic flashed by, I was fraught with despair at which direction to take next, but spotted a sign to Shiplake Church: '12th Century; Medieval Glass; Lord Tennyson married here 1850.'

Faced with another tree-shaded lane, I parked and started walking in the direction of the church, passing as I went hordes of school children from nearby Shiplake School. Paces later the church can be seen at the far side of a large churchyard, sited defensively on the edge of the valley no more than a kilometre, down a steep escarpment, from the River Thames. The church, 800 years old and of standard construction in 'Chiltern' flint, is unremarkable. Its graveyard is of interest only since it contains a scattering of obviously aged wooden grave markers, which I found unusual.

A plaque in the church was poignant, reminding me of Orwell's early writing. 'Awake, Young Men of England' was a poem published in *The Henley and South Oxfordshire Standard* shortly after Britain went to war, on 2 October 1914. It asked for young men to:

> *Awake! Oh you young men of England.*
> *For if, when your country's in need,*
> *You do not enlist by the thousand,*
> *You truly are cowards indeed.*

Bryan Osmond Dewes was no such coward, a '2nd Lieutenant Acting

Machine Gun Officer' in the 1st Middlesex Regiment, 'killed in action in France' on 30 July 1915 'aged 21 years'. His plaque ends: 'Fighting for GOD and RIGHT and LIBERTY.'

Orwell's views about the war had changed by the time he came to write *Coming up for Air*, one of his lesser-known novels about a childhood in the Thames Valley, with the narrator as the main character. It was written in Morocco, during a visit to Marrakech for winter sun to help his weak chest, and was published in 1939. George Bowling, a frustrated 40-something in the throes of a midlife crisis, returns to the town of his childhood to pay homage to fond memories of the past: 'In 1914 we thought it was going to be a glorious business. Well, it wasn't. It was just a bloody mess,' Orwell wrote.

From the church, a steep, stony path leads down to provide access to the river. George, whose nostrils sensed water was close, was released from his lead and darted off in search of a splash. I followed, apprehensively, since at the bottom of the path it was unclear where the river flowed. The meadows are flat; the river obscured here and there by the long, drifting branches of willow trees or thick clumps of rushes. At some time reclaimed from marshy riverside, Shiplake School has its rugby pitches here, the posts majestic white against a clear blue sky. I wondered what this spot would have looked like in the days before the yelling of the scrum, when the Blair children and their friends the Buddicoms would come here to play.

Here they would fish, and no doubt swim on warmer days, bird-spot or retrieve eggs from nests ('but you must only take one egg, and not disturb the parents', Jacintha Buddicom recalled). Her memoir is filled with idyllic recollections of summers which never seemed to end. She wrote: 'The spot we liked best was one of the little sandy bays along the riverbank of the gently sloping meadows', a place to be found still on the dry, windless Indian summer's day on which I found myself there. The stretch of the Thames here is separate from the main channel; one day it will surely be a little oxbow lake of its own. As such the water is listless, invitingly so, and fish-rich.

It came as no surprise that George began whining, awaiting my nod to throw himself in. The nod duly given, the only other people on the riverbank I could see were two men fishing. One was gregarious, apparently in need of a chat, having spent the day in silence. The other I could tell was there *not* to meet people, nor dogs for that matter. I am acutely aware that springer spaniels and fishing lines are not a good mix. As the speaking man distracted one of my eyes, the other was fixated on George. His tail navigated a circuitous swim, taking him precariously close to the line of the silent man, who gave dismissive glances in my direction. George's central preoccupation in the absence of a tennis ball was to paddle after the attractive, autumnal-yellow leaf fall of a nearby willow tree.

All three Buddicom siblings – Jacintha, Prosper and Guin – first met the young Eric Blair in the summer of 1912. Jacintha remembered they were playing French cricket in a field near the Blairs' home in Shiplake when they saw 'a boy rather bigger than Prosper standing on his head'. This was something they hadn't seen before and so asked him: 'Why are you standing on your head?' He replied: 'You are noticed more if you stand on your head than if you are right way up.' The siblings became instant friends with Orwell, spending their holidays more or less together until he left Eton.

Buddicom's book is delightful purely as an insight into an Edwardian childhood; dreamy days spent playing in the cornfields or fishing on the Thames. Many of these memories appear in Orwell's *Coming up for Air*, experiences which undeniably shaped the young Englishman, entwined from an early age in the bucolic pursuits to be found in a small English village. In general, it should be assumed – and many biographers agree – that the young Orwell was conservative, unwilling to compromise on a patriotism which, until his arrival at socialism at a much older age, was unaccommodating of radical politics.

After he adopted radical politics, his patriotism remained. To understand this blend of patriotism and socialism is to penetrate his life perspective truly. His love of what he described as 'the deep, deep sleep of England' – 'the fields and beech-spinneys and farmhouses and churches, and the villages with their little grocers' shops and the parish hall and the ducks walking across the green' – peppers his writing.

The Blair children became so ensconced in the Buddicoms' home life that they spent most of their summers together. Ida was not shy in regularly handing care of her children over to the Buddicoms' mother, an arrangement necessary with the unusual circumstances of the war. Orwell's father was fighting in France (said to have been one of the oldest recruits in the Great War, at 60) and, with Ida working in London, the house at Shiplake had been let. The Buddicoms seem to have adored the Blair children, and Eric especially. It cost Ida £1.00/week for Mrs Buddicom to take care of her children at intervals during the war, equivalent to about £100 in 2022.

Childcare was often further outsourced to the Buddicoms' grandfather and aunt at their estate in Shropshire. Again, access to the wealth of an English country house and its grounds is indicative of the exclusive social circles from which Orwell came. Ticklerton Court, a name which could so easily fall from a novel by Trollope or Thackeray, is close to Church Stretton in Shropshire, a beautifully hilly and curiously hard-to-reach county in the English Midlands. The west of Shropshire borders Wales, part of a region of Britain known as the Welsh Marches. Jacintha noted that this meant the area was little affected by the war, offering them the genteel pursuits of shooting and fishing. These fed them well, for wartime.

Ticklerton Court had an extensive library. Orwell and Buddicom were avid readers, as one would expect for a King's Scholar at Eton and a girl at Oxford High School. The library must have been a fantastic resource for them both. Advanced in their reading age, they exchanged books and discussed them, often reading aloud to one another. Buddicom wrote how they loved thrillers, but preferred Russell Thorndike to Arthur Conan Doyle's Sherlock Holmes; Conan Doyle's brother-in-law, Ernest Hornung; and G.K. Chesterton. Thorndike, Hornung and Chesterton are seldom read today but H.G. Wells, Orwell's personal favourite but of little appeal to Buddicom, is ever-popular.

Orwell was once disappointed 'to have just missed Wells' at the house of one of his aunts, who were members of the Fabian movement (they would meet, however, once his writing career had begun). Bowling, Orwell's alter-ego in *Coming up for Air*, recollected: 'now and again it so happens that you strike a book which is exactly at the mental level you've reached at that moment, so much so it seems to have been written specially for you. One of them was H.G. Wells's *The History of Mr Polly* ... Wells was the author who made the biggest impression on me.'

Orwell became a devotee of A.E. Houseman's *A Shropshire Lad*, which he loved so much he promised he would memorise every poem in it. He also met, through his aunts, E. Nesbit, author of *Five Children and It*. In this book, five children have adventures with a mythical wish-granting creature, the Psammead. Similarities can surely be seen between the Blair and Buddicom children and Nesbit's stories: both Edwardian, and dressed the part for the time, taking pleasure in hunting down risk and reward in and around Shiplake, or at Ticklerton.

Orwell and Buddicom also wrote for each other. He scripted plays but only read them out loud, and with plots Buddicom couldn't remember when she wrote about their friendship 50 years later. She recalled he was secretive about his writing, a tendency that stayed with him until he was well into his thirties if contemporaries are to be believed. He wrote a series of tales around a character called 'Mr Puffin', none of which survived. Likewise, most of the letters he sent Jacintha or the family are believed to have been destroyed when the Buddicoms' house at Shiplake was sold in 1964.

Ticklerton Court was primarily Elizabethan but had been modified heavily by the Victorians. With three storeys and ten bedrooms it must have been a playground for a group of children. The Buddicoms' grandfather and aunt sound deliciously eccentric, presiding over a house filled with stuffed birds, on which both were experts. This was surely the origin of Orwell's love of ornithology, notes on which he took all his life. Hunting, shooting and fishing were integral to estate life, with Orwell introduced to shooting for the first time there. On his first shoot he 'shot a rabbit on second attempt, which was very good', wrote the Buddicoms' aunt to his mother.

Aunt Buddicom seems to have kept the children busy, the Buddicoms' grandfather being aloof. She would take them to explore many of the Welsh Marches' ruined castles, to which they would bring a picnic and spend hours exploring the grassy derelict ramparts and pockmarked, denuded walls (a legacy of centuries of conflict between the Welsh and the English until union between the two in the 1530s). Orwell's favourite was said to be Ludlow. It could have provided the perfect inspiration for Orwell's unwritten ghost stories, a genre to which Jacintha was convinced he should have contributed.

From Ticklerton it was once reported he had 'a bit of a cough', said to be chronic. From this and many other sources, it can be gleaned that his health in childhood was never good – the origin of which was quite possibly his damp incubation as a baby in Motihari. His mother wrote in her diary that when he was aged just two, he had colds all winter. Buddicom also referred to 'the inherent delicacy of his chest', and he succumbed to pneumonia at Eton. Analysis of the extent to which his health affected his personality can only ever be conjectural, but it is possible it had substantial influence. Buddicom summarised his personality as 'naturally reserved [and] self-contained'.

〜

Central to the sentimental imagery of *Coming up for Air* is the River Thames. As for so many English writers, it was an enormous source of literary inspiration. In the novel, Bowling describes the water of the Thames as 'a kind of luminous green that you could see deep into, and the shoals of dace cruising round the reeds'. Today, even with encroaching urbanisation all around the area, the Thames retains its dreaminess: the classics, Jerome K. Jerome's *Three Men in a Boat* and William Morris' *News from Nowhere*, are both based on and around 'the river'.

Unlike the Thames, Shiplake has changed beyond all recognition since the 1910s. A process that was well underway when Buddicom wrote her memoir in the 1970s seems to have continued unrestrained over the period since. Many of the roads drawn on her map of the village are no longer there, built over or are now closed roads open only to their residents. In every direction large villas, each seeming to out-do the other in scale, inhabit the tree-lined lanes Buddicom recalled so fondly. Her map in the book may as well be discarded, though I could just about use it to locate the field where she first encountered the future Orwell.

The train station, a pub and a post office constitute the centre of the village. At the pub, the Baskerville Arms, there are photos of Shiplake in yesteryear. The photos show that the centre today differs from that of pre-1914, when it seems there were more shops housed in a colonnaded parade now on the site occupied by the pub. The parade reminded me of the sort so common to colonial architecture in India ('Raj vernacular'), and I am not sure this was just a coincidence. Shiplake and the surrounding area were home to many Anglo-Indians returning from the subcontinent. The colonnades and timber-framed homes were taken out of India and replicated in the towns these families usually retired to back in England. Great Malvern and Tunbridge Wells, other popular Anglo-Indian towns, are not dissimilar.

This evidently was not lost on Orwell, who described a house in *Coming up for Air* as carrying on the traditions of the Raj: 'As soon as you set foot inside the front door you're in India in the eighties ... The carved teak furniture, the brass trays, the dusty tiger skulls on the wall ... the Hindustani words that you're expected to know the meaning of, the everlasting anecdotes about tiger shoots and what Smith said to Jones in Poona* in '87. It's a sort of little world of their own that they've created, like a kind of cyst.' Orwell was open about the intensity of his interest in the choices of words he would use. The use of 'cyst' over 'bubble', or something more appealing, is suggestive of his lack of appetite for his own family's past.

At the small shop and post office in Shiplake I smiled at the sight of the shelves. It is remarkable how unappetising the sweets which filled my pockets at the age of ten seem to my mature palate. But the sight of those familiar yellow tubes of Liquorice Sherbet, or Dip Dab, or Refreshers brings to mind one's memories of childhood with which these concoctions are so deeply intertwined. Every generation seems to find the same attachment. Buddicom recalled: 'A penny would buy twelve caramels in separate paper', or 'large quantities of liquorice allsorts ... which Eric very occasionally bought'. She added he thought they tasted 'so beastly they were almost fascinating, and he wanted to make sure they were still as beastly as he thought'.

Rose Lawn, the Blairs' house at Shiplake, still stands, although most of what was a much larger garden has been sold for housing. Down the lane to the immediate right of the house, so close that the walls of Rose Lawn can almost be touched from the asphalt, is a warren of

* A hill station close to modern-day Mumbai.

newly built housing. The Blair house seems oddly sited in what is now too small a plot for a reasonably sized, black-timber-framed Edwardian villa. It is strangely shaped, especially at the rear, as if successive owners have imposed their grand designs and each of them has conflicted with the quaint simplicity of the original. Its present owners are sheltered by a large, above-head-height front fence and gates. These grand perimeter fences, now common in the village, are at odds with the historical style of housing.

Two things struck me as I approached the house and observed the surrounds, each entwined with my travels to come in the chronology of Orwell's life. The first was the rows of purple *Agapanthus Africanus* lining the front walls and fences of most of the houses on the Blairs' side of the road. This perennial bulb, I suggest later, is the modern-day equivalent of Orwell's Aspidistra; his middle-class status symbol once part of the décor of every Edwardian home. Plants generally still carry class status: they can also be found amid the prim front gardens of the large Georgian terraced houses in Hampstead, where Orwell lived in the early 1930s. It seemed apt that the plants' limp lilac flower heads drape down over their bright-green stalks so close to one of Orwell's childhood homes.

The second took me back to my visit to Moulmein, the old British capital of southern Myanmar, and the road where Orwell's mother and her family lived for well over a century. The Limouzin's family home was destroyed in fighting between the British and the Japanese during the Second World War. But further along from where it once stood are colonial houses that escaped war damage, each with names recalling places in England their owners missed so greatly. One house, an enormous teak-clad villa set far back from the road, retained its colonial name, Lyndhurst. As with the profusion of agapanthus scattered along the Orwell trail, it is appropriate that the house next to the Blairs' in Henley went by the same name. Both spoke volumes for me of Orwell's social class and upbringing: huge villas named Lyndhurst with agapanthus-strewn front gardens.

Rose Lawn was not the home of a great writer when the Blairs lived there, only the family home of an Anglo-Indian couple and their three children. While many of Orwell's former homes have some form of plaque, they are absent from the three main residences known to have been home to the Blairs in or around Henley. These retain a sense of the familial, surely a home today as then for large, affluent families similar in many ways to the Blairs. In *Coming up for Air*, Orwell predictably harks back to the memories of his childhood: 'A Sunday afternoon ... a smell of roast pork and greens still floating in the air ... And the soft feeling of Summer all around you, the geranium in the window, a starling cooing.'

~

The Blairs' homes in Henley are just a five-minute drive from Shiplake. At the end of the town closest to Shiplake, the houses are largely Victorian with smaller terraces of red brick at the bottom of the valley side, with houses of ever-greater size the higher one climbs. The terraced roads have American-derived names – 'Boston Road'; 'Montreal Terrace' – a fashion for the New World common in Edwardian England. The Blairs' houses were away from the main road reached by climbing sharply up a steep hill from the valley bottom.

One of the first, for which the exact years of occupation are not clear, was Ermadale. This is the huge villa outside which I came to appreciate Orwell's relative affluence, and it sits in a large plot with enormous mature trees: oaks, horse chestnut and ash. When Orwell and Buddicom were once in Henley together, he had mentioned to her it was named 'ErMadale' after Eric and Marjorie (Orwell's sister). True or not, this name hasn't survived.

The same can be said for much of the backyard of Ermadale. What would have been open countryside to the left and rear of the property has been replaced by mid- and late-20th century housing, 1960s style. It is possible to envisage how disturbed Orwell might have been by this, a process he condemned in the 1930s as a theme of *Coming up for Air*, super-charged in the decades since. One thing Orwell didn't live long enough to see, although he foresaw its application to other life necessities, was the use of cheaper materials in architectural construction. It is perhaps a good thing he didn't.

The Blairs' other known home, to which they moved after leaving Rose Lawn, is around the corner from the former Ermadale, on St Mark's Road. The tallest of their three homes, it is semi-detached, faced with red brick and five storeys high, with steep gables. It is unremarkable on a street accommodating equally extensive houses, but nevertheless attractive. It is a steep walk from the town centre, with the reward of one's perspiration the view across to the other side of the Thames Valley – no new estates there, only a prospect of forest-clad hillsides set against a misty autumnal sunset.

Henley might one day be home to an 'Orwell Museum' though plans for this seem to ebb and flow. A museum is unquestionably deserved. Of the same generation of writers, and an eventual winner of the Nobel Prize for Literature, John Steinbeck has several museums devoted to him in the United States. Orwell has none in England. One central observation of my travels in the footsteps of his life is that he is a curiously unrecognised author. Most of the places where he has lived bear the obligatory plaque, but not always even this. I hope that one day justice is done by Orwell, and a museum for him opened.

⤸

I drove back to Shiplake to eat supper at the Baskerville Arms and people-watched as I waited. I ordered fish and chips, long considered the English national dish. Orwell defended it staunchly in his essay 'In Defence of English Cooking', though it is rivalled today by chicken tikka masala. Orwell did not live to see the proliferation of Indian restaurants on British high streets, but I am certain he would have been intrigued by the biting back of the Raj. Orwell's taste in food, as embodied in the title of his essay, was traditionally English. In this way, he was no different to most people of his generation. I once bought a takeaway pizza for my grandfather, who poked at it in such a way as if to wonder what oddity I had brought home.

The food at Orwell's schools was almost certainly vile, but at home Orwell ate well. Buddicom described the comforting Edwardian diet they were rewarded with after a day's field-larking or fishing. Some of the dishes, such as pig's head, are making a comeback now that English food is gaining the reputation Orwell always believed it should: 'Our meals were always ready on the tick. Enormous meals – boiled beef and dumplings, roast beef and Yorkshire, boiled mutton and capers, pig's head, apple pie, spotted dog and jam roly-poly.'

One of the saddest aspects of the life of Orwell, ignored in most of the biographies, was what happened to his friendship with Jacintha. It is clear that they were close, but after he departed for Burma in 1922 she never saw him again. Dione Venables, Jacintha Buddicom's cousin, documents in an epilogue to *Eric and Us* just how tragically their friendship may have ended. An allegation to be forever unproven, but remaining likely and therefore distressing, is of an attempted rape by Orwell, leading to their immediate estrangement.

Later as an adult, following an unplanned pregnancy and the subsequent secretive adoption of her baby, Jacintha came to hear that the famous writer George Orwell was her childhood friend, Eric. She learnt this as late as 1949, as he lay dying. A brief flurry of letters between the two of them shows their fondness for one another, in spite of a 30-year break. Venables suggests Jacintha was in love with Orwell for three years, over 1918–21. To read Jacintha's book is thus to read reflections on a life marked by a deep sense of remorse. She ended *Eric and Us* thus: 'I wish that Eric were still here, now that I am already and he would be also, seventy, so that after all the years – even if it wasn't by our own united fireside – we could still say to each other, "Do you Remember?"'

Eton College, Berkshire, England

The greatest Old Etonian
(1917–21)

E ton was always in Buckinghamshire, but since 1974 has been in Berkshire. During a reorganisation of local government, Berkshire suffered as its borders were altered in an act of territorial re-shaping that must have made cartographers wince. Much of the north of the county was transferred to an enlarged Oxfordshire, and its gift in return was Eton, moved from its historic home of Buckinghamshire. Defined by its proximity to a school, a river and a castle, Eton is now a small town on the border between the two counties, with a population of just under 5,000.

Orwell would have been moving from one genteel, forested county to another. For visitors to England, the county system can seem confusing, familiarity being easiest for fans of cricket, since the premier league for the game uses the county names of England to compose teams. I have often come across bystanders in India, rickshaw-wallahs and the like, who know little about life in Britain other than possessing an encyclopaedic knowledge of English counties.

A 'public' school in the United Kingdom, confusingly, is a private fee-paying school that belongs officially to a special group: The

Heads' Conference, or HMC. Eton College is academically selective and requires new entrants to pass an interview and reasoning skills test aged eleven, before passing the HMC-wide 'Common Entrance' exam at thirteen. Among the public schools it is pre-eminent in status, arguably unrivalled in the ranks of popular recognition.

Eton was founded in 1440 by King Henry VI, a ruler of England for part of the turbulent Wars of the Roses. He established the school to provide scholars for his new college at Cambridge – King's College – and 70 poor boys across all five year groups would receive a high-quality education from his endowment. The 'King's Scholars' remain 70 in total today; Orwell was one of the 1917 intake. Fourteen of those achieving the highest marks in a scholarship exam are admitted each year, entitling them to adopt the abbreviation 'KS' after their name.

In the ways of the British Establishment, the award of honours endows those fortunate to receive an honour with an array of letters after their name. It is endearing, if puzzling, to see Eton introducing its boys to these traditions so early. Single-sex, and the school as a whole being 1,300 pupils strong, the Scholars are housed together in the same buildings of the original College, once also home to Orwell. Non-King's scholars, known as *Oppidans* (Latin for 'Townie') make do with boarding houses scattered around the rest of the town.

Eton is south of Henley-on-Thames, but sits on a stretch of a bank as attractive as that in Henley, although without the scenery provided by the Chiltern Hills. It is at the bottom of the valley as the river flows towards its broadest sections at London, rather than on the more dramatic cuts through the uplands of Oxfordshire. It is therefore surrounded by corridors of communication, both the Great Western Line – trains to Wales and the south-west of England – and the M4 motorway, providing a fast road to the same, skirting close by.

The river here is characterised primarily by its meadows, which being flat make Eton's buildings appear more elevated than they would be elsewhere. The Brocas is the name of the meadow separating the town from the river, and has been in the College's ownership since the 15th century. It joins Eton Common and Southfield as one of three large open areas surrounding the town. As in so much of the area, place names are derived from their royal connections. The Brocas is no exception, being named after a local family in the nobility.

Today residents remain entitled to use the grounds for pasture, providing 'Lammas Rights' for local farmers between Lammas Day on 1 August, which celebrates Lammastide, or the start of the harvest, through to 6 April. The right is still utilised even if the presence of cows is of grievance (as I was told by one resident) to the town's dog walkers. The meadows, river and rowing have long proved irresistible to pupils at Eton. One of Orwell's favourite spots, where he continued his passion for fishing, was 'Jordan', the College's name for a tributary of the Thames that flows to it from the town. At that time, it was a haunt for pike. Continuing the classical theme, his favourite spot for swimming (on the main river) was 'Athens', a place to which Orwell would often retreat for a solitary swim.

Like other public schools, Eton has its own dialect, a medley of strange words that have evolved down the centuries. They make it harder to understand life in these institutions; a deliberate or sub-conscious attempt to segregate pupils' lives from those outside. Any familiar school term is called something else within the confines of its walls: a teacher is a 'beak'; a lesson a 'div'; the College's prefects 'pop'; a bad essay a 'rip'; a good essay a 'show-up'; a rower a 'wet bob'. Even the three school terms – Autumn, Spring and Summer to the ordinary – are confusingly referred to as 'halves'. What is surprising, in one of the few insights into life at the school he ever wrote, is how Orwell believed the world of Eton was time expired and unlikely to last beyond the 1950s.

Writing a short book review of B.J.W. Hill's *Eton Medley* entitled 'For Ever Eton', in August 1948, he commented:

> *It's hard to disentangle admiration from dismay when one learns that Eton in 1948 is almost exactly what it was in 1918 ... The top hats and tailcoats, the pack of beagles, the many-coloured blazers, the desks still notched with the names of prime ministers had charm and function so long as they represented the kind of elegance that everyone looked up to.*

Orwell was given many invitations and opportunities to return to Eton, but it is believed he never did, making it clear he did not revere the college.* His closest engagement was a visit to his former Classical tutor, A.S.F. Gow, who by that time was teaching at King's College in Cambridge. This has not prevented Jeff Branch, a one-time Master of English at the college, concluding he is 'the greatest Old Etonian [OE] of them all' because, unlike Henry Fielding, Thomas Gray or Percy Shelley, '... his literary works continue to provoke and challenge universally in their attempt to probe the relationship between the individual and society'.

Orwell's style of writing was of course largely formed by his education. Eton has never been a school – it is formally named a college – but the education provided there matches that which any first-rate British university would offer young adults aged much older, and probably nearly as good as anything a college at Oxford or Cambridge might. Its class sizes are small, with an overall teacher/student ratio of 1:8, and many of its teachers also hold a doctorate or publish in their own right.

---

* I later learnt he may have once taken his future wife, Eileen, to watch the Wall Game.

It does, like the other very best schools in England, surpass possibly any other type of education in the world for a child of that age. When one considers Orwell did not go to university, it must be remembered that he profited from the very finest teaching available anywhere for five years. Indeed, the Provost of Eton at the time was M.R. James, the Antiquarian and writer of ghost stories, and Orwell's French teacher was Aldous Huxley, author of *Brave New World*. Had he fulfilled an ambition to continue to Oxford, the university would have been building on a mind fully formed by its tuition at Eton, rather than transforming an intellect that had struggled through lesser teaching.

Academically, Orwell was not successful. He came 117 out of 140 pupils in his year and the lowest in his election as a King's Scholar. The consensus seems to be that he switched off after entering Eton, contemporary Christopher Eastwood recalling: 'He just didn't try awfully hard at anything ... You'd never have thought for a moment that he was going to make his mark as a writer.' However, what evidence there is suggests he sought a literary career right from the beginning of his schooling.

Orwell wrote prolifically for the college's newspapers and founded a pamphlet (*The Election*) with two friends. The following titles, for which authorship by Orwell is confirmed, were written between 1918 and 1920. They offer some early insight into both his style and choice of subject: 'A Peep into The Future'; 'The Cricket Enthusiast'; 'Is There Any Truth in Spiritualism?' Each sounds familiar in style to the titles given to the very wide range of topics found among his later essays. Orwell is listed as the 'Business Manager' of *The Election*, a role sounding so modern it is puzzling to think of someone holding such a post in 1918. The paper was not professionally printed, and very few editions survive. What it demonstrates is that Orwell unquestionably sought to publish his thoughts from a young age, and in the certain honest style for which he would become famous.

The fact that he spent his education alongside M.R. James makes me consider what Orwell did not write as much as it might have inspired what he did. M.R. James was appointed Provost of the college in 1918, joining from King's College Cambridge, and was a perplexing character with a flair for dark writing. His stories remain read today, and an on/off tradition at the BBC since the 1970s is to commission *A Ghost Story for Christmas*, usually aired late on Christmas Eve, among which M.R. James' stories feature pre-eminently: *A Warning to the Curious* and *The Stalls of Barchester* among them.

James is less remembered for his medievalist work, which remains some of the best research ever undertaken in the field, such as his investigations into the lives of some of the old English saints, and England's abbeys. His academic research inspired the ghost stories; it may well have been hard for it not to have done given so much time spent in ancient libraries and ghostly cathedral cloisters. Jacintha Buddicom commented that as an adolescent: 'Eric's chief preference was for ghost stories; one of his theories was that half the people in towns were ghosts ... I am surprised he did not publish a collection of ghost stories himself.' Along with their exchange of so many other literary works, he gifted her *The Turn of the Screw* by Henry James and *The Room in the Tower* by E.F. Benson. He also gave her a copy of *Dracula*, which he discovered in the course of 1919, along with a crucifix to protect her from vampires!

Orwell was obviously impressed by M.R. James, and eagerly awaited his introduction to the provost, inevitable for the King's Scholars, with whom James lived in proximity and may have regularly eaten with. It is known that he rehearsed his stories to pupils, often in rooms lit with a single candle. It is enchanting to think of the young Orwell, enthralled by M.R. James' sonorous tones among the deep oak-panelled walls of a college study. Buddicom continued: 'Eric was particularly impressed by [M.R. James'] style, which was indeed impressive: never an unnecessary word, and un-withered by age. It was, I think, to M.R. James that the best of Eric's style is owed.' I think it a shame the world was deprived of a volume of Orwell's ghost stories, a diversification that would have enhanced his writing still further.

～

Driving towards Eton is enjoyable. Zig-zagging across the bottom of the valley of the river the drive is entirely flat, and in August the roads are quiet. This part of England is affluent, being so close to London and close to major roads, railways and Heathrow Airport. Post-war urban sprawl afflicts the area, however, and the distance between settlements is insubstantial. The village of Dorney becomes Eton Wick (Eton's poorer sister to the west) quickly, separated only by the ancient Dorney Common – presumably part of the only green buffer surrounding Slough that is legally protected by ancient writ.

In Dorney, even the service stations are not discreet at shielding the area's affluence. Out of the corner of one eye I caught sight of a blue-and-white MOT sign in the window of a beautifully ancient Tudor building. As my car approached Eton, passing under the remarkably long Windsor Railway Bridge, a viaduct that sequesters Eton from Eton Wick, my navigation declared: 'ARRIVED AT ETON COLLEGE.'

I was slightly perplexed since greenery and terraced homes surrounded me on both sides. I could see no grand entrance lodge. Later, once I had entered the college and gained my bearings, I realised Eton town *is* Eton College. The whole town more or less is owned by the college, and most of its buildings provide homes for its boarding houses, academic departments or other academic services ranging from its debating chamber to the careers service. If its operational buildings were lifted out of the town in one instant, leaving only those it did not own or which it lets, just the high street would remain (and most of its shops exist only by their service to the population of the college).

Eton's architecture is incredibly rich. The original college building resembles something like Hampton Court Palace and yet when passed on the road it can appear somewhat ramshackle, with various additions demonstrating its substantial age. It claims no less the title 'oldest school classroom in continuous use', dating back to 1443. The Georgians could hardly resist attempts to improve their Tudor inheritance, as they did with any house they found standing as their century unfolded in the 1700s, with additions from this era attached to both the original site and other new creations spread all over the grounds. In fact, an enjoyable study might be made in writing a history of architecture 'through the medium of the buildings of Eton College'.

The chapel, virtually a copy of St George's Chapel in the nearby castle, has an enormous vaulted ceiling in the medieval gothic style, which might suggest it predates much of the rest of the site. But appearances can be deceiving; a bomb hit it during the war, and a stone replacement was created in place of the wooden roof that would have existed in Orwell's school days. It smells like a typical school chapel – musty, with the scent of printed paper lingering from copies legion of *The Book of Common Prayer*; hymn sheets stuffed quickly into the rear of a pew and left there for eternity.

Entered by a side stairwell close to the Porter's Lodge, the centre of administration in the college, its main door is inauspicious. I turned what I thought could only be the handles into a chapel, enormous cast iron lungs of ancient metal, and entered. Above me hung the worn colours of various regiments and what seemed like a thousand brass memorials to fallen OEs across the centuries. A short walk to my left, passing under the enormous organ – as one might walk, head bent downwards, through a pergola – the stalls of the chapel and the altar appeared ahead of me. Passing yet more war memorials and wall paintings which, so detailed were they, resembled medieval tapestries, I absorbed much of the militaristic tradition of the Eton experience.

The college's enormous lead war memorial engulfs one entire side of the main, pebbled quad. Its losses from the Great War alone numbered some 1,157 boys. Given that most of these men will have been in their twenties or early thirties, each cohort of recent leavers in Orwell's time would have lost at least 100 OEs. In the second quad, entered after passing a statue of Henry VI, more war memorials line the walls listing campaigns from Crimea to the Boer Republics.

This militarism is common to most English public schools. A series of reforms pioneered by Matthew Arnold at Rugby School encouraged many other leading educational institutions to reform and adopt practices designed to produce a cadre of men capable of administering an empire. In reality, the number that went overseas was reasonably small in proportion, as an analysis of the college's leavers' register for Orwell's year suggests. Orwell's entry, club-sandwiched between 'Balliol, Oxford'; 'Business' and 'Trinity, Cambridge' is his destiny: 'Indian Police', neatly scrawled in dark black ink.

Any time Orwell had when he was not studying or playing on the river would be taken up in the O.T.C. (Officers' Training Corps). Many private schools and universities retain these organisations. There are inevitable risks of pretension, and I sense Orwell joined his O.T.C. begrudgingly, by compulsion of the war. In 1940 he wrote in his essay 'My Country, Right or Left' that at school: 'To be as slack as you dared on O.T.C. parades, and to take no interest in the war, was considered a mark of enlightenment.' By all accounts he used it as an excuse to play with compasses, maps and rifles, providing continuity for his shooting pursuits. He acquired useful skills that would prove helpful during his wild escapades on Jura, the Scottish island which would be his home at the end of the Second World War and until his final admissions to hospital.

Orwell's curriculum at Eton, much like at prep school, began with the academic pursuits required to deliver a King's Scholar into the universities of Oxford and Cambridge: classics and more of the classics. One of Orwell's biographers, Robert Colls, notes that as late as 1936 the college had just nine science teachers, but 39 classicists. Over his five years at Eton he became progressively less enthused with this path, commencing life as a Classical Specialist, before migrating to Classical General and then, finally, to the perceived-as-hopeless General Division.

At each level the academic expectations of the pupil became less and less, reflecting Orwell's increasing dissatisfaction with the nature of the education provided for him. The study of modern poetry or literature was neglected. Eton did not establish an English department until 1965, guided by Michael Meredith as Head of English, who was still working there at the time of my visit as librarian of College Library. The distinction from the College's Modern Library is important, since the latter serves as the College's conventional lending library, whereas the former is for use only by fellows or senior pupils. Meredith describes Orwell as 'the finest political writer in England since Swift', recognising the parallel of satire between Jonathan Swift's *Gulliver's Travels* and *Animal Farm*.

College Library includes the wealth of ancient texts and archive of documents owned by the college, which is fortunate to contain uncorrected proof sheets of the first draft of *Nineteen Eighty-Four*. Another item, donated to his House library and discovered randomly by a pupil in the 1990s, is a copy of *Misalliance; The Dark Lady of the Sonnets; Fanny's First Play* by George Bernard Shaw, inscribed:

Eric A Blair
June
1920

And in a different script, presumably by another pupil administering the House library:

Presented to
College Library
By E.A. Blair

George Bernard Shaw's plays were at the peak of their popularity after the First World War, but are today little known and seldom staged, with the exception perhaps of *Pygmalion*. Bernard Shaw's work is unlikely to have featured in any of Orwell's English lessons, at a time when classicists taught the subject. A book he gave Jacintha Buddicom, inscribed with the following, leaves us in no doubt of his views on the pre-modern literature he was taught:

E.A. Blair KS. Bought this book Much against his will For the study of Milton A poet for whom he had no love: but he was compelled to study or abandon English Extra Studies which not being Commendable to him He was compelled to Squander three and sixpence On this nasty little book.

Today, English is a celebrated subject at Eton, although the historical attachment to the classics remains, with each pupil still having two tutors – one classical, the other general. Orwell's works feature prominently in the modern curriculum, not because of his connection to the college, but since 'the boys enjoy his writing so much' and are '… inevitably pushed towards certain essays'. Michael Meredith, the almost lifelong English teacher at Eton, added that when Orwell was a pupil 'the Classics were taught in an extremely dull way. When I arrived here in the '60s, they were still learning verses by rote. Nothing had changed.' Science teaching was no better, even concerning traditional physics and zoology. The Masters had demonstrated their distaste with the college's dismissive attitude to their subjects by paying out of their own pocket for new laboratories at the turn of the twentieth century.

With teaching in Orwell's time ending at 11.30am, it is likely private reading time filled much of the rest of the day. His passion for history, frustrated by the teaching available to him, may well have been pursued in these free hours. In the time we spoke, Meredith evoked the passion and direction that are the hallmarks of every good teacher. I left jealous of the pupils in his instruction. To be ushered towards one of Orwell's essays, *at the age of thirteen*!

I was intrigued by Aldous Huxley's involvement in Orwell's education and wondered whether he influenced the young author's psyche. Huxley was remembered as a flamboyant schoolmaster walking around College with a hat and long, flowing scarf extending to the knees. His notoriously poor eyesight was subject to repeated torment by the adolescents, and he was hopeless at controlling his classes. Most people can remember those lessons at school – more common to some institutions than others – where baying pupils would reduce the vulnerable teacher to a forsaken wreck.

The conceptual similarities between *Brave New World* and *Nineteen Eighty-Four* are obvious, but it is unlikely Huxley pre-ordained his pupil to write a work so similar to that which he would publish in 1931. (At any rate, in my view, *Nineteen Eighty-Four* is the superior of the two.) However, in 'Why I Write', an essay published in 1946, Orwell wrote: 'When I was about sixteen I suddenly discovered the joy of mere words, i.e. the sounds and associations of words.' One of Orwell's fellow King's Scholars, the future highly accomplished medievalist Sir Steven Runciman, noted Huxley's:

> ... *use of words, the phrases he used, and that was a thing that Eric Blair very much did appreciate. You felt that you*

were with someone who enjoyed words, and compared to the ordinary Eton master it was a rare, rare joy to listen to him … I've often wondered if Aldous had any effect on Eric's later writing, just the sheer writing. I think probably he did have an effect.

With Huxley inspiring ingenuity, albeit through the medium of French, and M.R. James, brevity, there may be grounds to place these authors as having the most significant influence on Orwell's style. Whatever the case, and the role of James especially remains curiously unexplored, it cannot be denied he was privileged to enjoy the company of both.

⌒

The Eton Wall Game is a mysterious sport similar to rugby, in which, so the urban legend goes, a goal has never been scored. 'It's incredibly boring to watch', added Meredith. As with much sport in Britain's public schools, participation is exclusive. Fives is also played at the college, a game so precious six public schools have their own version of it. The Wall Game has greater recognition in the popular imagination, reflecting Eton's special status in relation to the British Establishment again.

I might suggest it is virtually impossible to understand the mechanics of it without seeing the wall. To access the site, the college grounds are entered to the far left of the Porters' Lodge, passing various formal gardens and the rear aspect of the accommodation for King's Scholars, before a prospect of playing fields leading down to the river opens up. The wall itself is the college's boundary with one of the main roads out of the town, leading to nearby Datchet.

White, cricket wicket-style markings indicate each side's base. Both are painted on the wall, and a gap of 400 yards or so separates them.

The two goals are a tree and a gate that lie at a perpendicular angle to the wall that lines the road. Contested on the one side by Collegers and the other *Oppidans*, the academic and physical virtues of the King's Scholars are put to the test in each game with the most important match played on the college's main feast day, St Andrew's Day, on 30 November.

The urban legend that a goal has never been scored is a myth – Orwell himself scored once – but it is not an easy endeavour. Each side aims to move the ball towards their opponents' end. In the last few yards of each end of the field is an area called the 'calx'. Here players can earn a 'shy' (one point) by lifting the ball against the wall with a foot. At the same time, a member of the same team must then touch the ball with his hand while the ball remains held to the wall, and follow with shouting out: 'Got it!'. Only once this has happened can scoring a goal be conceivable, worth a further nine points and achieved by throwing the ball at the door or the tree, depending on the player's side.

Orwell's contemporaries recall him enjoying the sport and revelling in the glory of scoring. Christopher Eastwood reminisced: 'It was Blair's sort of game. I think he rather enjoyed getting rather grubby ... I remember him coming in once looking rather pleased with himself for having got so very dirty!' The only known film footage of him shows him marching across some playing fields at Eton, arm in arm with his fellow team members.

Eton, and St Cyprian's before, provided the young Orwell with a network of influential people that would not only see him effortlessly comfortable among the rich in later life but positioned him well for gaining access to new opportunities the less fortunate would have been denied. As a King's Scholar he was lauded as one of fourteen pre-eminent academic candidates to be 'elected' to the scholarships at the College. Among the alumni of the King's Scholars are Harold Macmillan, former Foreign Secretary Douglas Hurd and Boris Johnson;

thus proving the well-rehearsed joke that above the school gates should be the motto 'Cabinet Makers to Her Majesty the Queen.'

Orwell was accompanied in his election as King's Scholar by literary critic Cyril Connolly and Alex Burdett-Money-Coutts, heir to the banking fortune. The future Lord Hailsham was a King's Scholar in the succeeding year. Even Huxley had been a member of this elite some twenty years previously. As a King's Scholar, Orwell was immediately cemented into this privileged group. Limited to fourteen every year and explicitly distinct from the mass of *Oppidans*, the rest of the college use the nickname 'Tugs' to label the scholars, a term which, used in conversation much later by friend Sir Richard Rees, caused Orwell to wince '... as if I had trodden on the tenderest corn'.

Some of Eton's traditions were a source of embarrassment for him, a man who one contemporary described as 'not being radicalised [to socialism] until the 1930s'. Sir Roger Mynors, a future classical scholar and another direct contemporary to be knighted, recalled their year group as being regarded as 'almost revolutionary' by schoolmasters. He added that this was an exaggeration and their year group's aspiration was just to 'get rid of excessive privilege' (presumably, extreme privilege within the confines of the college, rather than between the college and the mass of the broader population). Mynors concluded: 'I think [this was] the first side that really matured, and in this way he really made an impression on his contemporaries – this breaking up of prejudices and privileges and so on.' It is said that in Burma a woman once told Orwell he seemed a fair person. Orwell replied he felt that Eton made him so, along with a capacity to think for himself. In both respects, he was evidently grateful.

The college has such an embarrassingly illustrious list of alumni that it must find it hard to celebrate any alumnus especially well. When David Cameron became prime minister in 2010, it was claimed the clinking of sherry glasses could be heard from within the college walls;

celebrations of their 'nineteenth'. David Cameron was the nineteenth British prime minister to have been educated by the college, a man who had as many OEs in his cabinet as Herbert Asquith, who held the same office between 1908 and 1916.

Orwell is unlikely to receive similar praise, say on the date of his birthday. According to the archivist, I was the first person to visit the college on Orwell business in the two years they had been there. For a writer of his success, this surprises me, *The Greatest Old Etonian*. There was once an Eton Museum, hidden away in a corner of the college and now closed, where a wall of portraits helpfully reminded the visitor of Eton's contribution to the giants of British public service, culture and industry. Orwell's picture, the famous image of his wry smile in an elbow-patched academic's jacket, was positioned in the highest row.

Today he is revered informally by the Orwell Society, founded in the 1990s and open to all pupils. Among them, Orwell is very much possessed by the Left, with the society being a debating club for those sympathetic with ideas from that wing of the political spectrum. (Orwell once wrote in a review of a book about Britain's public schools dated 1940: 'Ninety-nine public school boys out of a hundred, if they had votes, would vote Tory.') That debating should be at the centre of his emotional legacy to the college is appropriate. Mynors recalled Orwell's love for: 'Endless arguments about all sorts of things ... I remember when we first did Greek and were introduced to Plato and the method of Platonic dialogue, in which Socrates argues like anything with a lot of other people, proving them endlessly wrong, really in order to get them just thinking. I remember thinking, "This man's just like Eric Blair!"'

The Orwell Society now organise events jointly with the Shelley Society, named after the romantic poet and contemporary of Byron. It is beguiling to imagine how many societies could be named after famous alumni at the college. As if when starting a new one a pupil might ask: So ... *who should we pick this time?* and pull out the name of yet another British worthy. It is likely that Orwell would be a member of his own club today. Records in the archive show he was elected to Eton's debating club only in his last year, however. The minutes of 22 July 1921 show 'E.A. Blair' proposed by 'Mssr Herbert'. Despite detailed notes of many debates, no substantive records survive for his year of membership. I am however certain he would have a view on some of the questions posed in the debates held before and after he joined. 'Whether, in the opinion of this house: The rich man's lot is happier than that of a poor man; Trade unions have a right to strike; The quality of college food is deplorable.'

⤻

I ate at the George Inn, an old pub in the direction of Windsor that was eerily quiet for a visit at the height of summer. Eton's high street is, the college aside, the whole of the town, and leads from the Porters' Lodge directly up to the river before a bridge crosses into Windsor, the bustle of which is apparent as soon as the end of the High Street is reached. Eton is a conservative place with shops and eateries to match. It has lost most of its banks, the Coutts branch lasting until 2017. Above its doors, a mere upstart compared to the College, was painted: 'BANKERS AD 1692'.

Some of the shops are functional but most reek of twee. There was no shortage of *Keep Calm and Carry On* mugs, posters and other assorted flotsam. There is a single bookshop, with tattered second-hand paperbacks and magazines stacked mile-high. Orwell's *Collected Essays, Journals and Letters in Four Volumes* were scattered casually at the back of a chaotic window display: an understated position in an understated bookseller's, a destiny of which he would surely approve.

Walking back to the college, I reflected on how Orwell developed a rebellious streak, formed well before he left school. This might suggest he was unsuited for colonial service, let alone as an officer in the Indian Police in the notorious backwaters of Burma. As a King's Scholar, the natural path would have been Oxford followed by entry into the elite Indian Civil Service: a path, it must be remembered, his father never attempted during his career as a mid-ranking official in the peripheral Opium Department. But his relatively unimpressive academic perform- ance would have made Oxford, let alone the ICS examinations, a hard ambition to fulfil.

Orwell left for Burma aged nineteen and returned grown in both body and mind. Of all the periods in his life, Burma more than any other built the George Orwell we read today. Leaving an imprint both culturally and politically on the author, Burma took a rebellious adoles- cent and turned him into an inquisitive, observant iconoclast. Debate still surrounds his ambition, or lack thereof, to attend University. As I have pointed out, the quality of his tuition, by the likes of Huxley and M.R. James, means the absence of a BA or BSc does not imply he failed to receive a pre-eminent education by any definition. His tutor Gow was surely misguided, however, in advising Orwell's parents that he would not be a suitable candidate for admission to Oxford. The university would have developed him further and permitted him to pursue topics hitherto unavailable in the stifling range of subjects at pupils' disposal at Eton. Buddicom insists that Orwell wished to study alongside her at the university, a privilege she too was denied since (as was common) the family's resources were prioritised for her brother. She goes as far as to claim that her mother tried her best to persuade Richard Blair that he should accept for his son an academic path rather than follow in his image.

It is easy to query today, when the choices of a school leaver are mostly made discrete from the views of parents, why Orwell did not fulfil his supposed ambition for Oxford. It is likely he could have made it into the university had he wanted to. Equally, his was an Anglo-Indian family of long standing, the links to Burma being exceptionally strong. Runciman shared: 'He used to talk about the East a great deal, and I always had the impression he was longing to go back there ... he used to say he didn't much want to go to a university.'

Of the many curiosities I saw during my time at the college, one above all remains fixed in my mind. A book, *Grey Beards at Play* by G.K. Chesterton, presented by Orwell to a friend and containing a bookplate that is inscribed:

Eric Blair
His Book

The bookplate is a sketch. Unmistakably tropical, one of the ancient southern ports in India, such as Cochin, could pass for it. It suggests to me that Orwell sought the exotic, a romanticism inspired by faint recollections of his earliest days in India. It is a plain drawing containing a mosque for certain, the rounded towers of what could pass for a castle and a scattering of swaying palm trees. Aden or a Trucial state perhaps, to be passed by his steamer under the glare of the sun or the silence of the night, during his passage to Rangoon.

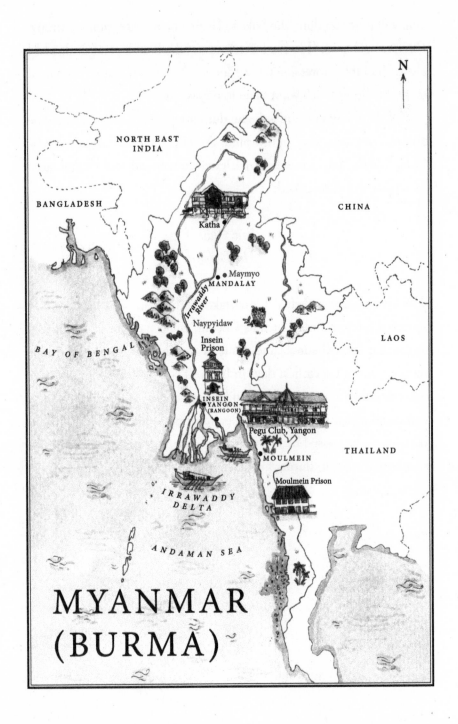

N

NORTH EAST
INDIA

BANGLADESH

CHINA

Katha

Maymyo
MANDALAY

Irrawaddy River

Naypyidaw

Insein
Prison

BAY OF BENGAL

LAOS

INSEIN
YANGON
(RANGOON)

Pegu Club, Yangon

THAILAND

MOULMEIN

Moulmein Prison

IRRAWADDY
DELTA

ANDAMAN SEA

MYANMAR
(BURMA)

Myanmar (Burma)

A Smoking Room Story (1922–7)

The title *Burmese Days* evokes sentimentalism. When Orwell's contemporaries heard it, they must have, like his family and neighbours in Southwold, anticipated a reflective work of a young imperial officer fulfilling his duty to the Raj: the sipping of gin under a *Topi** or multiple days of cricket accompanied by renditions of the National Anthem. On paper, Orwell was typical of the public-school-educated colonial administrator, but the titles of his essays, 'Shooting an Elephant' and 'A Hanging', should provide a decent enough foretaste of the unhappy nature of *Burmese Days* and the fate of virtually all its characters. They also say much of the feelings relating to his time there.

To my mind, the greatness of Orwell's writing is that, by-and-large, it does not date. Although *Burmese Days* abounds with anachronisms, it is precisely for this reason that the book still contains an important message: Orwell's courageous rejection of the logic and methodology of the imperialism then reigning for the most part unchallenged by his class. In its mighty damning of British colonialism, *Burmese Days* is an important contribution to anti-imperial literature.

* A pith helmet.

It is often compared with E.M. Forster's *A Passage to India*. While a fine book, Forster obsesses with orientalist mysticism to the extent it becomes the focus of the plot. *Burmese Days* wastes no energy at all in exposing the very worst attitudes held as orthodoxy among some of the British in India. The book has as its focus a timber merchant, Flory, leading a frustrated existence in a small up-state river-side port. It is readily apparent that the novel is semi-autobiographical, with the narrator and Flory having a deep insight into the culture and operation of the police.

Kyauktada, modelled on Katha, where Orwell had served, is Orwell's putridly tropical stage. It represents the yoke of the British presence in the town and the corrupting influence it has over all the actors of imperialism, demonstrated so clearly and pitifully by Flory's murder of his cocker spaniel and abrupt suicide at the end of the book. It is the desperate culmination of the many years Flory spent in the town, the book examining the relationship between the Burmese and the British community via the prism of its 'whites only' club and the repeated attempts of the civil surgeon, Indian Dr Veraswami, and the Burmese magistrate, U Po Kyin, to gain membership.

A brief (ultimately unsuccessful) romance with a niece of the Lackersteens, Flory's superiors in the timber trade, and his regular engagement of a Burmese mistress, against the backdrop of 'the strange rhythms of the tropical seasons', complete the novel. The book is not short of damning statements about the Raj:

> *It's a lie that we're here to uplift our poor black brothers instead of to rob them. I suppose it's a natural enough lie. But it corrupts us, it corrupts us in ways you can't imagine. We Anglo-Indians could almost be bearable if we'd only admit that we're thieves.*

> *My dear Doctor how can you make out that we are in this country for any purpose except to steal? It's so simple. The official*

holds the Burman down while the businessman goes through his pockets.

These extracts might appear stark to modern eyes, let alone those of the mid-1930s. The novel was considered so contentious that only an American publisher was prepared to issue it and, even then, the place names and people were changed to avoid inevitable allegations of libel.

The climax of the story, a riot and attack on the club following the death of a Burman and murder of a Briton held culpable, ruins the club building and the airs or graces of those within it. The shame continues when Flory's suicide is publicised as an accident, the dog hastily buried to hide all evidence, so that even this last act of defiance is subsumed into 'the system'. Flory's sentiment is in many respects not dissimilar to Winston's in *Nineteen Eighty-Four* – the uninspiring, final triumph of despotism.

Before his death, Orwell had identified three books he still intended to write. One would return his writing to the topic of Burma, being a summary of his observations based loosely on his passage by boat to and from Rangoon, and would be given the draft title *A Smoking Room Story*. In Myanmar today, the joke goes, Orwell wrote not one book about the country, but three: *Animal Farm* and *Nineteen Eighty-Four* continue the history of the state to present day.

Orwell arrived in India on the SS *Herefordshire*, now a popular diving wreck in Cardigan Bay, having foundered off the coast of Wales in 1934. Sailing to Rangoon from Birkenhead in October 1922, he spent his initial training in the Indian Police College at Mandalay. Orwell would later model the gruff Chief Superintendent of Police in *Burmese Days*, Macgregor, on the burly Scot in charge there. He was posted to the sweltering delta where the force's preoccupation was the security of the operations of the Burmah Oil Company, headquartered in Glasgow.

During a succession of posts, one took him to the town of Insein, north of Rangoon, now a suburb of the city, and pronounced 'Insane'! The town was then, and still is, home to Myanmar's largest prison. It was either at Insein or Moulmein prison in the south, where Orwell was number two in the police force, that he witnessed 'the' hanging so described in his famous essay of the same name.

Orwell's final posting after Moulmein was to Katha in the far north, the setting for *Burmese Days*. In the delta, he was within easy reach of Rangoon and especially enjoyed visits to the Scott and Mookerjee Bookshop, then the best bookshop in the country. Today, in a city broadly the same architecturally as it was in the colonial period, the bookshop is one of few sites to have been demolished. A five-star luxury hotel, the Shangri-La, stands in its place. Across the road, The Bible Society of Myanmar, at 262 Pansodan Road, survives as the sole tribute to the literary heritage of a corner of a city once famous for its bookshops.

Most of the world's famous port cities have long since introduced containerisation, removing from their heart so much of the activity that gave birth to them. In London the docks moved further east, now centred on Tilbury in Essex. In Hong Kong they were moved in the 1970s to a vast area of reclaimed land. Even in Calcutta the old warehouses stand empty in preparation for their demolition, as the boats now used are much too large to navigate the treacherous sandbanks of the Hooghly. Surprisingly no such fate has yet befallen Rangoon, whose chief characteristic is a waterfront still dominated by the arrival and departure of laden boats.

In many port cities, the embassies, banks and upmarket hotels are still located on, or close to, the docks they have always served. In today's Rangoon, their conservative, austere frontages peer down disapprovingly over the endless hive of activity: lorries laden with logs from up-country; fruit the size of basketballs departing by the thousand.

The city's Customs House, right down by the port's busiest pier, is as hectic as it has ever been, with an audience of traders entering in haste to seal the paperwork controlling the fate of their wares. Meanwhile an army of hawkers and stray dogs hover in the heat of the day, attending to whichever next arrival at the port will draw their attention.

The Irrawaddy Transport Company still dominates the operation of ferries on Myanmar's rivers but, like Burmah Oil, it is also no longer headquartered in chilly Glasgow. The local ferries, each day emptying people into the city centre from villages and towns across the undeveloped banks of the river on the other side, are deserving of a travelogue in their own right, such an experience is the crossing. On the far side several large passenger steamers stand ominously, half submerged, as unloved as much of the wealth of Rangoon's neoclassical architecture.

To the east of the city, among the broad, green avenues of the embassy district, stands the famed former Pegu Club. It is the most unnerving place I have ever had the misfortune to visit. Wooden for the most part – dark, elaborately carved teak – the bars, ballrooms and gymnasium of this vast ghost of the Raj haunt an otherwise bustling and attractive part of the city. The club was *the* place to be seen in colonial Burma, enshrined by the size and sophistication of its construction: intricately carved buttresses and, in the former ballroom, faint sky-blue paint drenching the panelled walls and Doric pillars, resting on what was once one of the finest sprung parquet floors in all of Asia.

The racquets, smoking rooms and cocktails (it pioneered its own, the 'Pegu', being a mix of gin, Curacao, lime juice and orange bitters) could not be further removed from the shell of the club today. Graffiti is scrawled over the wall containing the former bar; the loops and curved flicks, creeping above the Burmese characters resembling the head of a rearing python, distinguish the script. (Across the Bay of Bengal, the script of Kannada, of Karnataka state in India, is curiously similar.)

Such is the grandeur of the complex, visited in the early evening and the middle of the thunderstorm-to-end-all-thunderstorms, I felt as if I was meandering around some raised RMS *Titanic*. The columns of its walkways surround a courtyard, replete with stripped wooden decking above and below, resembling the twisted and tortured promenades on that great ship now lying some four miles under the surface of the Atlantic. The rainfall dripping and pouring from every orifice only heightened the effect of the club's sunken fortunes in the maze of the tropical jungle that now engulfs it.

A decision I made some years ago to travel by train wherever possible was vindicated by an experience on the Metro between Johannesburg and Pretoria, usually *verboten* for Caucasians in South Africa. Ten minutes or so into the journey, disparately spaced passengers in the carriage, undirected and simultaneously, sprang into gospel song. I often think what a performance I would have missed had I taken a taxi. Writing after the event, however, no sensible person would opt for the railway over a bus or flight to Moulmein. Myanmar's rail infrastructure is in an appalling condition – the roads are much better – and, as the crow flies, a plane can navigate an enormous inlet in the coastline separating the mouths of the Irrawaddy from Myanmar's long 'tail' of territory far faster.

I set off from Rangoon for my journey south, lasting twelve hours, just before dawn. Railway stations in the subcontinent are a hive of activity at any hour. At 5am passengers were darting as spectres, over the tracks and between trains, their faces decorated with the luminous white paste derived from tree bark the Burmese call *Thanaka*. The train passed out of the city and, for most of the next half day, passed stretch after stretch of paddy field, so drenched by the monsoon it was perplexing to see the continuous presence of villages and small towns, containing houses for the most part built on stilts. In the emptiest parts, I found myself recalling the vast wastes of Rannoch Moor, but with the Scottish heather substituted for elongated stalks of rice. The train never exceeded more than 30 miles an hour, often going at considerably less.

The trains are not only too large for the gauge, but as I was to observe by hanging from the window, the absence of ballast along sections of track leads to the energy generated by a train's passing being sent upwards. The result is a sensation I can only describe as riding horseback, the 'clickety-clack' of the wheels replicating the hooves of a horse galloping at speed. The entire carriage would erupt into laughter each time this happened, offset only by the crowing of the carriage's resident cockerel. The sensible decision to opt for Ordinary Class over the padded comfort of First was justified by the sense of natural surety wood has over the decrepit (and broken) leather seating available with the more expensive ticket. In both classes, the track was visible through the gaping holes in the floor. My meals were freshly steamed corn-on-the-cob, an abundant snack in the country, and a simple but delicious bowl of rice and roasted peanuts.

It is hard to put into words my impressions of Moulmein, the port in Myanmar's southern Mon state where Orwell spent two years as second-in-command in the city's police force. Sited where three enormous rivers meet, laden with silt from their passage from the uplands of South-east Asia, it was once a town of immense political and economic importance. Between 1824 and 1852, it was even the capital of British-administered Burma. My first impression was of a lush, green ridge, dotted with glittering gold pagodas and a town engulfed by swaying palm trees. The minarets of a mosque, the towering gaudiness of a Hindu temple or a crumbling church tower, as if copied and pasted from Surrey, emerge here or there, but it would be impossible not to describe the jungle as being firmly in control.

It has the aura of an Arabian trading port, its population influenced by centuries of exchange across the Indian Ocean, resembling what I imagine the Middle Eastern boom towns, Dubai and Doha, must have been before their rapid expansion. Its architecture is a blend of Arabic and colonial, all colourful facades and cool verandas, substantively unadulterated as if the Hong Kong or Singapore of yesteryear left a half-sister on the shores of the Andaman Sea and forgot to collect her. It is now a sultry town with something tepid about it. It is possibly the closest I have come to a frontier-style place, once so common but now largely found only among the pages of *Heart of Darkness* or a novel by Graham Greene.

The completely uninhabited green wastes visible from its long waterfront – distant hill ranges and just across the vast stretch of river, long islands forming an unbroken, flat mess of green – resemble the banks of the Congo or upper reaches of the Nile. A river too broad for the traffic it now receives means the four or five vessels anchored appear forlorn and uninterested in their surroundings. As a town, it felt well past its days of prosperity.

Even more perplexing is to imagine a British police officer, of all people George Orwell, administering the peace in this long-forgotten piece of living history. There are few surviving fragments of the town's long Anglo-Indian past. Local speakers of English asked to be spoken to in slow, short sentences and, even then, much of the meaning seemed to be lost among an archaic style of the language. I was addressed as 'Mister', and my replies were typically answered with words such as 'splendid'. The once-bustling Anglo-Burmese community moved en-masse after the military coup in 1962. None, I was told, ever make a return pilgrimage, and I appeared to be the sole tourist in town – a ghost-like curiosity for the impressively diverse medley of Burmese, Chinese and Dravidian residents.

The town was missing only a synagogue to complement its blend of creeds. Among Christians, nearly every denomination is present, including a substantial Catholic population and, corrected as I was by one bystander, no fewer than *two* Anglican churches (or 'English Pagodas' as they are known). This mix of identity in the ports that form the flotsam of the British Empire is unfashionable, but where the success of their tolerance seems still to flourish it should be celebrated, especially in Myanmar, where nationalism and Buddhist fanaticism has been whipped up by those for whom it has its uses.

The general Western impression of Buddhism is of a peaceful religion with purity and harmony at the core of its belief system. The West's media flocked to report demonstrations against the military regime in 2007, the sentiment of the reporting being the admirable contrast between the casually sedate mentality of the priests and their willingness to confront the might of the army, otherwise known as the *Tatmadaw*. It made for moving news, which rightly caught headlines. A warning in 'Shooting an Elephant' made me think twice, however, and one incident in particular – only taking place over milliseconds – but forcing an irrevocable and irreversible change in my perception of the faith, reminded me of it: 'The young Buddhist priests were the worst of all. There were several thousand of them in the town and none of them seemed to have anything to do except stand on street corners and jeer at Europeans.'

At the Kyaikthanlan Paya, Kipling's 'old Moulmein Pagoda, lookin' lazy at the sea', I took off my shoes, paid the entrance donation and began to explore the site. A monk, in his eighties and grandfatherly, was sitting beneath an ornate bell. Hastening to ask if it were possible to photograph, he replied: 'Mannay?' I answered that I had paid my entrance fee, but he snapped back: 'No mannay? Get out!' Later, at Mandalay, I was surprised by the subservience shown to a leading monk at a monastery I visited, to whom I was instructed to praise at least five times on my hands and knees. He was halfway through an enormous, twelve-bowl breakfast at the time – a healthy multiple of the average

Burman's first meal of the day. Another practice, in which the faithful line the side of the road beside passing cars, resembles a collection in a church. It is a strange sight to see some distance from any pagoda, and inevitably captures persons of any faith or none at all. Money is usually thrown from the windows of cars and grasped quickly by the standing priests. All faiths survive on charity, but never have I seen a religion's fundraising efforts to be so pervasive, or coercive.

❧

A colonial police officer's spare time was invariably spent at the Club, taking part in whatever sports were available, and drinking. In *Burmese Days*, Flory refers to booze as 'the cement of the Empire' but these orthodoxies, as far as we know, Orwell rejected. Few recollections by contemporaries in Myanmar exist (and none of Orwell's diaries) but what has survived suggests someone who felt he did not fit in, declining participation in the enormous expatriate 'team' to pursue what I imagine to be a private frustration in a climate which was not accommodating to his fragile health. In my short time in the country, scarcely a moment passed when there wasn't something crawling over me: a luminous green caterpillar that seemed to have dropped from nowhere, a cufflink-sized red ant or, of course, one of many legions of mosquitos.

Besides the occasional football match or game of bridge, Orwell sought solitude in books and, in Katha, in drafting the first chapters of what would become *Burmese Days*. After contracting suspected dengue fever, he began biding time until his leave of absence in England was granted and he would be free from the 'stifling, stultifying world' in which he had found himself for five long years. Visiting Myanmar in the monsoon, I could understand how the climate cannot have helped the lingering problems in his lungs. Sweat cascaded from my own body, joining the moisture that clings to everything. Flory described the water infiltrating 'everything until neither one's bed, nor even one's food, seemed dry. It was still hot, with a stuffy, vaporous heat.'

Orwell's desperation in these frustratingly intimate British communities whose 'great social event was the six-weekly church service' was at the root of his revolt against the Raj and the lazy, rent-seeking enjoyment of the people who served it. Orwell's frustration at the values of his contemporaries is shown in *Burmese Days*: 'Time passed, and each year Flory found himself less at home in the world of the sahibs.* So he had learnt to live inwardly, secretly, in books.'

A later dialogue with the Lackersteens' niece also reveals Orwell's true bookishness: 'What it means to meet somebody who cares for books! I mean books worth reading, not that garbage in the Club libraries. I think reading is so wonderful. I mean, what would life be like without it? It's such a – such a – such a private Alsatia.'

During Moulmein's heyday, the Limouzins, Orwell's maternal ancestors, were a significant family. Among the earliest expatriates to settle and enter the timber trade, Frank Limouzin grew his business to become one of the town's pre-eminent. As with many colonial trading houses, the activities of the Limouzins spread far beyond the sourcing, processing and export of teak and mahogany. They started a shipbuilding and repairs yard, even a spirits distillery. Their profits from these activities were immense, with some invested in an overbearing family house, where Orwell's grandmother was still living when the young police officer arrived in Burma in 1922. They are still remembered in the town for their indulgent parties.

It should be beyond doubt that Orwell would have joined these rendezvous and I imagine him nonchalantly sulking in a corner, or better still, arriving as the introvert holding a book to sit and absorb. Their house stood at the top end of the street in Moulmein that still bears the

---

* A respectful term for a male in British India and contemporary India.

family name, tweaked in the post-independence period to 'Lim Maw Zin Street' aiding pronunciation by the Burmese tongue. On a slight incline and perpendicular to the waterfront, today it is a quiet residential street of closely packed four- or five-bedroom villas.

The Limouzins' house, destroyed in the Second World War, was almost twice the size of those that exist today, and enjoyed a much more extensive plot filled with an impressive, decadent garden. Today two houses stand where theirs was, at the junction with the main road that connects the north and south of the town. But surviving villas from the same era can be seen close by: Lyndhurst, and Hill View. At one such house, now a Buddhist monastery, I was invited to explore the grounds. It being necessary to remove my shoes as I entered the compound, I became acutely aware of evading the reach of the scorpions that seemed to be lying in wait for prey at either side of the path.

Perhaps the most unusual influence of the priests is their effective lobbying to bring around the serial destruction of the country's Christian burial grounds. The Buddhist doctrine of reincarnation is at odds with the Christian rite of burial, causing the leadership of the faith in Myanmar to campaign for the destruction of Christian cemeteries wherever they find them. As a consequence, most of Myanmar's graveyards have been destroyed, on the grounds that they harbour 'evil spirits'. A double tragedy, since the government's practice of often removing just the graves' headstones will be a cause of unease for anyone familiar with the film *Poltergeist*. Moulmein's historic Anglican graveyard is now built over with a police station. Since its obliteration, the graveyard's headstones have been moved twice.

At the time of the second movement, parishioners from the more historic of the two Anglican churches, St Matthew's, tried to retrieve as many headstones as they could. They now stand at the forlorn rear of the (literally) crumbling red sandstone church, which was visited, in common with my visit to the Pegu Club, in the midst of a violent thunderstorm. As I brushed soggy red dust and cobwebs off the gravestones, in a place that had the aura of a subterranean crypt, I was moved by inscriptions on the surviving, chipped fragments of gravestone that remain. I recalled the chill of the North Sea when comparing the final resting place of 'ROBERT WOODSPRY', lying there in forgotten Moulmein, with his hometown of Kingston-Upon-Hull.

One Limouzin headstone is entirely intact, belonging to the first wife of Orwell's grandfather, Eliza, and her two infant children. With lightning flashing through the grills of the shutters lining the walls, my only company the intermittent lapses of darkness between strikes, this was not a place I wanted to stay for long. I hastily jotted the inscription, and left as quickly as I could.

In memory of

ELIZA EMMA,
WIFE OF F. LIMOUZIN
WHO DIED ON THE 18TH JANUARY 1865
AGED 23 YEARS AND 4 MONTHS
AND OF THEIR CHILDREN
ARTHUR FRANK
AGED 2 YEARS AND 11 MONTHS

AND EMILY FALLON
AGED 1 YEAR AND 4 MONTHS

THEY LIE RESPECTIVELY BY THE SIDE
AND AT THE HEAD OF THEIR MOTHER

The legacy of colonialism is everywhere in Myanmar, peculiarly so, such that there are observations one makes that would not be apparent in other former British colonies. For instance, in no country I have visited has the local prison been considered as worthy for inclusion in an itinerary, let alone feature in the maps of every town in the guidebook (Alcatraz; the Tower of London; and the Bastille excepted, though they have long ceased to be operational). Yet in every Burmese town and city they seem to be centre-stage: sinister, barb-wired enclosed fortresses that are as full today as when they were built by the nascent colonial administration.

The *Tatmadaw*, Myanmar's ruling 'junta', have ruled the country since a coup in 1962. On occasion they have permitted forms of 'civilian government', but ultimately ensuring their pre-eminence in their control of the country. Myanmar's brief period of democracy just before, and after, independence was not a happy one. Aung San Suu Kyi's father, nationalist General Aung San, had sided with the Japanese after their invasion, but after seeing his countrymen treated with even more disdain than they had been by the British, switched allegiance back. Shortly before independence, scheduled for January 1948, acting prime minister General Aung San was shot dead during a cabinet meeting in Rangoon's Secretariat Building, now an enormous crumbling edifice at the heart of Myanmar's former capital.

The assassination, plotted by the pre-war prime minister of Burma, Galon U Saw, was a violent beginning indeed for a country on the precipice of its post-colonial future. Revered as 'father of the nation', his imagery is everywhere and is also a major source of his daughter's popularity. General Ne Win, dictator from the 1962 revolution until 1981, pursued what was known as 'The Burmese Way to Socialism' which, combined with idiosyncratic superstition (in 1987 he ordered that the country's banknotes be reprinted in denominations divisible by nine), caused untold damage to the country's standard of living.

Investors fled, export markets collapsed and in due course economic disruption was complemented by the persecution of anyone who had the nous to ask awkward questions. The universities, as usual, suffered most and would be closed, opened and re-closed on a whim in the decades to come. Paralysis continued after the 1988 reforms which enabled a civilian election but, despite being won by Aung San Suu Kyi's National League for Democracy, the junta's response was to place her under house arrest for almost all the period until a liberalisation, of sorts, began in 2010.

Although the joke runs that *Animal Farm* resembles the outcome of the 1962 revolution, and *Nineteen Eighty-Four* Myanmar under Ne Win, I think, as is often the case, these two books are used for purposes for which they are not appropriate. The case is perhaps stronger for *Animal Farm*, although my observation is that the *Tatmadaw* only installed themselves as the rentier class enjoying the fruits of Myanmar's wealth, as the British Raj did, and a pretty tyrannical monarchy had before it. As Flory notes in *Burmese Days*: 'There is a prevalent view that the men "at the outposts of Empire" are at least able and hard-working. It is a delusion. The real backbone of the despotism is not the officials but the army.'

A form of administration that relied so heavily on the armed forces will have gifted these men the influence and stature to do as they wished once Britain had conceded independence. The surviving British (now Indian Army) cantonments, a feature of every town in the subcontinent, and the post-independence trajectories of former British colonies everywhere, from Uganda to Fiji, is further evidence of this sad legacy. The comparison with *Nineteen Eighty-Four* is overstated: the regime in Myanmar is an unpleasant one, although in practice its techniques differ little from those adopted by the British colonial administration and the army was, of course, trained by the UK before independence.

Myanmar is also a primarily agrarian country where, outside the largest towns and cities, the state's powers of control are invariably limited. The mass rural population, diversified by an enormously rich ethnic fabric and preoccupied chiefly with feeding itself, is mostly oblivious to the sophisticated administration erected by the Raj, which remains in-situ. It was probably always thus. In general, the Burmese appeared to me as an optimistic, industrious peoples whose objective was to get on with their lives in the best way they could within the means available to them. Amusing phrases appeared here and there, a source of comedy for me and the Burmese I was with. Inscribed on the entrance to military buildings were:

'TATMADAW AND THE PEOPLE, CO-OPERATE
AND CRUSH ALL THOSE HARMING THE UNION'

'DEFENCE SERVICES ACADEMY:
THE TRIUMPHANT ELITE OF THE FUTURE'

The second can be found at the entrance to the Sandhurst-styled institution founded by the British outside Maymyo, an old hill station and a Raj-era cantonment. These phrases could quite conceivably be heard as instructions via a telescreen, the two-way TVs that are installed in every home in *Nineteen Eighty-Four*. But the junta strikes me as being desperate to emulate totalitarianism. As for the British before them, total control of a diverse and impoverished agrarian nation is an impossible endeavour. Big Brother could not survive long without technology, a privilege of an industrialised society. Without a country absorbing the cost of investing in it, the outcome is a population on low incomes left standing as the rest of the world progresses.

My journey to Katha by road from Mandalay was unconventional. It began in a minibus providing 'shared taxi' services between the two towns, rammed with items ranging from sacks of flour to crates of toys, filling the space from floor to ceiling. The roads in Myanmar are excellent and include a sophisticated system of tolls with booths and automatic barriers that would not look out of place on a French motor-way. The terrain was flat to begin with but steadily became more varied, resembling the gently rolling hills of the border between Germany and France: Alsace-Lorraine but without the neatly pruned contours of its vineyards. Occasionally a more massive ridge would appear in the distance, grander in scale than anything surrounding it.

The landscape started to become drier, more like African savan-nah, while along the way the minibus stopped at the small farming communities which line the road. At a pick-up one of the few other younger members of our group, a student studying in Mandalay, left. Standing at the edge of the road ready to take his seat were an elderly couple. There being just one spare seat – barely that for all the sacks of rice – someone would need to go on top of the minibus, and the driver intoned a passenger would need to volunteer. With the mindset of a Briton intent on minimising fuss, I motioned to the expectant face of the driver that I would make the sacrifice.

I had travelled on the top of a train before, during a journey on the now-defunct line connecting Khartoum in Sudan with the border with Egypt in the far north of the country. I might suggest riding atop the train feels safer since the movements of a train are so much more predictable. However, after some time on the roof of the minibus, my body adjusted to the new rhythm and it was no longer necessary to grip the bars of the roof rack, as I had after I'd first hauled myself atop. Ten minutes later, the minibus came to an abrupt halt, two passengers unwrapped and handed up to me a folded polythene sheet, ostensibly for use as a cushion. I imagined in my head the chatter that must have preceded this act of benevolence: *We must ensure the foreigner is comfortable. Has anyone got some polythene sheeting?*

The views were, of course, much better as hour followed hour. A cloud-topped Kilimanjaro-style mountain, in whose direction we appeared to be travelling, only became more distant. The sight of me on the top seemed to bemuse locals lining the road, their heads turning, like the neck of a swan, to reveal a perplexed expression and in quick succession, a broad smile. Later we entered maize country and came across buffalos and their wagon-wheel carts, almost resembling the midwest frontier country of North America. By dusk we had penetrated into dense jungle, accompanied by the audio provided by its orchestra of insects.

In Katha I had the good fortune to become acquainted with Nyo Ko Naing, a local historian and campaigner. He demonstrates the alacrity of a child anticipating Christmas the moment the words 'George Orwell' are uttered, his thoughts about the author so rapid he must interrupt his speaking intermittently to draw breath.

Ko Naing first heard of Orwell when working the boats that drift on the long stretch of the Irrawaddy that lies between Katha and Mandalay. In 1998 an Irish man, referred to only as 'Patrick', told him of Orwell's time at Katha. This led to his exploration of the works and especially their pertinence in nurturing Myanmar's eventual freedom from British colonial administration. Like my own, Ko Naing's admiration for Orwell only grew the more he read, and I knew within moments of meeting him that the two of us would have a lasting friendship.

Impressively for a small provincial town, Ko Naing helped to establish, and is secretary of, the recently formed Katha Heritage Trust. It has already made tremendous progress by encouraging local authorities to defend the town's heritage, and especially the links to Orwell. In one of his many bouts of passion he told me 'We have to defend it. It all began here.' Sure enough, the first sheets of the handwritten draft of

Burmese Days were penned on Government of India-headed notepaper. Almost every location referred to in the novel still exists, the exception being the cemetery (destroyed on the instruction of the local Buddhist establishment) and the house belonging to Lackersteen, the manager of one of the major timber firms based in the town. The demolished mansion has been replaced by the 21 houses that now stand on its once extravagant plot.

Each prop Orwell used – the Club; the District Commissioner's House; the Maidan – survives such that, in the way of an amateur dramatic society in England, *Burmese Days* could be rehearsed and exhibited safari-style. Indeed, if Ko Naing's literary ambitions for the town are fulfilled, I suspect his zealous drive will mean it is. Until recently, a house used by a superintendent in the Indian Civil Service was mistaken for Orwell's, but research by Ko Naing, validated during an afternoon the two of us spent pouring over land registry maps, has since revealed that Orwell's house was actually next to the Anglican Church.

Approaching his house, I almost expected to find Orwell on the veranda. It is as if he might never have left – a 1920s-style jeep emblazoned 'POLICE', smothered in dust and the dead leaves of the overgrown tropical garden that engulfs the two-storeyed teak structure, being parked on the drive. Most of the Raj-era houses are home to the Burmese successors, in positions handed down by the sahibs of yesteryear, a European community in Katha that never exceeded 30.

Of the largest houses, the deputy district commissioner's is the most impressive. Still owned by the General Administration Service, part of the government of Myanmar's Home Department, it is cared for by the Heritage Trust; in time, they hope it will become a museum. A photograph that greets every visitor who arrives in the entrance hall shows a young, moustached Orwell, sitting as the sole expatriate in Katha's police force of seventeen. But the house was home to the most senior Briton in the town, not Orwell, and one holder of the post is remembered affectionately by residents. Bernard Houghton, who served 1892–1900, was a refreshingly liberal colonial administrator and published many articles and books questioning the imperial project. Orwell would never have met him but would have heard of the man and the unorthodox views he espoused. It is a source of possible influence on Orwell's writing that I have not seen recognised before.

The club, set back along a dusty lane now home to stray dogs, is straddled by a single, hard-surfaced tennis court. While the tennis still flourishes ('Katha Tennis Club: Established 1924'), the club ceased its activities in 1973. It has since been home to a trade association-cum-co-operative, which only half-occupies the forlorn, single-storey fronted building resembling a cricket pavilion. The grounds are scrubby, the borders with their 'swathes of English flowers – phlox and larkspur, hollyhock and petunia ... rioted in vast size and richness' replaced by several burgeoning warehouses, containing for the most part sacks of rice. Inside the building, still 'teak-walled' and 'smelling of earth-oil', the Club's old furniture is stacked to ceiling height and the old bar is boarded.

Virtually everything (including, it seemed, the cooperative's elderly staff) is covered in jungle-dust. The downstairs, hidden from the front since the club was built hanging to the side of the riverbank, is approached down a grandly carved staircase. At the base of the pad-locked grille that now forms the entrance to the former billiards room, an enormous spider the size of my hand, but slighter, was sitting comfort-ably in its web. It was consuming what must have been its lunch with the aid of two grey, furry paws. The spider's solitude seemed at odds with the mayhem Orwell describes engulfing the building in *Burmese Days*, the shrieks of Mrs Lackersteen accompanied by the shattering of glass as a riot against the British unfolded.

I did seek confirmation as to whether these events were based on any real history. The riot in the novel was a fictional creation, and there is nothing on record to suggest it ever happened. The stereotypical Anglo-Indian club was not imagined, though. Ellis, another character in the novel, is painted as the very definition of 'those Englishmen, common – unfortunately – who should never be allowed to set foot in the east'. Verrall, a newly arrived member of the British community seconded from the Indian Army to Burma is accosted by the 'grey, furious' Ellis after Verrall had hit the butler of the club after some easily forgivable misdemeanour. Ellis states: 'What's it got to do with you if he needed a good kicking? You're not even a member of this Club. It's our job to kick the servants not yours.'

꒱

I was determined to leave Katha by boat, as Orwell would have, reflecting that the flow of the Irrawaddy through the expanse of Myanmar and into the Indian Ocean was a metaphor for the police officer's exit from empire. The river at full flow in Upper Myanmar is more like some vast lake. The water has a green-blue hue, something like the light green in army camouflage. At 4am it was as still as a mill pond. As I made an early start for the boat down the river, I woke to find the waterfront – usually bustling – eerily quiet. A single light on the far side, close to a mile away, dominated the scene, as if the North Star had been plucked from the sky and attached to a moored fishing boat.

Passengers boarded with their possessions one by one, wearily negotiating the pirate-ship-style wooden plank that bridged the gap between the bank of the river and the long, narrow raft that would somehow navigate the currents south. Capsizing is common, and the transient sandbanks of the Irrawaddy are notoriously treacherous. Like the minibus that took me to Katha, the boat called at villages along the route, people and goods leaving and joining. The camaraderie of the river is joyous to watch, the boat being a lifeline reminding the communities it serves that the world continues outside them.

At one village a gaunt, stick-insect like woman walked onto the boat, assisted by a younger woman. The gaunt woman's face expressed the agony of the dying, her right arm clasping feebly a saline drip that hung precariously at her side. Having fallen asleep shortly after, the uninterrupted jungle passing on both sides and the monstrous flow of the river unimpeded, I woke when I received a prod from the passenger lying beside me. Her index finger pointed in the direction where the lady with the drip had been slumped. The dead patient lay wrapped in crisp white linen; now just another piece of cargo accompanying us on the sweltering passage south, to the endless chug of the boat's weary engine.

Southwold, Suffolk, England

Church and State
(1927; 1929–32)

S outhwold is a small port clinging to the extremity of the East Anglian coastline. Orwell had, it seems, great affection for Southwold's seaside position. At the end of the summer term in 1933 he wrote to Eleanor Jaques, one of several women he was pursuing in the town: 'perhaps we can go and picnic again as we did last year. I am so pining for the sea again; ... it would be so nice if we could go and bathe and make our tea like we used to do ... along the Walberswick shore.' Much like land-locked Henley-on-Thames – Orwell's other hometown – Southwold is an affluent place, a concentration of wealth and privilege which is not common around the UK. It is a reflection on his social background that it is Henley and Southwold – rather than, say, Paisley or Doncaster – that he knew as home.

A *Clergyman's Daughter*, Orwell's second novel, was published in 1935. It explores the conflicts of the soul in a woman in her twenties as she juggles the responsibilities of running the rectory in a small East Anglian market town, Knype Hill (a proxy for Southwold). She questions her faith, with the novel transcending her 'down and out' experiences of hop-picking in Kent, 'tramping'* in Trafalgar Square and teaching in suburban London before the resumption of life at the rectory under her irritable father. It is easy to identify the hop-picking, 'tramping' and teaching as resembling Orwell's activities in his late twenties and early thirties, described elsewhere in his travelogue *Down and Out in Paris and London*.

There are strong grounds for presenting *A Clergyman's Daughter* as not only being loosely autobiographical, but also the story he wished to tell of his journey from a very conservative background to a radical, agnostic philosophy. Many writers, among them Graham Greene (*The Power and The Glory*) and Thomas Hardy (*Under the Greenwood Tree*), explore faith and life in the church, Catholic or otherwise. *A Clergyman's Daughter* is Orwell's contribution to the fictional canon of church life, focussing primarily on the Anglican Church which, being protestant and reformed, lacks the colour of its Catholic mother. It is the national state church of England, with around 1 million members.

Orwell looked back on *A Clergyman's Daughter* with regret, a book he thought not worthy of a second printing (his later *Keep the Aspidistra Flying* also joined this list). While it is not comparable with his best writing, it is hard not to read it without feeling great sympathy towards Dorothy as her sad life and its tragic circumstances move from slighted hope to absolute despair. As a book that centres on this single character, it is undoubtedly a success, above and beyond any deeper resonance as a semi-autobiographical work and its perceptive insight into homelessness. She lives with her father and a housekeeper in a rambling Suffolk rectory. Her father is the youngest son of a 'Lower Upper Middle Class' family, following the tradition of the youngest son entering the church.

---

* Possibly having wider colloquial usage in the 1920s, a word used often by Orwell for his activities among the destitute for his *Down and Out in Paris and London*.

With few assets and on an ecclesiastical income, her father often refers to his time at public school or Oxford, and the grander aspects of wealthy living he is no longer able to afford. Her mother dead, Dorothy assumes the role as matriarch of the Anglican Church in Knype Hill, running everything from errands for needy parishioners to the Mothers' Union, the Church of England's fellowship for motherhood.

Dorothy's father, remote and disdainful of daily parish life, expects her to run not just the parish but also the Rectory as their home on his behalf. The parsimonious vicar is infamous among all the town's traders for being in debt to his creditors, with whom Dorothy spends her days pleading to extract just enough supplies to keep her life, and his, functioning. Single and accepting a life of spinsterhood, she dutifully fulfils her role before an alleged elopement with an older man, a trader in the town, following a possible loss of memory. The loss of memory is never explained between sections of the book; she is left stitching a costume for a forthcoming play she is organising for the school, before re-appearing scantily dressed on a London street, oblivious to any part of her former life.

As a novel, its message is of a woman accustomed to comfort, being the daughter of a rector, thrown into a world of tramping, rags and subjection to those who do not love or respect her, among the hop fields of Kent and London's underworld. Written during the Great Depression, it is just as fascinating a report of poverty in 1930s Britain as *The Road to Wigan Pier*. Four aspects of the book provide lasting insight for the reader: the culture of Church life and a rural English parish; the hardship of Dorothy and the friends she acquires in worlds so different from her own; a pointed critique of England's small private schools; and the loss of faith.

Dorothy's existence in Knype Hill, so English in the traditions of a spinster in service to her church, is mocking of the parochial world Orwell designed for the novel. It is known he had mixed feelings for

Southwold, at once mesmerised by its timelessness and loathsome of its narrow-mindedness. This is evident at various points of Dorothy's journey, especially once her father agrees to her return to the rectory and her re-establishment in Knype Hill, a town of '2,000 inhabitants, where everybody knows everybody else's private histories and talks about them all day long', and where residents have 'only a very dim conception of anything that happens more than ten miles from their own front door'.

Those who have lived in a village will see the reflection of their own experience, where news travels and changes faster than the weather. Knype Hill's insatiable gossip, Mrs Semprill, goes out of her way to create a scandal where there is none. She inflates Dorothy's disappearance to an affair with Mr Warburton, an older man with grown-up children, which leads to the scandal spreading across the gossip columns of the national press.

⌐

Orwell returned from Burma to his parents in Southwold, later using it as his base as he travelled to and from London, Kent and Paris. The quaint rectories and village greens must have seemed distant from the realities of poverty he witnessed at home and abroad. This poverty he sought to report – either the economic costs of British imperialism or the damage to fairer living standards caused by what he once described as England's 'shadowy caste system' – was far removed from Southwold, a town popular with retirees from the Raj and containing a decent number of native plutocrats. The settings chosen – the village green with its 'little general shop with some newspaper posters outside'; the 'commons and ... buried villages with incredible names ... lanes that led nowhere ... and dry ditches smelling of fennel and tansies' demonstrate, like much of his writing, his love of England.

Orwell's longevity as a writer, testimony to the quality of his analysis and powers of observation, seems to appear in the occasional sentence, which, much like the works of Dickens, summarise the human condition and its emotions so perfectly. They remain applicable to life irrespective of the age in which they are read. One note by the narrator relating to Dorothy's trawl among the homeless of central London explains her arrival 'by the same process of gravitation that draws all roofless people to the same spot, at Trafalgar Square'.

Anyone who has visited or worked for any length of time in the vicinity of Charing Cross should acknowledge the poverty of its only permanent inhabitants: the 'roofless' who sleep in the vast open-air homeless camp provided by the doorways of Coutts & Co. or South Africa House. Orwell's descriptions of poverty are transformed into eerily impressive contrasts with Dorothy's former life by a de-frocked clergyman, now as homeless as she, who transforms the liturgy into haunting proclamations that fold Dorothy and her companions into their makeshift beds: 'Our destiny is the pauper's grave, twenty-five deep in deal coffins, the kip-house in the ground. It is very meet, right and our bounden duty at all times and in all places to curse (him) and revile (him). Therefore with Demons and Archdemons (and all the company of hell, etc.).'

The apparent hypocrisy of organised religion appears to Dorothy alongside her painful and hunger-filled days picking hops in Kent, insights borrowed directly from Orwell's own experience in the hop fields between August and October 1931. Here an eclectic group of down-and-outs join gypsies and East Enders, who made a summer pilgrimage to the hop-fields on pitiful wages where their hands would bleed until flesh-raw. 'Misery Farm', where Dorothy concludes her hop-picking before returning to London, was the apt name for the farm on which she worked. Although Dorothy becomes genuinely friendly with some of the pickers, her interactions are awkward and stilted: reflecting perhaps the difficulty Orwell had in mixing with persons removed from the social security of Eton or Southwold. Their plight during the Great Depression is indicative of social conditions widespread in Britain before the evolution of an expanded welfare state after 1945.

Inspired perhaps by Mr Gradgrind's uninspiring teaching of 'facts facts facts' in the school of Dickens' *Hard Times*, or the pathetic education provided by Dotheboys Hall in *Nicholas Nickleby*, Orwell rescues Dorothy from hop-picking to a small private school in a London suburb. Modelled on the parts of Middlesex where Orwell taught at two different boys' schools, Dorothy's wealthy uncle (a branch of the clergyman's family where there was some money remaining) found her a job in a school there to minimise the scandal of her disappearance.

'Ringwood House Academy' is based in the fictional suburb of Southbridge. Its headmistress, Mrs Creevy, is a widow and headmistress of the school which has only one class and employs Dorothy despite her not having any teaching experience. Mrs Creevy has no time at all for children or providing a rounded education. She queries whether Dorothy happens to have a degree or master's, which would make her name 'look so much better on the prospectus', the fees and means to attract new pupils her sole interest.

When Dorothy, excited by the opportunity to inspire young minds, begins to innovate, Mrs Creevy becomes irritated, and insufferable when the primarily low-church or non-conformist parents complain at the prospect of their daughters learning of the 'man who was not of woman born' in Shakespeare's *Macbeth*. She explains to Dorothy: 'Handwriting. That is something [parents] can see the sense of ... plenty of neat copies that the girls can take home and that the parents will show off to the neighbours and give us a bit of free advert.'

The narrator is damning in descriptions of the school, Orwell happy to condemn the 'vast numbers of ... second-rate, third-rate, and fourth-rate [private schools that] exist by the dozen and the score in every

London suburb and every provincial town ... started in exactly the same spirit as one would start a brothel or a bucket shop.' Snobbish perhaps, and not the first time Orwell was accused of snobbishness by his critics, but the truth as he saw it.

Orwell, who was an occasional communicant in the Church of England, came from just the sort of family where the youngest son would enter the Church. He also insisted on being buried in an Anglican churchyard by its traditional rites in his will, carried out to his wishes after his death. His belief in God, or formal religion, I suspect was placed into some form of abeyance during his transformative experiences in London, Paris, the north of England and Spain. But it would be a mistake to consider that his churchgoing by force of habit (as Dorothy's becomes following her return to Knype Hill) was disingenuous. Possibly ending his life an agnostic, I suspect that he would have avoided concluding that there is no God, or that all of the mystery and elaborate procedure of the formal churches is a vast waste of time and effort, best put to other uses. It is hard to fully grasp the measure of such a mercurial personality as that of George Orwell.

The most interesting observation when it comes to Orwell's faith I have found originates from the philosopher Roger Scruton, who explained that for Orwell the Church of England was not '"church", but "England" ... a sanctification of the land, its boundaries, its language, and its law'. For Dorothy the two appear inseparable; her way of life is devotion to her church and the section of English society that forms this community.

Dorothy's reasoning for returning to her old way of life after the loss of faith echoes Orwell's philosophy as a church-goer:

> It is a mysterious thing, the loss of faith – as mysterious as faith itself ... But however little the church services might mean to her, she did not regret the hours she spent in church ... in all

that happens in church there is something, hard to define, but something of decency, of spiritual comeliness. It seemed to her that even though you no longer believe, it is better to go to church than not; better to follow in the ancient ways, than to drift into rootless freedom.

∽

The Blairs had moved from Berkshire to Southwold in 1921, soon after Orwell had left Eton and was shortly to embark on his career in the Indian Police. It is an isolated town, without the easy accessibility to London enjoyed by Henley or Shiplake. For those returning from the Raj, certain market towns became fashionable places for retirement, retaining vestiges of the grandeur of their residents' lives in British India, with large houses, gardens and attractive vistas. Tunbridge Wells in Kent, Great Malvern in Worcestershire, and Surrey were popular; seaside towns too. Suffolk, Aldeburgh or Southwold provided natural continuity for those wealthy Londoners with second homes and family links there – a feature of these places still today, with the former's nickname being Chelsea-on-Sea.

Orwell spent little time in Southwold during his parents' first years there, being permanently based in Burma 1922–26. No letters nor diaries survive from this period, so it is not clear what reports were sent from Southwold or Burma. However, during a family holiday in Cornwall upon his return from the East, he concluded he would not be returning to colonial service; initial curiosity evolved to blithe tolerance and then unabashed hatred of the system he had served and then turned on.

Orwell's distaste for the Raj extended to the many former sahibs and memsahibs* of Southwold, who replicated their snobbery back home.

---

* Respectable term for a female, used during the Raj and in contemporary India.

Biographers conclude he had little time for the inhabitants or the way of life in the town, but its scenery and sheer undisguised Englishness, which continues to be a feature almost 100 years later, became irresistible for his psyche. He not only chose to live there, on and off for five years, but visited frequently too: 'The high street forked, forming a tiny marketplace with a pump, now defunct, and a worm-eaten pair of stocks. On either side of the pump stood the Dog and Bottle, the principal inn of the town, and the Knype Hill Conservative Club.'

The high street still forks, and the marketplace with its tea rooms and Conservative Club (actually, the 'Southwold and Reydon Constitutional Club') are as alive today as they ever were. Southwold remains a bustling and conservative market town, although one with decidedly fewer retirees from the Indian Civil Service.

But numerous figures in the high street still resemble 'Sir Humphreys', the name for an eponymous British public servant, one could imagine wandering around Writers' Building in Calcutta, or a government department in Nairobi or Whitehall. One such figure, a retired civil servant named Anthony, was exceptionally interested in George as I passed him on the high street and showed fussiness, in the way only an older retiree can, when explaining which tearoom would be best for refreshment. 'I know where to avoid. There's always Suzy's of course,' he said, dressed in a Panama hat and the sort of thin, merino wool jumper grandparents wear. It was the *'of course'* that I liked most, the emphasis that Suzy's would be instantly familiar to anyone, resident or visitor, since it was so much a part of the town's fabric. The fabric that would be familiar to a visitor to any affluent provincial market town, the usual delicatessens and smart pubs.

Denny's, Orwell's tailors, remains in business in the same building it has occupied on the market square since 1851. It no longer tailors – this ended in the 1980s – but it is still a family-owned business selling clothing, and the present owner is the daughter of the last generation of the family to have made clothing in the 'proper way'. Orwell visited the store to have his clothing made for Burma just before he made his passage East of Suez, and he had attended a local crammer (a school called Craighurst, long closed) to prepare for the exams he needed to pass for entry to the Indian Police. His measurements are still recorded in the tailors' books. Today, Panama hats, or hats of any type one could imagine, seem to sell well at Denny's; as do brightly coloured shorts or chinos in the usual pinks, reds and sky blues.

Older oak or teak furniture is scattered throughout the shop – a grandfather clock; a chair upholstered with William Morris fabric. I was determined to leave Denny's with something. I'm too young to wear a Panama hat, and neither a belt nor wallet was required. I started flicking through the ties (a man can never have enough ties!) and past the generic green and white or blue and silver stripes I found one with a curious figure, repeated across the silk and appearing like the medieval figurines that might feature on a coin or the crest of an old school. I asked a shop assistant who the figure was, and they answered: 'Oh that's Jack of Southwold. Haven't you heard of him? There'll be a pamphlet about him in the Town Museum if you make it there before it closes.' I smirked on the presumptive 'Haven't you ...?'

I found Denny's manufacture of a Jack of Southwold tie odd, but of course, it couldn't have better fulfilled my ambition to purchase a curio. I set off to find out more about this figure, a character of the sort that many other towns and villages in Britain find they commemorate, but aren't entirely sure why. Predictably, on further investigation, conflicting stories emerge, and the origins of Jack of Southwold (now also an emblem of Adnams brewery) are confused.

Named Jack the Smiter officially, his statue stands in the Church of St Edmund, four-feet-four-inches tall, with armour resembling a soldier from the Wars of the Roses. Made from wood and as old as the church, his purpose is to strike his bell to inform the congregation to rise for the entry of clergy. One legend claims he was a local boy who went to fight for the House of York in the civil war of the late 1400s, between the royal houses of York and Lancaster; another that he was sent to the town to protect it; and, for those possibly tired of the bell's tinging, that he was part of a force attacking the town. Whichever, if any, tale is right he is a survivor of both the reformation and puritan damage during the Cromwellian period; one of few wooden statuettes in an English church to survive into the 21st century.

The church and a search for the rectory absorbed much of my time in Southwold since both were bound so intimately with *A Clergyman's Daughter*. Orwell worshipped at St Edmund's and wove architectural details into his description of the fictional St Athelstan's. Maybe this is a strange choice of patronal saint, since there has never been a Saint Athelstan and no church in England is dedicated to anyone of this name. But King Æthelstan was an Anglo-Saxon king (AD 924–939) and the first to have united England under one crown after defeating the last Viking kingdom at York.

The man who created the territorial definition of England was possibly worthy, in Orwell's eyes, of sainthood; the Church's name also serving as a mechanism to educate readers that Æthelstan is a monarch deserving of greater recognition than history has given him. Orwell loved such subtleties: they appear throughout his writing, from the flotsam of the lost world found in the junk shop in *Nineteen Eighty-Four*, to his use of the aspidistra to epitomise the suburban middle class.

᠍᠊᠍᠊

'The church was very cold, with a scent of candle-wax and ancient dust. It was a large church, much too large for its congregation, and ruinous and more than half empty ... [with] the roof over the chancel sagging visibly ... upwards, to the headless roof-angels on whose necks you could still see the saw-cuts of the Puritan soldiers.'

With delicious irony St Edmund's church was wrapped in scaffolding during my visit, 'Save our Roof/Nave/Tower' campaigns being a hardy perennial for church congregations across England. The structure must have been in an even worse state of repair during Orwell's visits in the 1920s and 1930s since his time in Southwold preceded a major renovation of the roof in the 1940s. Still, Dorothy's fears of the costs of restoration remain relevant for the clergy and congregations of many present-day churches.

I searched for the damaged angels referred to in the novel, being reliably informed by the present rector, the Reverend Simon Pitcher, that during the last Civil War Cromwell's henchman Lord Dowsing butchered the wooden angels that lined the nave by destroying their heads, hands and wings – the 'saw cuts' that the narrator in A Clergyman's Daughter refers to. The bodies of the angels could not be removed since they were built into the structure of the roof but, in any event, the angels' limbs were restored during works to the roof in the Victorian period.

Assuming that the present-day rectory was the same as in Orwell's time, I searched around the streets close to the church. The churchyard, virtually absent of trees, is large and surrounded for the most part by Edwardian terraces. Nothing came close to resembling the imposing building, with its drive and conservatory, I had expected to find. I asked one passing pedestrian who pointed me in the right direction, actually to the other end of town, on the ridge that looks down over the valley, towards the nearby coastal village of Walberswick.

Southwold's present rectory (I later learnt from the rector that its location had shifted several times since the 1920s) is a detached, late-Edwardian house, almost hidden from the road at the end of a short drive. In fact, it resembled what I've always imagined the suburban home in Keep the Aspidistra Flying might look like. I'm sure I could even see an aspidistra plant on one of its window ledges. The rectory's sweeping drive encircles a prim front lawn and is approached via the crunch of gravel. At the porch, a pair of heavy, black, beetle-crusher-type shoes, the sort that clergy England-wide seems to wear, like an army's standard issue, lay in a corner before a huge, stained-oak and cast-iron braced front door.

The rector's study resembled the office of a person who doesn't have time to file paper: pile on pile of theological books and papers scattered over filing cabinets; occasional chairs; a large table; and several old but what look like incredibly comfortable armchairs; the sort that every rectory in England seems to have, covered in 'tea dress' style fabrics. A parish priest in a small community serves as much as a helpful counsellor for parishioners as for their usual ecclesiastical duties of, say, two or three fixed services during a working week and multiple communion services or 'evensong' on Sunday. The 'fixed' demand on the rector's time might be managed quite easily, since a small village church may have only one Sunday service a month. But the expectations of counselling and support to those sick or in need of moral support (who may not necessarily be Christian, let alone Anglican) means the time pressures on a rector are substantial.

Providing a run-through of his duties, the rector later explained to me how the house came into the ownership of the church, having moved several times since the 1920s from a large Georgian property on the high street. The present house was gifted to the church by the three spinsters who had built it and lived there. I thought this of interest, given Dorothy's spinsterhood. I re-imagined the John Major-invoked 'old maids cycling to Holy Communion through the morning mist' – a phrase the prime minister pilfered from Orwell's essay 'England Your England' and which seems to have passed into history as his own.

⌣

The Blairs lived in three different properties in Southwold. Their first home was on Stradbroke Road, an Edwardian terraced house overlooked by the town's pretty, white lighthouse. This was followed by a larger Georgian house on Queen Street (close to the market square, and surrounded by shops) and, finally, to another Georgian terraced house, albeit a less imposing one, at 36 High Street. Having asked at the small Tourist Information Centre how to find the Blairs' home, I did query whether many people came to Southwold for its Orwell connection. I was told that the traffic is steady, but like many of the places on the Orwell trail, Southwold has not done its best to advertise its most famous former resident.

The information bureau told me there was once an 'Orwell Bookshop', but it closed in 2011. The only bookshop in the town, Southwold Books, is part of a national chain and housed a fairly pathetic shelf of new-but-slightly-foxed Orwell novels at a height no greater than the head of a young toddler. The person behind the till feigned interest when I said how proud the town must be to have been home to such a famous author.

Other shops seem to prosper. The trend for 'vintage' has very much taken off in the town's marketplace. 'Squires of Southwold' was selling sweets the old-fashioned way, in tall glass jars alongside Romney's Kendal Mint Cake, Fizz Wiz and Candy Sticks. One vintage shop, selling old rope at extortionate prices and other flotsam bought for a song at the house clearance of a late memsahib or two, had three Penguin book cover postcards on display with the titles *Siamese White* by Maurice Collis, *Good Potato Dishes* by Ambrose Heath and *Murder Incorporated* (a comic subtitled 'Crime Never Pays').

Each, I am sure not the least bit deliberately, paralleled Orwell's adventures in Burma (*Siamese White* being an account of Collis's experience as a civil servant in Rangoon in the 1920s), and the other two postcards his essays 'In Defence of English Cooking'; and 'Boys Weeklies'.

One of the first things I remarked, entering the town from the fields to the south after crossing by the 'passenger ferry' (a rowing boat: fare £1.00) were the names of the houses. Each one was indiscreetly labelled like garish offers in a supermarket, with signs made from driftwood or some other homely material.

Reminded of the town's Anglo-Indian heritage, I expected to find names such as 'Simla' or 'Rawalpindi', but despite a reasonably thorough search (the temptation to keep going was tremendous), I could not find a single house name showing any connection with India. The best I could manage was 'Adelaide', another retirement town monopolised by the Raj in South Australia. But clear themes emerged; an analysis would be an enjoyable endeavour for the idle statistician. Curiously there is a very strong emphasis on Scottish place names: 'Staffa Cottage'; 'Caithness House'; 'Iona Cottage'. The very strong prevalence of Scots in the Indian Civil Service and (British) Indian Army may account for this; retirees from India naming their retirement homes with memories of their childhood. It would be interesting to see whether other seaside retirement towns have a similar tendency to evoke the Highlands or Hebrides.

The Blairs' last residence in Southwold, Montague House (36 High Street) sits among a much more conventional run of English house names, such as Rose Cottage and The Old Post Office. It is a two-storeyed Georgian townhouse, now split into two holiday lets and hosting a stone plaque inscribed:

The author

GEORGE ORWELL
(Eric Blair)
1903–1950
Resided in this house.

Living in Southwold only periodically, much of his time there was spent recovering from hop-picking or tramping and relaxing during the school holidays. The best description of the house I can find, in a letter from his recently married wife Eileen to her friend Norah Myles (a contemporary from her time at St Hugh's College, Oxford) is of a home, 'very small and furnished almost entirely with paintings of ancestors', a down-at-heel and once affluent family, 'on the shivering verge of gentility. In spite of all this the family on the whole is fun & I imagine unusual in their attitude to me because they all adore Eric & consider him quite impossible to live with.'

Presumably as another form of escapism, Orwell enjoyed fishing on Southwold's pier. Constructed during the heyday of English seaside piers in 1900, it has suffered from a succession of violent storms, deliberate sabotage by British forces arising from the fear of a German invasion and then bomb damage during the Second World War. For a flat landscape and sedate population, the tide is uncharacteristically aggressive. The water is a luminous green and opaque, much more like a giant river than a sea, and the waves lash the beaches even on days of calm weather. To celebrate the 100th anniversary of the pier, it was completely refurbished with funding coming from the purchase of dedicated brass plaques. Screwed to the promenade's railings, these are an eclectic mix of personal dedications and amusing idioms:

Heaven is a pier on earth

Peerless not pierless

My favourite was 'Living here in your mind', since recalling the pier's benign decking and blustery air under the broad East Anglian sun is as good a way as any of ignoring the maelstrom of life and London.

The pier is one place in Southwold that does give proper acknowledgement to Orwell's time there. Not visible from the road, on the rear wall of the head of the pier, the famous image of Orwell sitting behind his BBC microphone is painted within an enormous, two-storey-high graphic. Created by the artist and contemporary of Banksy, 'Pure Evil' (real name Charles Uzzell-Edwards) it will be in-situ for the foreseeable future. Some of the author's most memorable phrases loom down over visitors – *All animals are equal but some are more equal than others* – reminding them of the precarious footing on which their liberty rests.

The town's museum, a small red-brick building with a Dutch-style parapet close to the church, is only open for two hours a day – between 2 and 4pm. I've seen branches of banks with better opening hours, which is saying something; but, being run voluntarily, it does an excellent job of telling the story of the town on probably a very restricted budget. A photo of Walberswick Church displayed there jogged my memory of the lonely spot in that church's graveyard, where in the summer of 1931 Orwell believed he saw a ghost.

To discover that Orwell wrote convincingly that he once saw the apparition of 'a man's figure, small & stooping, & dressed in lightish brown; I should have said a workman', passing in the corner of his eye in the desolation of a Suffolk churchyard, comes as a surprise. But this is what he described in a letter to a friend in August 1931. Walberswick, a village to the south, back across the River Blyth, is as busy as Southwold with its daily invasion of visitors, but its church, at one time evidently subject to substantial damage and subsequent repair, remains seldom frequented. This is curious since it is so close to the road, the same road that Orwell walked to, after:

[Following] it out into the churchyard, [where] there was no-one in the churchyard, & no-one within possible distance along the road ... & in any case there were only 2 figures in the road, and neither of them at all resembled the figure. I looked into the church. The only people there were the vicar, dressed in black,

& a workman who, as far as I remember, had been sawing the
whole time. In any case he was too tall for the figure. The figure
had therefore vanished.

Lucian Freud, the artist who became close friends with Orwell towards
the end of his life, was startled by the writer's rationality, seemingly at
odds with the concept of him claiming to have seen a ghost: 'I used
to meet him in Café Royal, and though some of his opinions seemed
extreme, what I liked about him was that he always had reasons for
them. But what an extremely unaesthetic person. When you said that
such was a beautiful work of art he seemed quite put out. He would
say: 'What do you mean? Prove it!'

∽

The dunes of Walberswick, vast and once wild but now tamed by lines
of garishly coloured beach huts, were often visited by Orwell for crab-
bing – a pastime that continues to flourish – and long walks with female
friends he was intent, usually unsuccessfully, on courting. George, bored
by several long days traipsing around town, delighted in riding the rough
waves that crash on its pebble beaches, and bounding over a succession
of sand-swept ridges, held together precariously by the invasive roots of
Marram Grass (*Ammophila*), that provide the perfect playground for
a springer spaniel.

I wondered whether it was here, in between the journeys to London
and Paris, that this great man reached the same conclusions as Dorothy,
the clergyman's daughter from a small Suffolk town, following her return
to the safety of an English rectory:

Those things don't really matter. I mean, things like having
no money and not having enough to eat. Even when you're

practically starving – it doesn't change anything inside you ... mere outward things like poverty and drudgery, and even loneliness, don't matter in themselves. It is the things that happen in your heart that matter.

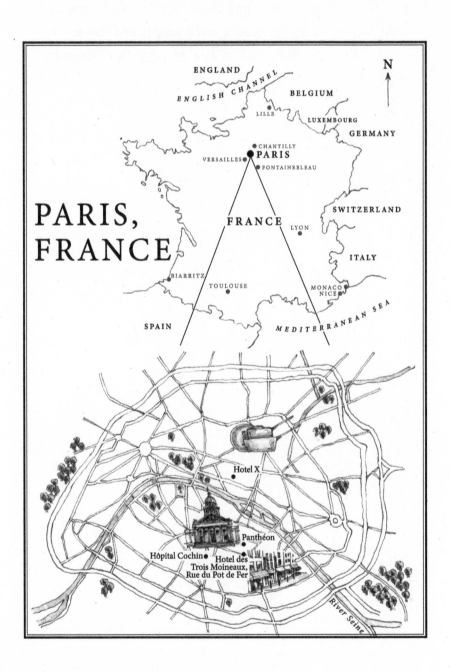

PARIS,
FRANCE

Paris, France

A tale of two cities (1928–9)

L ondon's St Pancras station replaced Waterloo Station in 2007 as the main departure point for most Londoners to Paris. In 2007 I lived nearby, in Barnsbury, and remember sneaking in to see the restored station a week after it opened. It is a testimony to the standard of renovation that more than ten years later it could pass for a recently restored building.

In 1927, when Orwell visited Paris for the first time, the primary means of transport to Paris was a train from Victoria, and by 'night boat' transfer across the English Channel to France. There was a scheduled commercial air service, but it was heinously expensive. There was no Channel Tunnel and certainly no motorways. I often think we forget how easy it is to get to most places, how simple journeys today (two hours and 15 minutes from London to Paris by train) were once so arduous.

The Channel Tunnel opened in 1994, although the ambitious Victorians had designs for one throughout their century. Even though construction of the tunnel had numerous false starts, this did not stop Victorian railway investors splurging on a north of London continental line – 'The Great Central Railway' – which would have connected the English Midlands to the continent via the Channel Tunnel. It was closed for the most part in 1966, 28 years before England was finally connected to France.

I reflected, as I boarded my Eurostar to Paris, that Orwell would have had something to say about Great Britain no longer being an island, the connection such an obvious statement of Anglo-French and Anglo-European relations. An engineering feat it is undoubtedly, but it is also a geopolitical one representing partnership between Britain and France. Orwell began writing as thousands of former pupils from his school were being killed in the First World War, and achieved widespread fame during the Second World War, at the very start of which, at Dunkirk, his brother-in-law was killed.

The principal book Orwell wrote about Paris was actually his first – a travelogue of sorts, part fact and part fiction. After his first extended stay at Southwold and before moving to London wholly in 1931 to teach, Orwell spent two years in Paris, and spent bouts of time tramping in London or Kent. How an Eton-educated Indian Police officer ended up homeless on Trafalgar Square, and then more or less living hand-to-mouth doing menial work in Paris, is just one of many perplexing aspects of Orwell's character.

Down and Out in Paris and London is written in two parts, the first a part-summary of the time he spent in Paris, and the second (shorter) section of his time tramping in London. *A Scullion's Diary* was considered as an alternative title, and it was from the publication of this first book that the name 'George Orwell' was invented. English literature was bequeathed this world-famous name not by any decision of Orwell's but through the choice of his agent, Leonard Moore, from a shortlist of four. The name change happened because Blair thought that the content of the book might prove an embarrassment for his parents who, it must be remembered, were conservative members of the Anglo-Indian tradition. It is unlikely *Down and Out in Paris and London* would have been read with much relish in the clubs of Calcutta or Rangoon. Later, his first novel, *Burmese Days*, would be met with opprobrium for its anti-colonial sentiment.

The route to publication was a long and arduous one. In fact, there was a very good chance *Down and Out in Paris and London* would never have been published at all, and the phrase 'down and out' not have been immortalised for being so quintessentially Orwellian. It was rejected by several major publishing houses, including by T.S. Eliot at Faber & Faber. But a friend Orwell acquired in London, Mabel Fierz, was handed the manuscript with an instruction from Orwell to bin it after reading. Fortunately, Fierz did not bin it, passing it to her friend and literary agent Leonard Moore, who secured publication with Gollancz's 'Left Book Club'.

Other than his writing from school and some draft chapters of *Burmese Days* written possibly in the last days of his time at Katha, Orwell's career as a writer began in Paris, where over the two years he contributed articles to a scattering of periodicals. Some were in French, and signed 'Eric Blair'. He wrote non-fiction, possibly producing draft manuscripts for a novel or several, but he considered them to be of poor quality and they were destroyed. Orwell's obsessive self-criticism meant he heaped scorn on some of his work, which is lost forever. I do wonder about these lost works – to think that, in a dusty attic somewhere in Paris, they may lie waiting to be found.

It was only toward the end of Orwell's two years in Paris that his 'down and out' episode was undertaken. This was not forced on him but was undertaken out of choice. An aunt, one of the Limouzins from Moulmein, lived in Paris, and it goes without saying she could have provided a roof and sustenance as required. Orwell sought the poverty he described, both his own and that of others. He sketched out in his travelogue the characters he met in the tradition of one of his literary heroes, Dickens' *Sketches by Boz* being the Victorian parallel from which Orwell drew inspiration.

Relative poverty exists all over Paris, as it does in London. But living standards in both cities are immeasurably higher now than when Orwell was writing about them. The Fifth, the 'quarter' of Paris in which Orwell chose to live and find the subjects of his sketches, is no longer a poor district. Like so many parts of both cities – London's Islington for instance, where Orwell would live in the 1940s – places which were once decrepit now provide homes for those on the very highest incomes.

⌒

I chose to walk to Rue du Pot de Fer, the real name of the street Orwell's lodgings, the *Hotel des Trois Moineaux*, was on. One can always feel the excitement of Christmas in Paris, and so on a dry, cold December day, I thought I would take a walking tour across the south of the city from *Militaire* to the Fifth. Paris is a beautiful city to walk around, but not the most practical. What would have been a reasonably long stroll drawing a piece of string between my points of arrival and departure, turned into a lengthy trek as a consequence of walk-arounds through a myriad of boulevards.

Forty-five minutes or so later into my walk, Orwell's address was in sight. Following several wrong turns, I spotted a busy, pedestrianised alleyway which resembled what I had seen in photographs: a narrow thoroughfare, gloomy from the steep buildings on either side and characterised most obviously by a succession of bars and restaurants. Curiously, even in winter, French restaurateurs lay the outside tables. I immediately gained the impression that Rue du Pot de Fer would be noisy at night; it felt noisy even though it was mid-morning because it is so claustrophobic a space. Restaurant staff busied themselves as I walked along it, polishing the generic menus of third-rate restaurants ubiquitous in Paris: known for the sale of gallons of Stella Artois, sinewy steak and under-cooked *pommes frites*.

One of the jobs Orwell took in Paris was as a waiter, at the famed 'Hotel X'. One among many of the cynical observations he made in *Down and Out* was to suggest that the more expensive a restaurant is, the filthier the conditions of the food's preparation: 'Roughly speaking, the more one pays for food, the more sweat and spittle one is obliged to eat with it,' he wrote. After reading the book as a twenty year old, it was the one lesson from its pages I have never forgotten.

After the book was published, a minor spat occurred on the letters' pages of *The Times*, with a Parisian restaurateur, one Humbert Possenti, writing: 'as a restaurateur and hotelier of 40 years' experience', it was inconceivable French kitchens were as Orwell described. Orwell, at risk of being accused of exaggeration (not for the first time in his reporting), responded: 'In spite of his 40 years' experience, my evidence in this case is worth more than his.'

Orwell's training as a waiter – it is amusing to think of nonplussed diners being served coffee by such a famous writer of the future – stayed with him. His knowledge of wine, not least how to treat it, was remarked on by friends. Rayner Heppenstall, who lived with him in Hampstead, reflected in his memoir *Four Absentees*: 'Eric would order red wine, feeling the bottle and then sending it away to have the chill taken off, a proceeding by which I was greatly impressed.'

Having been a reasonably well-paid colonial police officer, it seems that waiting tables came as a bit of a shock to Orwell. Throughout his life Orwell found it hard to understand how so many people could do such boring jobs – usually jobs described using the words 'fearful' or 'beastly'. He echoed similar opinions when he went on his tour to the north of England, the diaries from which became *The Road to Wigan Pier*.

Some of Orwell's commentary seems intolerant to me today, not helped in the knowledge that he was a public schoolboy from a very comfortable background by any measure, and did these jobs out of choice. He did not find them to be boring from having done them for a lifetime, in which position many people find themselves, without the leisure of choosing a job that might not be as creative as the pursuits of a writer. His analysis also omits the obvious fact that boring jobs still need doing; as a means of income for those without the skills needed to find better employment if nothing else.

To Orwell's credit, however, he was at least able to write about 'beastly' jobs from the perspective of having done them, which offered him more credibility than people who talk as if they can represent unskilled workers from their luxury of having only ever held a pen. The first review for a book written by Orwell was remarkably prescient, identifying from the start the style for which he became so famous, and remains admired the world over. Muriel Harris, writing for what was then known as the *Manchester Guardian*, noted that: 'Mr George Orwell ... tells of things which to most people are horrible in a quiet, level tone which enables him also to use a vocabulary suited to his subject. No-one ... can fail to be deeply moved by the truth which is evident in every sentence.'

∽

Off the street from where Rue du Pot de Fer leads is another narrow lane, along which a car could just about pass. Lined with twee shops rather than restaurants, I caught sight of a bookshop. It is hard to resist visiting any bookshop in the vicinity of somewhere with Orwellian credentials, giving the shelves a quick glance and seeing whether his books are stocked. His works are published in all major languages and plenty of minor ones too, but the French have their own intellectuals to borrow ideas from, and the nuances of Orwell's Englishness don't necessarily translate well.

The lady at the counter, which was awkwardly some way above waist-height, was wearing a blue-and-white, fine-striped, long-sleeved cotton t-shirt, thin-rimmed spectacles and bore an expressionless, nonchalant face of the sort so typical of booksellers. 'Book Shop Memories', an essay whose observations remain valid 80 years since Orwell himself worked in a bookshop, explains that they are one of the few shops people can walk into and leave without the intention of buying anything. They thus attract a certain type of clientele which, Orwell pointedly remarked, is not always bookish!

Even more appropriately, for it brought to mind another of his essays – 'Books vs Cigarettes' – she stank of tobacco. It was the sort of stench one comes across visiting a *tabac*, from the round-bellied owner across the counter. I asked, humbly, for 'Orwell'. She extended in return an arrogant glance and pointed to the bookcase below the large shop front windows labelled '*Littérature anglo-saxonne*'. I felt, bearing in the moment, a shame of my Anglo-Saxon culture, as if I had been relegated to some forgotten corner.

I knelt down and noticed all the volumes were more or less the same size, save for what looked like a *Tintin*-style cartoon version of *Animal Farm*. It stood out from all the other books on the shelf, a beautiful crimson blue. Few cultures in the world, save for perhaps the Scandinavians and the Swiss, match the French in production quality. *La Ferme des Animaux*, published by L'Echappée, is the most impressively artistic edition of *Animal Farm* I have come across. I purchased a copy, wrapped by the tobacco-smelling bookseller in a thick, brown-paper sleeve.

The book's font is that scrappy cartoon type the French seem to love – the sort which is scribbled as graffiti all over the Metro, and used for the satirical magazine *Charlie Hebdo*. The book and translation is a curious insight into Anglo-French relations, in the same way the Eurostar terminus in London was 'Waterloo' for thirteen years. Napoleon, the hegemonic pig in *Animal Farm* named after the French dictator, is rechristened 'Caesar' in the French edition. It is a nice footnote in Orwelliana, but despite my best efforts I have been unable to reveal the origins of the change, or whether it was an amendment approved of by him. It is just the sort of trick Orwell would have liked, however.

To my surprise, *Down and Out in Paris and London* was unavailable. This perplexed me, given the logical tourism value of the book to Paris and the man who wrote it more or less across the street. When I worked in a bookshop there were certain books which we automatically restocked; *The Good News Bible*, dictionaries and that sort of thing. It seemed to me that *Down and Out* should be such a book in this shop, a whole pile of them – but nothing, and neither any other Orwell merchandise. Perhaps the spat across *The Times* letters pages did Orwell for good in Paris, or to stock him would give his work the credibility a particular type of French intellectual objects to an Anglo-Saxon writer achieving.

﹌

At this stage in his life Orwell felt dejected, following his aimless return from Burma, faced with the bewilderment of his parents and their pressure to force his settling down into something respectable. In *The Road to Wigan Pier*, he noted that at the time of his departure for Paris, 'failure seemed to me to be the only virtue'. In *Down and Out* itself he emphasised the attractions of the world he was eager to join: 'The Paris slums are a gathering place for eccentric people – people who have fallen into solitary, half-mad grooves of life and given up trying to be normal or decent.'

Out of choice, he had sought, via his tramping in London and hop-picking in Kent, to participate in situations different to his lodgings at Eton or his grace-and-favour homes in British India. Characterisation, as in Dickens' *Sketches by Boz*, was what he wanted to observe, writing in *Down and Out* that: 'It would be fun to write some of their biographies. I am trying to describe the people in our quarter, not for the mere curiosity, but because they are all part of the story ... poverty is what I am writing about.'

Both Orwell's desire to go tramping and hop-picking can surely be traced back to his exploration of Dickens' works – his essay on Dickens is often praised for being one of the best literary analyses of the author's writing – and also his admiration of H.G. Wells' *History of Mr Polly*, an influence from his teenage years. What Orwell discovered was an underworld, and one he enjoyed participating in, if only momentarily. He could never bring himself to realise that so many people were forced into 'fearful' jobs not as a luxury, but out of sheer necessity. Orwell wrote in *Down and Out*: '... washing up was a thoroughly odious job – not hard, but boring and silly beyond words. It is dreadful to think that some people spend whole decades at such occupations.'

The *Hotel des Trois Moineaux* has since been demolished, replaced by a nondescript apartment block. I was thus unable to explore the 'dark, rickety warren of five storeys, cut up by wooden partitions into forty rooms. The rooms ... [are] small and inveterately dirty.' 'Madame F' administered this shambles, the sort of shady slum landlord who thrives off the hard cash return from a pathetically dishevelled asset. They are still a common part of the rental market in India, and no doubt, in the shady quarters of the underworld in England and France too.

Much of his time in the Parisian slums seems to have been spent in bed, chatting among the medley of residents and plotting to find work, typically in restaurants and hotels. Since the time he spent in the Fifth was no more than six months, none of these jobs lasted for very long. He sought purposely to maintain the same shabbiness as his peers, and pledged on the second day under Madame F's tutelage to pawn his overcoat, although of course – given that his aunt lived in the city – this was hardly necessary. It is not difficult to feel the story is a little embellished.

I got the sense, as I walked up and down Rue du Pot de Fer, that no one working in the bars and restaurants lining the street enjoyed in the least any of their jobs. There was sullen brushing-up of fag ends and pigeon droppings; the hasty cleaning of the surfaces of the outside tables; the sort where the smears show half of the table has been missed. A sign for *'Delirium tremens'*, a beer marketed using a pink elephant as its emblem, declared itself to be 'elected as best beer in the world', the only thing cheering up an otherwise desolate winter morning in Orwell land.

On a short winter's day such as it was, the sunlight was already fading, and I began to organise my thoughts to plan a route for the long walk back. I decided this time to take the easy route, to head for the river and follow it all the way home to *Militaire*. Quickly out of the narrow streets forming Orwell's old quarter there emerged grand roads with six-storey apartment blocks, smart shops and posh pharmacies; the sort one finds in London in Holland Park, or in the vicinity of Oxford Street.

Fiddling around with my smartphone to find the precise path to the Seine, I paused at a junction only to do a double take at the sight of an Islamic-style tower down the side road in the distance, shrouded by greenery even in mid-December, at Place du Puits-de-l'Ermite. In my visit to Marrakech, chronologically after Paris in Orwell's life, but taking place before my visit to Paris in *The Orwell Tour*, I had visited the Koutoubia Mosque. It is the definitive sight of the Moroccan capital, the sun always reflected in its blue-tiled ceramic shell. I enjoyed making the connection between one place Orwell called home and another.

I had intended to visit the hospital Orwell stayed in during one of his bouts of illness, the experience of which formed the content of 'How the Poor Die'. This essay, another insight into the ways of the underclass – in this instance, how they end their days – led from his disappointing experience of French nursing. His essay displays aspects of a John Bull-tendency never to waste an opportunity to take a hit at England's old rival. The hospital he stayed in – Hôpital Cochin in the Sixteenth Arrondissement – is now a multi-storey, glass and steel behemoth, the sort of thing that looks like it should form part of London's Canary Wharf. I couldn't imagine there would be much evidence of Dickensian hospital conditions there, so had no intention of wasting a Metro fare.

Fortunately, my walk home did not disappoint in my search for something resembling what I imagined the hospital would have looked like, in the same way that, if you search hard enough, it is still possible to find reasonably decrepit former workhouses forming parts of British hospitals. I walked past a grand, dishevelled building, surrounded by the usual flurry of activity – patients and nurses dressed in their habitual garb, smoking their cigarettes; hurrying families visiting relatives; the odd ambulance. Its name was Hôpital Necker.

It is strange how, what one hopes to find is what one does, and it did not disappoint. Set back from the road, like a château plucked straight out of the Loire Valley, and with all that pride the French invest in their civic buildings, Hôpital Necker appeared just like the sort of 1920s Parisian hospital in which the twenty-something Orwell could have found himself incarcerated. Hospitals are supposed to not only be clean but to look clean, and this building was anything but: on the upper storeys the windows were broken, with pigeons flying in and out, and the building gave the impression of a struggling *grande dame*.

Orwell did not think much of his stay in a French hospital, which he described with its 'gloom and bareness, its sickly smell, and above all, something in its mental atmosphere', which he noted stood out in his memory as 'exceptional'. He did not like hospitals, which is unfortunate since in his middle age he would spend so much time in them.

Likewise, 'How the Poor Die' explains how a good death would mean to 'die violently and not too old', rather than a natural death, which, 'almost by definition means something slow, smelly and painful'. His demise was very much the latter.

Orwell's experience of French hospitals led him to view English ones as being superior, although I sense that, in a patriotic rather than a nationalistic sense, he believed England was best at most things: this was the Edwardian attitude of the world in which he was raised. Even in death he observed that the English wish to see things disguised, disgusted by his French hospital leaving a person to die and then leaving the body in full view: 'You certainly would not see that in England, and still less would you see a corpse left exposed to the view of the other patients.'

The 'sickly smell' of Hôpital Cochin revived for Orwell his recollection of Tennyson's *In the Children's Hospital*, which put in black and white the filthy conditions of Britain's Victorian hospitals. Orwell's brief life, of just 47 years, saw the transformation of his country from a patrician Edwardian society, where no women and only a proportion of men had the vote in General Elections, to Britain's first socialist government able to effect a programme of social transformation. Orwell lived just long enough to see the creation of the National Health Service (NHS) in 1947 and died in it in January 1950. For him, as for the independence of India which he also lived to see, these were progressive acts which contrasted with the political stagnation of the interwar period. *Coming up for Air* satirised what he believed to be two lost decades, Britain being led in his view by an inept political class for the duration of the 1920s and 1930s. He reminded readers that before the NHS it was common for 'free' patients to have their teeth extracted without anaesthetic: 'they didn't pay, so why should they have an anaesthetic – that was the attitude'.

'How the Poor Die' is important because it exposes the root of the common fallacy present in most caste-based societies, that in life (if not in death) there is a hierarchy of worth. Social egalitarianism is a significant theme of his writing, in everything from *The Clergyman's Daughter* to his polemical essay about the class structure, 'England Your England'. He shared this value with the prime minister of 1945–51, Clement Attlee, who oversaw the creation of the health service and independence for India. Attlee and Orwell also believed in a sense of fellowship between the same citizens of a country, acting as a unifying force. It would seem they had mutual respect for one another, although it is unclear whether they ever met.

Orwell's return from Paris was by third-class train across the channel between Dunkirk and Tilbury, in the days when trains were carried by ferries. Until the growth of cheap air travel this was the most common way to travel between London and Paris, and even after commercial air travel had expanded, British Rail continued running its night sleepers to Europe until 1980. It seems to have been a romantic journey, although owing to the attachment of metal clasps required to clamp the trains to the floor of the ferry most passengers, I read, rarely got much sleep! Orwell commented it was 'the cheapest and worst way of crossing the Channel'.

Britain and France are two nations bound together in a mix of love, hate and rivalry – of comedy, competition and confounded communication spread over a shared history of well over 1,000 years. It seems to me *Down and Out in Paris and London* was an attempt to explore the differences between the two nations, by someone whose lineage was almost as French as it was British. It matches Dickens' *Tale of Two Cities* in its assessment of this contrast, a feast of insights from the nearest match to Dickens readers in the 20th century could discover.

Hayes, Middlesex, England

Schoolmaster (1932–3)

One of Orwell's lesser-known forays into employment involved his eighteen months teaching. Between 1932 and 1933 he taught at two schools in Middlesex, historically the county immediately west of London, now absorbed into the capital. He went into teaching as a means to earn an income, rather than it being something for which he had any special interest. He enjoyed the process of teaching, but resented the confines of the structure of schooling, as well as the arduous hours.

Orwell had spent the time back in Southwold engaged in various forms of private tuition, but was lured to Middlesex as a result of his accepting a job at The Hawthorns, a small boys' school in Hayes. Hayes was one of a profusion of market towns in Middlesex which, by process of agglomeration, slowly merged into one enormous suburban jungle. Middlesex was formally abolished in 1965, a fact resented by the poet John Betjeman. He wrote:

> *Dear Middlesex, dear*
> *Vanished country friend,*
> *Your neighbour, London,*
> *Killed you in the end.*

Hayes and its environs were a change from the socially exclusive towns of Henley and Southwold, being home to people much nearer to the 'average' Briton's standard of living. At this point in his life, Orwell had, for the most part, experienced the highs of the upper-middle class – all shooting and British India – and also, albeit fleetingly, that of the underclass as he tramped across London, southern England and in Paris. But he had little understanding of the lower-middle class.

Then, as today, the lower-middle class constituted the bulk of the population of Britain, as much as 40 per cent depending on which survey is followed. These are the skilled and semi-skilled mainstay of most industries: office assistants, call centre workers, retail managers. It is a social group now concentrated in towns which are home to light industry – provincial towns all over the UK – and the less desirable parts of the Home Counties such as Crawley or Slough.

In Orwell's time, Hayes was 'clerksville', a lower-middle-class haven. Close to London but also, at that time, not London. This 'suburbia' spread, as those with the aspiration to live in cleaner and greener locales moved out to anywhere within reasonable, easy reach of London. London Underground promoted the idea of the rural idyll within reach of the city's centre: the District Line, coloured green, and the extension of its lines took the ever-hastening spread of London into its surrounds.

The expansion of London came to an abrupt halt after the Second World War, when the new Labour government passed laws to stop construction on a 'greenbelt' enclosing London, and most of the large conurbations. Urbanisation, which seemed at the time to know no end, slowed. I am not sure whether Orwell was well enough to notice the passing of these new laws – he was in a hospital for most of 1949 – but they came as a result of a growing consensus that the spread of London had to be curtailed. Orwell's *Coming up for Air* played a part in achieving these controls, with its emphasis on the regret felt for lost rurality.

⤳

Catching a train from Paddington Station always feels slightly more exotic than the other major London stations, all of the mysterious West before one. Paddington feels much the most spacious station in London, and never seems crowded. The eclectic mix of characters is also amusing; it is usually possible to identify all the suspects of an English murder mystery story. On this occasion, there was a vicar in a dog collar, trailed by a Miss Marple-type carrying her small Jack Russell in a wicker basket.

My romantic view of Paddington, which I would hope most passengers passing through share, dates from the age of Agatha Christie, who was writing at a time when the Victorians' culture of ambitious engineering was still in the national consciousness. Isambard Kingdom Brunel, who co-designed the station and built the line, made a railway as flat 'as a billiards' table' out into western England and Wales, the line operated by the famous Great Western Railway, aka 'God's Wonderful Railway'. There is not much of this legacy left today. Britain, in general, has traded on the giant legacy of its forebears too much; a diktat which applies more than anything to the nation's railways. Dirty diesel intercity trains, whose filthy fumes toxify the air, have been moving in and out of the station for 50 years – a sad reality for a major European railway line, and a London terminus.

There was little exotic or mystical about my short trip to Middlesex. I have travelled past Hayes and Harlington station hundreds of times en-route to the West Country. This part of the journey is usually a blur of medium-rise modern apartment blocks – all glass and steel – and a hotchpotch of industrial sites. The industrial buildings, in contrast to the new apartments, are in various states of repair. Some are vast modern industrial plants, such as Nestle's. Others lie derelict, a sad remnant of heavy industry which has moved away and left its handsome Victorian buildings to decay.

Hayes was once a dormitory area, a place where commuters lived within easy reach of London. Since Orwell's time this has changed, with most of its residents now living and working locally. Slough, which is only a few stops further west, is the capital of 'light industry UK', manufacturing consumer goods from chocolate bars to household paints. This development of light manufacturing, which took place in the 50 years after the war and at the same time as the old heavy industries declined, demanded a supply of cheap, generally unskilled labour.

So now Hayes no longer houses employees of the city seeking their suburban haven. Instead, these fly by on intercity trains from affluent Berkshire, including Orwell's old hometown of Henley, to their offices in London. As they developed these new industries, Hayes and its close neighbour Southall, attracted immigrants from South Asia who were encouraged to move to Britain to fill labour shortages in the 1960s and 1970s. As data on households collected by the census shows, this was accompanied by a move away from Hayes by white Britons, and by the 2000s the profile of the town and its environs had changed hugely.

Southall, just fifteen minutes from Paddington, is one of the main centres of the South Asian population in Britain, alongside others including Leicester, Bradford and Tower Hamlets. As the doors of my train opened, a delicious waft of Asian cooking filled the train and a rush of women in prettily patterned saris departed and boarded. A large factory producing South-Asian food occupied almost the entire view to my left, partially obscured by a row of attractive red-brick arches, which brought to mind the heavy Victorian railway station architecture in India. To my right was a vast Sikh temple.

The South-Asian community here – rather, I should say, the Punjabi community – is so large that the station sign has been translated to list its name in Punjabi as well as English. There are few places in England, to my knowledge, where the settlement of Asian immigrants has been quite so all-encompassing. At the next station, Hayes and

Harlington, I would find for myself the enormous extent to which the area has changed since Orwell arrived here in 1932.

I suspect Orwell, whose knowledge of the rest of the world and especially the Indian subcontinent was strong, would be surprised by the extent to which so many parts of England have been transformed by immigration since his death. He would also, I am confident, comment on the observation that rather than Britain being 'two nations' – as opposed to the socially cohesive 'one nation' championed by liberal Conservatives such as Benjamin Disraeli – it now seems to be 50 nations and more, few of which seem to have much interest in interacting.

The station at Hayes, as for Southall and Paddington, is Victorian, but at the time of my visit was in the process of being demolished. Hayes must have been recently designated to provide thousands of new homes to cope with Britain's booming population since, as one arrives at the station, huge new blocks of soulless modern flats appear. The station exit felt scrappy, and the usual mix of permanent station dwellers – tramps and drug dealers – hovered.

From the station I turned right, in the direction of Hayes' High Street, and crossed a large canal – now quiet, save for a few leisure barges – which preceded the railway as the highway for trade in the 18th century. A beautiful old pub, the sort one finds typically by the side of a canal in the middle of the countryside, greeted me as I crossed the bridge. The Old Crown, in common with the rest of old Hayes, is a remnant of a changed residential and demographic landscape.

The high street looked forlorn, as what I prayed would not happen on one of those typical days of British weather when the risk of rain is touch-and-go – a downpour – began to dampen my clothes. I am not sure what Hayes' High Street looked like in the 1930s, although with a bit of imagination and based on the older period buildings which remain – half-timbered mock-Tudor bank branches, a graceful war memorial and so on – I thought of a suburban bliss of flower baskets and slow-moving trams. Today the high street is typical for multicultural London, noticing as I passed along it, distinct groups of Nigerians, Afghans, Somalis and Pakistanis congregating outside of their respective bars, bakeries and grocery shops.

The architecture of the high street was depressing, the surviving Edwardiana offset by obtrusive blocks of concrete and cheap single-storey retail parades housing betting shops and fast-food outlets, bustling on a Sunday afternoon. Some of the buildings have had mansard extensions added to their roofs, generally unsuccessfully. Among a motley collection of scrappy retail outlets, each with their wares spilling out onto the pavement, there remained the traditional high street banks. Almost all the other British chains seem to have gone. One former clothes store now houses a Pound Plus Shop and, in the not-too-distant future, I can see the banks being turned into pawn shops, as is the usual pattern of the decline of the high street. I heard 'Acha' often – a word for 'yes' or 'agreed' in Hindi – and momentarily had to remind myself I was, in fact, in dreary, rain-sodden England.

⌒

From the high street I walked in the direction of the Fountain House Hotel, now housed in the building once home to The Hawthorns, the small boys' private school at which Orwell taught for a year before moving to another school, further to the north, in Uxbridge. The walk from the bowling green to the hotel was a no-man's land of suburbia: row after row of semi-detached housing, most dating from the 1930s, 40s and 50s.

Coming up for Air was an exploration of the changing character of London's hinterland in the 1930s. George Bowling, the main character and narrator, returns to the town of his childhood to find it altered beyond recognition by the sprawl of the city, the effects of which Orwell observed first-hand in and around Hayes. I guessed that many of the homes there date from the period, with names like 'Chamberlain Close' betraying its naming during the interwar hubris of 1930s England. Some had over-manicured front gardens, inch-to-inch covered in garish annuals and garden gnomes. Others had fake plastic front lawns, an effort-saving asset I am sure Orwell would have detested. He disliked the ever-prevalent mechanisation of the 1930s enough, without living to see these fake lawns pepper suburbia in the same way the motor car was so invasive during that decade. Most of the houses however, perfectly formed two-up two-downs, had their front gardens concreted over – the ultimate triumph of the automobile, described by Orwell as 'nasty, smelly things' among the pages of *Coming up for Air.*

After a walk of twenty minutes, over what would once have been open countryside, I came to a break from the interwar estates and spotted much older Victorian housing. I glanced to my right and saw the Fountain House Hotel sitting to the left of a junction – a road towards yet another interwar estate – and immediately felt as if I was somewhere melancholic, a place where the sun doesn't want to shine.

On a small patch of green across from the hotel, in every direction in which I looked, the civic assets were neglected. The grass was fist-height, the street lamp flickered in the grey of the afternoon sky and litter was strewn across the pavement. All the surrounding trees, presumably nice enough in high summer, had been pollarded, leaving their trunks and branches contorted and twisted, almost hideous.

My first impressions of the Fountain House Hotel was that it did look like a school, the sort of tiny Victorian school one can find in villages across England. I imagined Orwell standing at the front of one of its classrooms, streaking chalk across a board or reprimanding his pupils for misbehaviour – recalling his policing skills from Burma, which no doubt would have been of priceless value in a school.

The hotel advertises itself idiosyncratically, with a sign shaped like the bow of a ship sticking out in the direction of the street, the misshapen characters of a 1970s font publicising 'vacancies'. The front garden has been paved over and the fountain, after which the hotel is named, is dry. It is surrounded by miniature concrete statues of fairies, frogs and such like. George lurched forward to a concrete bulldog, sniffing at its face, to force a reaction I told him wouldn't be returned.

The blue plaque – in this instance, a green one – was erected by 'The Hayes Literary Society' and, unlike any other blue plaque I have seen has morphed into a much larger Orwell shrine, with 'GEORGE ORWELL LIVED HERE' emblazoned on a white board just below the main plaque. A collage of photographs was attached to the board also, inappropriately framed as a picture hung indoors might be, and water-stained from the infiltration of rain.

Was this to attract guests? I could not understand, and the more I saw, the more the place seemed to resemble something like Fawlty Towers. I peered through the downstairs windows, at rows of little tables laid with crockery, and snooped around the rear to see if I could find any evidence of it having been a school. Not much was forthcoming – the back was filled with gas canisters and a modern extension housing more rooms.

～

The Hawthorns was a tiny institution, the inspiration for the school taught at by Dorothy in *A Clergyman's Daughter*. It was one of the once incredibly common small private schools favoured by the aspirational middle class, those not able to afford a public school but who could afford to take their children out of the state sector. These types of school were run as businesses, typically prioritising fee income over the quality of education they provided. Orwell disliked the headmaster and owner of the school, hemmed-in just as Dorothy would be by a restrictive curriculum meeting the needs of parents, rather than education in its truest sense.

Geoffrey Stevens, a pupil at the Hawthorns interviewed in the early 1980s, explained that Orwell was 'without a shadow of a doubt' the best teacher he had ever had, adding: 'He was also the oddest man I ever met in my life. Even as a lad of thirteen I could discern he was no ordinary character. He was a man who lived within himself.' Stevens recalled that he used to paint a lot – something which I haven't seen coming out in other periods of Orwell's life – and had once shown Stevens a self-portrait. Had this survived it would no doubt be a decidedly valuable item.

Orwell's teaching style was evidently borrowed from the tradition of Eton. He encouraged essay writing and learning by exploration. Stevens remembered him being frustrated at how weak their efforts at essay writing were, Orwell writing 'Bilge!' in his remarks on their work. As during the rest of his life, his obsession with the natural world took him and the class into the open air. He taught the sciences outside, visiting nearby nature reserves to explore insects' habitats: 'We used to walk about two-and-a-half miles to a little stagnant pond ... we used to probe the bottom of the pond with long sticks and hold jam jars above to catch the marsh gas, as he called it – the methane. Then we used to cork up the top and put a hole through it and set light to the gas. That's the kind of thing he really enjoyed.'

Reflecting on the job, Orwell noted his thoughts to Eleanor Jaques and Brenda Salkeld, the women he was pursuing back in Southwold. He advised that teaching itself wasn't 'uninteresting', but lamented the fact that he was exhausted at the end of every day and had no time spare to write. He was no fan of Hayes at all, which he described as a 'foul place' and 'one of the most God-forsaken places I have ever struck'. In common with many teachers, he was glad to be away from pupils after the end of the school day: 'It is a day school, thank God, so I have nothing to do with the brats out of school hours,' he wrote to Jaques.

Across the junction from the Hawthorns is a squat, prefabricated chapel. Housed in a compound hemmed in by chicken fencing, it appears temporary, as if part of a war-time barracks. I suspect it was this simple Unitarian chapel that received Orwell's opprobrium when he noted, again to Jaques, that: 'The population seems to be entirely made up of clerks who frequent tin-roofed chapels on Sundays and for the rest bolt themselves indoors.' This seems to be a tradition which has ended in Hayes – I couldn't tell whether the chapel was still functioning, but it did not appear welcoming.

From the school I wandered on up into the area of older housing, curving around a slight bend to reveal a perfect English village green, with a lych gate shielding a path that led up to St Mary's church, a church hall and a red Gilbert Scott telephone box. On my left, as I followed the pavement, I passed an elaborately fronted former butchers and one or two other erstwhile shops, which presumably once formed the basis of a village community.

There was a war memorial, butting out from the church onto the pavement, and behind this a churchyard, filled with yew trees and enclosed by other large mature trees, allowing little natural light to shine through onto the gravestones on an already gloomy day. The Church Hall, the sort that reminded me of Women's Institute halls, was across the road from the church's lych gate, but seemed to be derelict, the windows clouded up with dust and brambles inundating its side passage, heaving with ripe blackberries.

⌁

This corner of Middlesex, the centre of a village subsumed into London even by the 1930s, was Orwell's stamping ground for around a year.

He admitted to Jaques that he made no friends, apart from the curate of St Mary's, Ernest Parker, whom he described as 'High Anglican but not a creeping Jesus and a very good fellow'. I could visualise his lean, lofty figure crossing to and from the Hawthorns up to the lych gate and on up through the churchyard to the entrance of the grey, flint-faced church. Orwell spent a lot of time at St Mary's, assisting the curate in the care of the church and using it as a nearby overspill facility for the pupils at the school. He wrote and directed a play about Charles II, which was performed there. It is unusual for a London church – more like the church at Walberswick or Southwold than the lofty Georgian or Victorian churches more commonly found in London – and it was perhaps its East Anglian-ness that attracted him, a slice of home in a place he took no liking to.

The church porch of St Mary's is built in a similar style to the lych gate, worn lengths of what could easily pass for enormous logs of driftwood so tortured was its surface, like lumber beached from a ship-wreck. The site is said to have been a place of Christian worship since AD 846, with the present structure dating from the 12th century (the same age, incidentally, as the churches at Walberswick and Southwold). I wondered whether the wood from which the porch was made had been standing here happily for all of 900 years.

A printed sign where the ink had run from the damp was stapled to the door: 'PROBABLY THE OLDEST BUILDING IN HILLINGDON BOROUGH'. For some reason, the word 'building' was coloured red, contrasting sharply with the wood-engraved etchings of a good nine centuries of graffiti – 'BD 1880' and suchlike – on the wooden door behind it. As I imagined Orwell drifting through the porch and into the church to assist the curate in the polishing of the brass, I walked back out of the church and into a small, enclosed part of the graveyard opposite.

Attached to some of the graves were tents, and the grass was strewn with the detritus of what seemed to be some form of homeless encampment. At the boundary of the churchyard, which was thickly lined with shrubs, a homeless person seemed to have created an outside bathroom: there was a full-length mirror, and a battered sink perched on an old-fashioned suitcase. There might be worse places to be down and out, I reflected, a home in God's harbour for the dead.

Orwell did not write much in his time at the Hawthorns, nor at Frays College in Uxbridge. This he joined in September 1933, only to leave on the grounds of ill-health halfway through the academic year. (The Hawthorns closed after the war; Frays College in the 1970s.) But one momentous change to his life and works did take place as part of the publication of *Down and Out in Paris and London*: the adoption of his pen name 'George Orwell', which was selected by his agent, Moore, from a choice of four. The other choices for an alias were 'P.S. Burton', the name he used when tramping; 'H. Lewis Allways' and 'Kenneth Miles'. How funny to think that this famous name should have forever defined Eric Blair's writing; neither 'Burtonellian' nor 'Allwaysian' quite work. Moore was prompted into his choice by Orwell noting to him: 'I rather favour George Orwell'.

Strangely, in spite of not finding time to write, he seems to have invested significant time in growing produce. This tendency, which appears again during his and his wife's time during the lease of a Hertfordshire cottage, and on Jura, might seem quaint to 21st-century eyes, but Britain has a strong tradition of allotment-tending and it became for Orwell an outlet of genteel solitude, much as his reading was. He grew shallots and broad beans at Hayes – both of which failed – but produced 'enormous quantities of peas', alongside a pumpkin. He told Brenda Salkeld, one of his dates in the period, that: '[this] of course requires much more careful treatment than a marrow', illustrative of his developing skills in horticulture at a still youthful age.

It is not clear where his garden or allotment was. The rear of the Hawthorns, as for the entire plot surrounding it, has been concreted over. I like to think that after his pupils had left the classroom he could retreat outside to his vegetable patch, strip away the bindweed and fork over the soil, as he contemplated ideas for writing based on his past, and a future with whomever – at this time, more likely to be a romantic connection from Southwold – he was likely to settle with.

Later, at Frays College, he picked up fishing again. One incident very possibly led to the worsening of his health, forcing his departure. A Mr and Mrs Stapley taught alongside Orwell at the college – Mr Stapley would later become headmaster there – and when interviewed in the 1960s he recalled Orwell fishing in the river at the bottom of their garden, where there were trout, roach and gudgeon. Mrs Stapley remembered him coming in from the garden during an enormous storm, dripping from the rain, and asking her to cook the mess of fish that hung from his clammy hands!

As for his reading, there is little on record to know what his habits were. He wrote to Jaques in July 1933 that he was reading D.H. Lawrence, author of the scandalising (and banned) *Lady Chatterley's Lover*, whose *Collected Letters* he described as 'very interesting', producing a quality of prose he could 'not define'. It was published for the first time in 1932, with an introduction written by Orwell's old French master, Aldous Huxley. Lawrence is another literary influence on Orwell's work, an author who also attempted to explore the effects on society of modernisation and industrial change.

⌒

Coming up for Air's main character, George Bowling, is stuck in a managerial job and, in his forties, escapes his wife and children to travel back to his hometown, Lower Binfield. He hopes to rediscover his lost childhood, returning to a pond he remembered was stocked with great big fish. Bowling states: 'The very thought of going back to lower Binfield had done me good already. You know the feeling I had. Coming up for air! Like the big sea turtles when they come paddling up to the surface, stick their noses out and fill their lungs with a great gulp before they sink down again.'

The countryside of Bowling's childhood had disappeared under new housing, however – 'Long, long rows of little semi-detached houses ... the stucco front, the creosoted gate, the privet hedge, the green front door' – and the pond, drained of its water, was half filled with tin cans. The pond Orwell took his pupils to for their science lessons went the same way as the pond of his imagination; destroyed this time by the new M4 motorway. It is possibly a good thing Orwell did not live to see the growth of the motorway network, of enormous airports and the jet engine.

Orwell's character was forged principally in the Edwardian period; an era of steam trains and branch lines, 'King and Country' and Gilbert and Sullivan. Bowling states in the novel that: 'the civilisation which I grew up in ... is now, I suppose, just about at its last kick'. It might be said that every generation sees itself swept away by change, and Orwell's defeatist narrative of the march of irrepressible change is that there is not much that can be done about it.

I caught the train back to Paddington in the midst of another downpour. Thirty of us, awaiting the usual delayed train to sweep us into central London, shivered in a stiff breeze lashing the roof of the plastic shelter with rain. I was the only white Briton under the canopy, surrounded by a large family of Sikhs standing proudly in their smart, colourful turbans, and a group of elderly women dressed head to toe in their bedazzling multicoloured saris. To fight off the chill I imagined myself back on a station platform in India, awaiting the sleeper at Muzaffarpur Junction.

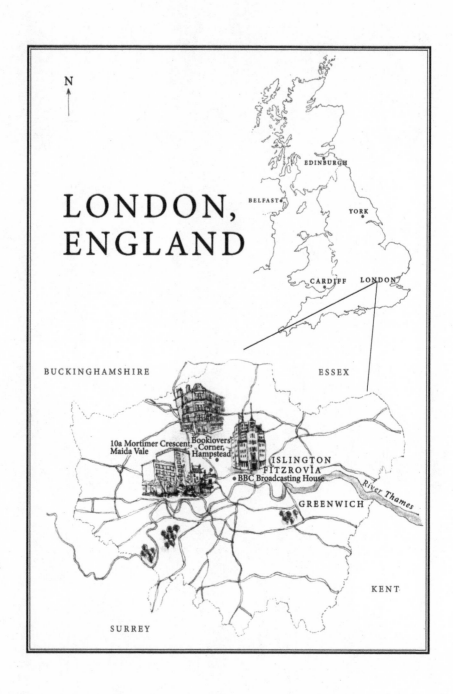

N

LONDON,
ENGLAND

EDINBURGH

BELFAST

YORK

CARDIFF LONDON

BUCKINGHAMSHIRE   ESSEX

10a Mortimer Crescent, Booklovers'
Maida Vale   Corner,
                        Hampstead
                                ISLINGTON
                                FITZROVIA
                                • BBC Broadcasting House
                                                River Thames
                                        GREENWICH

                                                        KENT

SURREY

Hampstead, London, England

Booklover (1934–5)

The lasting impression left by Orwell on many who met him was his bookishness. Ever-present, his literary knowledge informed how he perceived the world. Throughout his novels and essays, the works of those he had read or by whom he had been inspired appear page after page. At Eton, at home during the school holidays, in Burma, his love of reading was observed first hand, and appears all over the historical record. But it was his experience of working in a bookshop, in north London's Hampstead, that shaped his literary prowess more than any other period of his life.

Orwell's two years working at Booklovers' Corner, a bookshop owned by friends of his French aunt, provided the inspiration for his third novel – *Keep the Aspidistra Flying* – and a short essay on life in the trade, 'Bookshop Memories'. Good authors introduce their readers to new writers, especially those neglected or long forgotten. Orwell's gift of this has been an unexpected benefit to my Orwell tour, causing me to pick up books and pursue reading or lines of thought I had never considered.

As a literary critic in his own right, irrespective of the quality of his journalism or fiction, he is first rate. His essay on Charles Dickens alone, first appearing in the *Inside the Whale* collection, both blesses and curses the author. It is a delight to read and, unusually in literary criticism, almost impossible to put down. Other powerful and original insights can be discovered in his analyses of the life and works of Rudyard Kipling; Leo Tolstoy; Shakespeare; T.S. Eliot; Arthur Koestler; Tobias Smollett; Jonathan Swift and Evelyn Waugh.

During a later spell of recuperation in Morocco, in the winter of 1938, Orwell, deprived of the easy access to books in the English language to be found in London, requested a selection of books by the Victorian greats. This list included works by Henry James, Anthony Trollope and William Thackeray; George Gissing, a 19th-century author who wrote about the condition of the working classes in London from the perspective of a working-class man, and D.H. Lawrence, are authors he admired in his thirties. Even on his deathbed, he read profusely, his choice of reading likewise offering insight, as they might anyone with finite time to revisit old favourites, into Orwell's literary passions. These included more Henry James – reflecting the love for ghost stories described by Jacintha Buddicom – Hesketh Pearson's *Life of Dickens*, and both Hardy's *Tess of the D'Urbervilles* and *Jude the Obscure*. Orwell wrote in one of his last ever letters: 'Tess is really better than I had remembered, and incidentally is quite funny in places, which I didn't think Hardy was capable of.'

Keep the Aspidistra Flying is possibly Orwell's least successful novel. But it still triumphs on two counts: an articulate revulsion to what he describes as society's 'money God', and descriptions of London and its characters that demonstrate further his powers of observation. As ever in Orwell's writing, some form of critical message is delivered to readers. The book can be placed down with happy recollections of the breadth of persons encountered within. The central character – the Flory of *Burmese Days* and the Dorothy of *A Clergyman's Daughter* – is Gordon Comstock, an aspiring writer struggling to gain recognition for his work. It is no coincidence that Gordon, like Orwell, resigns from a stable, 'respectable' job, begins working for a bookshop and spends years despairing as his writing is rejected by publishers.

Where *A Clergyman's Daughter* examines the life of a single young woman, *Keep the Aspidistra Flying* does the same for a young man at the same age (the late twenties, approaching the age of 30) through the prism of the central character's dislike of middle-class identity: since Victorian times the aspidistra plant had been a middle-class icon to be found in many a suburban home. Unlike his first two novels there is no incident, no blackout, no riot, which might be the cause of the novel's unravelling. Much to Orwell's distaste it was heavily edited by the publisher, and does not hang together well.

Keep the Aspidistra Flying is however a funny book, especially for anyone who has spent a reasonable time in office work or a corporate hierarchy. Gordon longs for creativity, loathing the monotony of office life and the people who inhabit it – especially those who reach that stage of life where the only intention is to coast and preserve whatever rewards are given to them for as long as they can with the absolute minimum of effort. Echoing Orwell's own transition to the freedom of his writing, following so closely in the footsteps of his father's work in India, Gordon describes: 'His uncles and aunts ... talking dismally about "getting Gordon settled in life". They saw everything in terms of "good" jobs. Young Smith had got such a "good" job in a bank, and young Jones had got such a "good" job in an insurance office. It made him sick to hear them. They seemed to want to see every young man in England nailed down in the coffin of a "good" job.'

Even in the 1930s, the City of London and Britain's financial services industry represented the pinnacle of achievement for the over-educated leaving its universities. It is a compliment to Orwell's foresight that other remarks in the novel remain as valid today as they were in 1935, though the bowler hats must surely be substituted for conference call headsets: 'As for the types around him, the little bowler-hatted worms who never turned, and the go-getters, the American business-college gutter crawlers, they rather amused him than not. He liked studying their slavish keep-your-job mentality.'

The theme of money and how it corrupts humanity can be observed so frequently in Orwell's work that I am not confident it has been analysed sufficiently. It is not a subject that immediately comes to mind when thinking of his works. In *A Clergyman's Daughter*, for instance, a conspicuous reference in a novel centred on faith is made to 1 Corinthians: 'In fact, it reminded her of a favourite saying of Mr Warburton's, that if you took 1 Corinthians, chapter thirteen, and in every verse wrote "money" instead of "charity", the chapter had ten times as much meaning as before.'

The title page for *Keep the Aspidistra Flying* goes further, leaving the reader in no doubt as to the focus of the book and demonstrating apparent continuity in the writer's method, with 1 Corinthians published beneath the author and title of the book:

GEORGE ORWELL

Keep the Aspidistra Flying

Though I speak with the tongues of men and of angels, and have not money, I am become as a sounding brass, or a tinkling cymbal. And though I have the gift of prophecy, and understand all mysteries, and all knowledge; and though I have all faith, so that I could remove mountains, and have not money, I am nothing. And though I bestow all my goods to feed the poor, and though I give my body to be burned, and have not money, it profiteth me nothing. Money suffereth long, and is king; money envieth

*not; money vaunteth not itself, is not puffed up, doth not behave
unseemly, seeketh not her own, is not easily provoked, thinketh
no evil; rejoiceth not in iniquity, but rejoiceth in truth; beareth all
things, believe all things, hopeth all things, endureth all things...
And now abideth faith, hope, money, these three; and the greatest
of these is money.*

I CORINTHIANS XIII (adapted by George Orwell)

Even greater prophecy is revealed by his analysis of money as religion,
an accurate forecast given the near-universal decline of worship in all
parts of the United Kingdom since Orwell's death. Time once used
for worship has been replaced by shopping, with malls and shopping
centres replacing churches and cathedrals for many people on Sundays.
The commercialisation of Christmas also, apparently, seems to have
no end.

Orwell critiqued the money god further in his 1942 essay 'Money
and Guns', evaluating the impact of the war on attitudes to material possessions and the value derived from them. But it is a passage from *Keep
the Aspidistra Flying* that remains arguably his most potent observation
on the making of the modern world:

*Money worship has been elevated into a religion. Perhaps it is the
only real religion – the only really felt religion – that is left to us.
Money is what God used to be. Good and evil have no meaning
any longer except failure and success ... the Decalogue has been
reduced to two commandments. One for the employers – the elect,
the money-priesthood as it were – 'Thou shalt make money'; the
other for the employed – the slaves and the underlings – 'Thou
shalt not lose thy job'.*

My journey to Hampstead began on one of those very dark autumnal mornings, where the inhabitants of London seem to be ignoring the world that awaits them outside. Their beds entice them to slumber still, or having already risen, a cup of tea is taken in a cold kitchen where only the boiling of a kettle, or the radio, break the silence of dawn. They are days when it never seems to get light fully; the winds begin to pick up and 'leaves on the line' or the 'wrong type of rain' begin to disrupt rail timetables.

Every line on the Underground has its peculiar smell, which changes even as one crosses from the foot tunnel of one line to the foot tunnel of another in the same station. As for most Londoners, I feel the tube is a comforting, never-changing presence in a city whose capacity for regeneration is surely matched only by New York. The black-coloured Northern Line is one of the busiest on the network, the busiest for most of the 2000s but now second to the Central Line with 280 million unique passenger journeys in 2016–17. Even on a Sunday, tube carriages are crushed full of people. However, the Underground can still be found deserted at certain hours, as I discovered beginning my journey to Hampstead.

George and I descended into the Bank branch of the Northern Line from London Bridge station at 5.40am, a time when the network seems to be inhabited only by its engineering staff going home to sleep. The stations passed in quick succession, as familiar as the passing of night for day, the pre-recorded announcer echoing throughout the empty carriage.

There is no Underground station close to the part of Hampstead Orwell lived in for two years. The choice is between Belsize Park or Kentish Town, both some distance and a good walk from either Booklovers' Corner or one of the two flats he occupied during his time in the area. Settling for Belsize Park, we arrived just after 6am to the usual maze of Underground tunnels. The spiral stairwells of the tube lines built during the Edwardian period are brilliant for dogs, since while the smells and winds waft up or down the void intermittently, a dog is left in a perpetual state of bewilderment as the stairs twist up and out of sight. It is the only place on the Underground where I will let a dog off their lead: they proceed cautiously on the basis of the unknown, and always totter up or down by six steps or so, before halting and peering back to their owner.

I felt the first blast of cold air as we neared the top of the stairwell, the endless swirl of maroon red and cream tiling eventually breached by the algae-green floral tiling of the ticket office. Designed by architect Leslie Green, who had been commissioned by the 'Electric Underground Railways of London Limited' to build their lines' stations, the ticket offices represent an imaginative application of the 'arts and crafts' style. Few remain intact across the network now.

Belsize Park is an affluent area of North London, and even at 6am there was a steady stream of commuters still scurrying, as Orwell described more than 70 years ago, as 'black hordes ... like ants into a hole'. At that hour, in autumn, their faces were obscured in the dark, and as I walked away from the station their flow towards the subterranean world of the Underground became greater and greater. My task was to find the site of Booklovers' Corner, a kilometre and more away, through the maze of Edwardian terraces which sprawl over this area south of Hampstead Heath.

Most of this part of London was built rapidly, chiefly in ostentatious red brick. This was a status symbol contrasting with the ever-sooty yellow brick in which older parts of London were built. It also escaped large-scale bombing, meaning the often-enormous villas, well into four storeys, stand there solidly still.

The late Victorian period, and Edwardiana, was obsessed with decorative details which sometimes went into excess. St Stephen's Church, at Rosslyn Hill, just at the junction down on to South End Road and completed in 1869, is the epitome of this: a heavily gothic church in the French style, built from a myriad of coloured bricks from

Indian red to tallow. In the ominous dawn light of that hour, the profusion of exceptionally foul gargoyles looming down from on high is not an attractive spectacle. I can't imagine how much more eerie the building would have appeared when derelict, having been out of use since 1977, and deconsecrated in 2002.

Booklovers' Corner lay towards the bottom of South End Road, down a steep incline from St Stephen's, where a small traffic island appears amid the chaos of a London Borough's attempt at effective traffic management. Several busy roads meet here, and there is the constant puffing of gigantic, red, double-decker London buses, with the effect of the traffic mingling like a herd of elephants unsure which direction each of them is to take next. The dominant feature architecturally is a brutal, modernist NHS hospital – The Royal Free – which would look more at home in a Stalinist model town somewhere in the foothills of the Ural Mountains, than among the lanes of genteel Hampstead. Before it was completed in 1977, two other hospitals were based on the site, Hampstead General Hospital and The North Western Fever Hospital, suggesting that in Orwell's time as a bookseller the staff of the hospital were as common a sight in these parts as they are today.

I would struggle to think of a better name for a bookshop than Booklovers' Corner. London is a little less civilised a city for the absence of its name, a place where I imagine lovers of literature encountered each other amid the bustle of a busy London interchange: a backdrop of red buses and George Gilbert Scott's scarlet telephone boxes. For most of the 80s and 90s the site, a conventionally sized shop at the base of a red-brick tenement block known as Warwick Mansions, was a down-at-heel pizza parlour open until 3am. Later a hamburger bar, today it is a bakery. A hair salon and upmarket flooring company are its neighbours.

A plaque on the wall, featuring a bust of Orwell that is a replica of one owned by his adopted son, Richard, is attached to the left of the main entrance. An enduring mystery is the repeat disappearance of the Orwell bust, only recently restored and dedicated for the third time. Across from the shop, on the small wedge of land that sits in the middle of the interchange, is a gothic Victorian water fountain, installed by some wealthy benefactor.

A remodelling of the pavement around the fountain thoughtfully engraved the following quotations into a literary heptagon of paving, coincidentally (and I am unsure whether intentionally) including a quotation from D.H. Lawrence, one of Orwell's favourite writers, and another from Herbert Asquith, the former Liberal prime minister who is buried close to Orwell in the graveyard of All Saints' Church, at Sutton Courtenay in Oxfordshire. A famous phrase from Orwell's great novelette, *Animal Farm*, faces the direction of Booklovers' Corner:

'"All animals are created equal,
but some are more equal than others"
George Orwell (1903–1950), *Animal Farm* 1945'

'"The living moment is everything"
(1885–1930) D.H. Lawrence'

'"Youth would be an ideal state if it came a little later in life"
Herbert Henry Asquith (1852–1928)'

⌣

'Bookshop Memories' is Orwell's account of life in a second-hand bookshop, and it is characteristically accurate of the nature of the work in one, and of the observations one might make. The first time I read the essay, published in 1936, I photocopied and posted it to the second-hand bookshop I worked in as a schoolboy, The Old Hall Bookshop in

Brackley, Northamptonshire. Such was the rapture of laughter when it was read by the staff, it was posted to the shop's noticeboard:

'The thing that chiefly struck me was the rarity of really bookish people ... I doubt whether ten per cent of our customers knew a good book from a bad one'.

'Vague-minded women looking for birthday presents for their nephews were commonest of all'.

'Scarcely half the people who ordered books from us ever came back'.

'As a rule a bookshop is horribly cold in winter'.

'... and the top of a book is the place where every bluebottle prefers to die'.

Orwell seems to have enjoyed his time there, commenting to Cher Monsieur Raimbault (the translator of *Down and Out in Paris and London*), not long after he started at the bookshop in November 1934, that he felt it was a job that suited him much better than teaching. Jon Kimche, who worked with Orwell at Booklovers' Corner, recalled that he rarely sat, preferring to 'stand in the centre [of the shop], a slightly forbidding figure ... a very tall figure almost like de Gaulle, standing'.

The descriptions of customers and their features are captured in *Keep the Aspidistra Flying*, I think possibly the best descriptions of characters to be found anywhere in his fictional work:

'The old woman made off, mumbling, with malevolence in the hump of her shoulders, and joined her husband ... the two old creatures shuffled away, beetle-like in the long greasy overcoats which hid everything except their feet.'

'The door-bell clanged. Two upper-middle-class ladies sailed noisily in. One pink and fruity, thirty-fivish, with voluptuous bosom burgeoning from her coat ... the other middle-aged, tough and curried – India, presumably.'

One interaction in the shop, between Orwell and a sales agent from a publisher, cannot help but break a smile. Charles Pick, a renowned literary agent who discovered among many well-known writers Graham Greene, John le Carré and Roald Dahl, began his career in publishing as an office boy for Victor Gollancz, Orwell's publisher. Responsible for navigating the Capital's bookshops to drive up sales, he took copies of *Burmese Days* to a 'bookshop in Hampstead'. Trying to persuade the shop to stock the new novel, he said to the bookseller he met: 'I know you don't stock a lot of new books, but there's a marvellous new book called *Burmese Days* coming next month by George Orwell.' Orwell, to whom Pick was speaking, replied in the laconic fashion for which he was known: 'How interesting!'

It cannot have been the only occasion Pick met Orwell, since numerous terse letters exist illustrating the toing and froing that led to Orwell's publisher significantly altering the text of *Keep the Aspidistra Flying*. Orwell was summoned on more than one occasion to Gollancz's offices in Covent Garden, which Pick's son, the publisher Martin Pick, recalls as being 'pure Victorian in its austerity. Gollancz didn't believe in heating it and there was just one lavatory in the basement. Until the 1960s it was in the middle of the market and on summer afternoons, rather smelly.'

Orwell lived above the shop in Warwick Mansions for a time, in a bedsit leased to him by Booklovers' Corner's eccentric owners, Francis and Myfanwy Westrope. This comfortable existence meant that bed-to-desk travel time was minimal, and Orwell was able not only to find time to write in the shop (on occasion, it is documented his typewriter was with him in the shop) but the arrangement for his working hours gave him the time to both earn a living and write. A letter to Brenda Salkeld dated 15 January 1935 explained: 'My timetable is as follows: 7am get up, dress etc., cook & eat breakfast. 8.45 go down & open the shop, & I am usually kept there until about 9.45. Then come home, do out my room, light the fire etc. 10.30am–1pm I do some writing. 1pm I get lunch & eat it. 2pm–6.30pm I am in the shop. Then I come home, get my supper, do the washing up & after that sometimes do about an hour's work.'

Later he moved further away, to a flat off the southern part of the Heath, at 77 Parliament Hill. The bottom of this steep road is found by walking over the humped bridge above a railway line, and turning right at the Hampstead Heath London Overground station. We walked halfway up before I spotted a black-and-white 'STOP TTIP'* poster in the window of a house five-storeys high and worth well over £4 million. I reflected how comforting it was to find Hampstead Socialism alive and kicking ferociously.

In search of breakfast, I turned around and discovered, back down at the parade of shops, another refreshingly familiar constant of the British way of life in Polly's Tearooms, an old-school cafe ('CAFF'), with brown-and-cream lino tiling, and a transparent refrigerator unit full of substantial carrot, fruit and chocolate sponge cakes. No matter what new technologies advance, places like this will always survive in England (incidentally, this might explain Orwell's choice of a tea shop as the location of the final chapter of *Nineteen Eighty-Four*).

Eventually, heading back towards the Heath I saw a sign directing the pedestrian towards 'Keats House', home of the Romantic poet John Keats (1795–1821), another of Hampstead's literary heroes. I find

---

* The Transatlantic Trade and Investment Partnership, once to be signed between the European Union and the USA.

monuments of any sort – churches, or follies especially – hard to resist visiting and so relenting, was led by a boisterous George up the quiet, green lane. At the top of it stands a New England-style parish church, St John's, Downshire Hill. New England vernacular is a fashionable architectural style in these parts of London, and in the autumnal colours, evocative of Providence or Boston. It may explain the attraction of Hampstead for American expatriates, though 'the New England' style actually began in England, being replicated in the American colonies, and has not changed much since – just like the archaic style of the English language to be found in India. The houses lining the road, renamed Keats Grove just to avoid any doubt that Keats once strode along it, are all set back from the lane with beautiful, English cottage-style gardens.

The country-cottage style can be found all over the wealthier streets of residential London; the very definition of the English middle-class obsession with the bucolic in one of the world's largest urban centres. It is something emulated by wealthy immigrants and expatriates, a status symbol of affluence and respectability no less. In the 1930s the aspidistra embodied the same. Only to very few people will the aspidistra have resonance in 21st-century Britain, however.

In the novel, the principle remains: certain possessions, brands and habits obliquely state one's belonging to one class or another. It still applies to plants in my view, and still one beginning with the letter 'a'. Almost every garden along the lane, and most of the front spaces across Hampstead maintain the agapanthus rather than the aspidistra. *Agapanthus Africanus* is a bulb plant with upright stalks growing each summer into a striking green, and bulbous purple or white flowers which lean into the sun in a chic, unobtrusive style; just as middle-class rules of conduct might dictate.

The psychology of the English middle class, as defined by Orwell, and their marriage to the traditions of the countryside, is a complex one, but is a prerequisite for understanding this social group's attitudes to so many topics. Possibly a hand-down from the aristocracy, which begrudgingly decamped to London townhouses 'for the season' before squirrelling back as fast as they could to their estates or Scottish hunting lodges, it is a phenomenon defined best by the popularity and longevity of London's parks and tree-lined roads.

⌣

At the top of the steep residential road we had already half-conquered before breakfast, and a good half-mile from Booklovers' Corner, Orwell was further away from the shop with his move to Parliament Hill. No longer 'living above the shop', his time commitment at the bookshop became less of an interference with his writing. In one letter, again to Salkeld, he described his new landlady somewhat enthusiastically as 'the non-interfering sort, which is so rare among London landladies'. Shortly after moving there he met, at a friend's flat in Primrose Hill, the woman who would become his first wife.

South Shields-born-and-bred Eileen O'Shaughnessy had studied English at St Hugh's College, Oxford, and after a brief period teaching was studying for a master's degree in psychology at University College London when they met. It does not seem to have been love at first sight, and it was said by friends that the future Eileen Blair only accepted Orwell's offer of marriage because she was determined to accept the first proposal she had after reaching the age of 30 (she was 29 when they met).

Kay Ekevall, a customer of the bookshop who became acquainted with Orwell after complimenting the giant man's ability to 'reach all the shelves nobody else could without hauling a ladder out', said of O'Shaughnessy: 'She was gay and lively and interesting, and much more his level. She was older than me, she'd been to university, and she had an intellectual standing in her own right.' In an interview in the 1980s one of her friends from Oxford, Lydia Jackson, reflected pointedly in the other direction that:

> *After that party in London she told me that Eric Blair 'sort of' proposed to her, saying that he wasn't much good, but even so perhaps she would consider him ... I was rather appalled, I must say, because I felt Eileen really should find someone much more suitable, more attractive, younger perhaps. More physically attractive. Because George didn't look well even at that time ... George talked in a way that intrigued her, interested her, because he was an unusual person. I'm very doubtful if she was in love with him. I think it must have been his outspokenness that attracted her.*

For Orwell, so long engaged in hopeless trysts and forever thrown by his estrangement from childhood sweetheart Jacintha Buddicom, his meeting O'Shaughnessy was transformational. Rayner Heppenstall, a fellow novelist and future BBC producer who soon after shared a flat with Orwell in nearby Kentish Town, was informed by Orwell in a letter dated September 1935, that: 'She is the nicest person I have met for a long time. However, at present alas! I can't afford a ring, except perhaps a Woolworths' one.' The relationship advanced, however, and before long they would be living together and married. Their life was centred, for the time Orwell was not in Spain, on a cottage in the small Hertfordshire village of Wallington.

⌒

Parliament Hill is usually far less frequented than the viewing point out across London from Greenwich Observatory, although on this occasion I had the pleasure of observing the naturalist Bill Oddie darting in and out of the bushes which engulf the steep descent on its southern side. The view from the hill gives a better perspective of London, even with the Shard now framing the dome of St Paul's Cathedral in a way that causes the skyline of London to look just that bit more muddled. Walking up to the site, past steel-framed wooden benches and more dogs, I always find it impossible not to feel excited in anticipation of the view that awaits. Misty autumnal days are best, and for some reason – no matter how many times I see it – my eyes are distracted by a strikingly tall tower, at this distance looking built in a Japanese-style, cast-off to the bottom left of the panorama.

Leaving the Heath behind us we walked in the direction of Kentish Town, in search of Orwell's third and final home during the second of the three periods he spent living in London over the course of his life. Another flat, this time a smaller townhouse split into maisonettes, on leafy Lawford Road. Orwell shared with Heppenstall and Michael Sayers (an Irish poet), both new friends made among the literati of Hampstead he had now joined. There can be no question that this period of his life led to the establishment of George Orwell the author, as opposed to Eric Blair the writer.

The publication of *Burmese Days* during this time established him as capable not only of writing impressive journo-fiction, but also of building on the acclaim of *Down and Out in Paris and London*. It also propelled him to explore the poverty of interwar Britain in the next project following his departure from London, *The Road to Wigan Pier*. The house on Lawford Road, number 50, is a large, semi-detached, Victorian villa and the epitome of middle-class respectability, both in 1935 and at the time of writing. To illustrate its status, the front door is reached by climbing no fewer than thirteen steps; a tradesman's entrance to the rear the point of access for lesser mortals.

Orwell's work in Wigan and the north of England, at the age of 32, was a significant part of his political awakening, with his commitment to democratic socialism not complete until his experiences in the Spanish Civil War. However, his appreciation for England – England, not Britain – in the context of its social and economic history is clear and demonstrated by his love of literature where, in his description of the bookshop: 'A little above eye level, already on their way to heaven and oblivion, were the poets of yesteryear, the stars of his earlier youth. Yeats, Davies, Housman, Thomas, de la Mare, Hardy … shall we ever again get a writer worth reading?'

The historical sweep of English literature is a theme especially present among Orwell's essays, and the synthesis of history and literature I sense was an obsession for him. Ekevall, his closest friend during his time in Hampstead, reflected after his death: 'We talked about Chaucer quite a lot because we both liked him. He wanted to write an epic on Chaucerian lines about the history of England from Chaucer's time to the present day.' The epic, like the ghost stories, never came. But both Chaucer and another of his favoured authors, D.H. Lawrence, are referred to glowingly in *Keep the Aspidistra Flying*. As if to suggest: I think these are good authors and if you try them, you might think so too.

Wallington, Hertfordshire, England

Animal farm (1936–45)

Hertfordshire straddles a part of England lying between industrial Bedfordshire, with its tradition of brickmaking, and agrarian Cambridgeshire. Orwell sought somewhere archetypically rural, somewhere to seek relief from his dislike of the spread of London, articulated in *Coming up for Air*. Much of what he loved about Wallington revived memories of summers he'd spent as a child in Shropshire, his love of the exotic vegetation and creeping jungle observed in Burma and, later, his self-exile on Jura. His time in Wallington might easily have inspired the TV sitcom *The Good Life*: all land-living and allotment-tending.

My journey, by car, began from Milton Keynes and then went cross-country, over north Buckinghamshire, Bedfordshire and finally into Hertfordshire, a confusion of A-roads and dual carriageways. Poorly signposted, a sharp right-hand turn off a main road lands the motorist on a quiet country back road, immersing the driver in a rural idyll of twisting lanes and sunken hedgerows. Wallington is then discovered, perched atop a gently sloping hill at the northern extremities of the Chilterns.

It is, in general, an undeveloped village, quite free from post-war and modern housing. Very little has physically changed here since Orwell moved to the village. The houses are invariably large, and the sense that this is an agricultural settlement is apparent from the number of farm buildings and equipment passed on the first stretch of road, the main thoroughfare. The gardens are big too, so any poverty that once existed there must have been ameliorated by access to home-grown food. The genteel rural poverty of the past is a far cry from the affluent commuter village Wallington has become, all chic shades of paint and fast cars.

Rural poverty exists still, but is of a very different form to that found in urban areas. In rural Britain, there is no shortage of homes that still lack central heating. Unlike people living in poverty in urban areas, who remain freezing most of the time in the colder months, rural dwellers have to be good at making fires. Orwell's small cottage, the Stores, typified the decrepit condition of much housing in rural England at that time. Orwell even confessed to a friend that it was a 'bloody awful' place. But it still benefited from an enormous garden few slums in the city could dream of. Today the property rests in around a quarter of an acre of land, backs onto open fields and even has a swimming pool.

1936 was a formative year for Orwell, the first full year of his relationship with his future wife, Eileen. Wallington would be his refuge in between his visit to the north of England to write *The Road to Wigan Pier*, and to Spain, the findings from which would lead to *Homage to Catalonia*. No substantive work relates to Wallington. *Animal Farm* was written when Orwell was living back in London during the war, although he drew inspiration from the village and its farms. Essays and letters from this period abound and were likely to be written here in his small, two-storey wattle-and-daub, thatched cottage. Arguably his most famous essay, 'Shooting an Elephant', was written in Wallington over the autumn of 1936.

Sunk deep into its setting, on a sharp bend of the main thoroughfare, the Stores was once the village shop and is undeniably one of the older houses in the village. Like the ancient roads that lead to Wallington, old houses can be dated by how big a step is taken down to enter them. In the Stores' case, this is more or less a whole foot, and its upstairs windows are much closer to the ground than any two-storeyed modern property would be. Together with its thatched roof, it is Hobbit-like. No doubt such a quirky building was the source of appeal for Orwell, a man who made an art out of seeking distinction in individuality. A plaque on the Stores reads:

Herts County Council Centenary 1889–1989

George Orwell
1903–1950
Author
Lived here 1936–1940

Its garden fulfilled his desire to grow his food and to rear animals. Wallington also reflected the tendency of Orwell's homes, as in Burma and on Jura, to be shared with four-legged friends.

In addition to the garden, which was vast, Orwell leased a section of Kitt's Piece, which was an area of land across from the Stores. Here Orwell and his wife grew vegetables and kept their goat, Muriel. She inspired the naming of the endearing goat of the same name in *Animal Farm*, whose responsibility it was to read the farm's seven commandments. A second goat, Kate, later joined Muriel and, after he and Eileen built a hen house, nineteen hens arrived in the autumn of 1937. Eileen was confident enough to write: 'There is probably no question on poultry keeping that I am not able and very ready to answer.'

Orwell developed an attachment to goats, providing a home to one in Marrakech, too. In one letter he gave his view that goats' milk tastes much the same as cows' milk, an observation I've enjoyed echoing, to my host's concurrence and my amusement, when offered it. Villagers would spot Orwell enjoying a walk with his goats, but his own animal farm at the Stores must have been nightmarish to manage. If he was not away researching, Eileen was, or they both were. Over his lease of the Stores, Orwell travelled to the north of England for his *Road to Wigan Pier*; Spain for *Homage to Catalonia*; spent six months at a sanatorium in Kent, followed by another six months' recuperation in Marrakech. And during the war, the Stores was for weekends only.

Goats were not the only animals to receive earthy human names. A cockerel was named Henry Ford, on the grounds that he was so industrious, and their dog, a poodle, was called Marx. It has been hard to find out much about the dog, when he died and in what circumstances, but after his purchase in July 1937, he is described as 'appealing' by Eileen. Marx was so named because they wanted a reminder that neither of them had read much Marx, but once they had, they took such a dislike to the writer that Eileen mentions they found it hard to look at him. With 'black and white hair, greying at the temples', Marx joined Orwell when he went into the sanatorium in Kent, and various photos show them together there and on the beach at Southwold.

The condition of the cottage had never been good. Like most of the houses in the village it was the product of centuries of addition by generations of owners. Likely to date from the turn of the 18th century or just before, the cottage once had large open fireplaces. Known as inglenooks in England and topped by a huge, thick trunk of hardwood, these were replaced in the Stores by smaller iron grills in the late Victorian period. The largest had a side oven for baking but is unlikely to have been used by them for making bread. The Blair's regular order from the travelling baker, J. Walker and Sons, was 'two small brown loaves', recalled their delivery boy as an adult. Even the cottage's sources of heat will have made little difference to the warmth of the house, since there was no damp-proof course. When the home was renovated in the 1980s, many of the bricks in the foundations were found to be disintegrated.

The damp, exacerbated by absences, will not have helped Orwell's lungs. But with so many trips away over their time in Wallington, he would ferociously produce new written work during the periods he was back. Villagers, who could purchase non-perishable items only from Orwell and Eileen, in their scheme to re-open the village shop, recall the tapping of the typewriter upstairs. Eileen hesitated to disturb him; in one letter she wrote she was scribbling in the dark because he had hogged all the candles. A pamphlet on war for the Peace Pledge Union was written there and is among the small volume of Orwell's work to be lost. But the most avoidable of all losses took place when Orwell surrendered the lease in 1946, with the cottage sold a few years later.

Esther Brookes, the headmistress of the nearby junior school, bought the cottage after Orwell ended the lease. The kitchen walls were described as grimy, the stench of Calor gas lingered, and the floor was covered in old boots. The presence of boots, probably unintentional, is fitting: Orwell wrote in a letter a memorable description of the many boots he dug up in the garden when they first took it. Brookes also found papers scattered over the floor, said to be mouldy or illegible. When interviewed years later she recalled a name on one of them: a letter to, or from, Ethel Mannin, the anti-fascist campaigner. One couple who helped clear the cottage after Orwell moved out remembered the smouldering remains of a bonfire outside, and a letter bearing the name 'O Henry', the pen name of the American writer William Sydney Porter. Had they survived, they would have filled gaps in Orwell's *Collected Letters*.

Orwell's observation of the changing seasons and flora and fauna feature in his writing throughout his life. Wallington, shorn of the urban jungle, let his love of the natural world prosper. Villagers were thankful, as for more than 40 years after he left, the Albertine Rambler rose he had planted in the front garden opened into flower every summer. His diary and letters for periods spent at the Stores are marked by his jottings on the transition from winter to spring. He wrote after returning from Morocco in April 1939:

> *The spring on the whole seems backward. Flowers now in bloom in the garden:* Polyanthus; Aubretia; Scilla; *grape Hyacinth;* Arabis; *a few* Narcissi. *Many daffodils in the field ...* Bullaces *and plums coming into blossom. Apple trees budding but no blossom yet. Pears in full blossom. Roses sprouting fairly strongly. Peonies sprouting strongly. Crocuses just over ... bats everywhere.*

And in March 1941:

> *Crocuses out everywhere, a few wallflowers budding, snowdrops just at their best. Couple of hares sitting about in the winter wheat and gazing at one another. Now and again in this war, at intervals of months, you get your nose above the water for a few moments and notice that the earth is still going round the sun.*

During the war, and also when Orwell and Eileen were in Morocco just before it, the Stores was sub-let. This was not without complication, given the primitive living conditions. Guidance instructing friends who they sub-let to noted to avoid 'the use of thick paper in the W.C.', on grounds it would block the cesspool. One comment, indicative of a dark sense of humour, explained the kitchen was likely to flood if there was sudden rain in winter, but that the house was 'otherwise passably dry'. The sub-lets were not a success, residents being bewildered by the vast garden and its zoo. From September 1939 onward the animals were sold, and the allotment wound down.

The area behind the cottage, accessible via a short footpath, is known as the Plantation. It is a wide grass field interspersed with large mature trees and does not seem to have been ploughed for some time.

This is probably for the best since the weight of a tractor would mean the field's rampant rabbit warrens and foxholes might collapse in on themselves. It seems an unloved area, the sort where rabbits and foxes have been allowed to take over, and clumps of rusting barbed wire fester. Orwell enjoyed walking at the rear, where Marx would course hares.

～

A short walk from the church, via a driveway that peels off from the metalled road, a farmhouse appears just as one might imagine the farm from *Animal Farm* would look, aping the house from the animated Christmas classic *The Snowman*, or an accessory for a child's train set. Although there is doubt over which of the three farms in the village can lay claim to the title of *the* 'animal farm', it is likely Orwell used artistic licence to combine the features of Bury Farm, next to the church, and Manor Farm back down on the main road which passes through the village. Confusingly, although not unexpectedly for an English village, both have at one time or another been called Manor Farm. It is the current Manor Farm which has the traditional Great Barn, however, and it is here where villagers hold the occasional *Animal Farm* barn dance.

Orwell seemed to be broadly fond of the villagers he met, and they retained favourable memories of him. In autumn 1938 he wrote: 'The village people are really very nice', but his description of them – as a collective noun – is indicative of a sense of separateness. Eileen sounded much less attached, writing at around the same time that 'one gets hysterical with no one to speak to except the village who are not what you could call soothing'. In spring 1938 Orwell's health deteriorated, with heavy bleeding on the lungs, and he was accepted temporarily to a sanatorium in Kent. This episode is what led to the trip to Morocco, or at least a bout of recuperation in somewhere with a kinder climate than that of the English winter.

Before Orwell's health worsened, he had been considering a return to India, to work as a journalist at a weekly journal in Lucknow, the north Indian city famed for episodes in the Indian Mutiny in 1857. *The Pioneer* was edited by a Desmond Young, who wrote to Orwell out of the blue to invite him to become his assistant editor. The newspaper was liberal, advocating self-government for India (albeit, 'towards the end of the century'). Orwell was positive, writing: 'My object in going to India is, apart from the work on *The Pioneer*, to try and get a clearer idea of political and social conditions.' From this might well have developed a *Road to Wigan Pier*-style investigation, of which we were deprived when the (British) government of India blocked his appointment. So alas there was no '*Road to Lucknow Ghat*', and the rationale for the government's objections remain murky.* *Burmese Days* had been banned in British India, so it was a little ironic that he should later be employed by the BBC to broadcast to India from London.

⌐

Wallington could be a case study in the decline of the English village. Orwell's revival of the village shop at the Stores was his attempt at reversing the process of economic decline. They took nineteen shillings in the first week. He caustically noted that there was none of the 'hanging around' he observed in the book trade. But the shop did not last long, impossible to sustain with their toing and froing. The village pub, The Plough just next door (a villager, Rene Stacey, remembered serving Orwell his last pint there, and she kept the jug she served it in until her death), and the all-age elementary school once so common in England, closed in the early post-war period. The farms have undergone

---

* A *ghat* is a river-side wharf, common to the Indian subcontinent.

a process of amalgamation, meaning that one landowner now owns most of the fields surrounding the village.

Orwell would often cycle down to Baldock, the nearest market town, just two miles distant, and his journey was very much 'down'. At the other end of the village, the opposite to the side I entered, a winding country road descends quickly to cross the dual carriageway, a bypass to Baldock, and then enters the town. Baldock is an ancient medieval market town fairly typical of a country town in England. Many, especially in the south and east, have broad central streets onto which a jumbo jet could comfortably land. These served a practical purpose, the trading of cattle and the hosting of a weekly market, hence the soubriquet *market* town. Most in the south of England, especially those closest to London, have long since lost their cattle and many their markets, too. Being reasonably close to London, just 40 minutes by train, Baldock shares with Wallington the same dormitory status, providing homes for commuters to London.

The best choice for lunch in an off-the-beaten-track market town will typically be its coaching inn, although some menus have not changed since the 1970s: all prawn cocktail or breaded scampi. Holding George tightly on his lead, I entered The White Lion and, like I always do, asked whether dogs were welcome. In London this approach is hit-and-miss. My default position is to consider they will not be allowed entry, so it was refreshing to hear the landlady say: 'We prefer dogs to children', and a barmaid add: 'Absolutely, go and sit by the fire', in a tone which was surprised to think any other response would be plausible.

The rain was lashing down as we arrived and left. I had forgotten to bring an umbrella so was drenched twice. But my stomach was pleasantly lined with sausages, mash and real ale, ensuring I at least had the energy to continue exploring Wallington for the rest of the day. I had hoped to visit the town museum before leaving, in anticipation of finding some long-lost Orwelliana, but was disappointed. Housed in a small part of the town hall and with a tiny entrance, it seemed to be closed indefinitely. Had it been open I would have needed to spare the entrance fee – an inexpensive, curiously low 25p. Even then, its opening times are hardly convenient for the tourist:

BALDOCK MUSEUM
OPENING TIMES

SUNDAYS 2–4PM
WEDNESDAYS 11AM–1PM

Glumly returning from Baldock to Wallington, I drove back towards the village via the steep lane that connects it to town. There was no traffic in either direction, and on a bleak midwinter day the hedgerows were barren, the withered branches of the occasional tree the only break in my line of sight. Orwell, who traipsed this lane often by either bus or bike, may have enjoyed the descent to town, but surely not the climb back up. Even the engine on my car was pleased by the plateau once we passed the signposts and entered the hilltop village once more.

It is not clear whether Orwell regularly attended church in Wallington, although if his habit in the rest of life held right, it is likely he went on occasion. It is recorded that when Orwell was shot in Spain, he was entered on the list of the sick or invalided to pray for during services, suggesting he was known to the Wallington congregation. The church, St Mary's, was also the venue of his wedding on 9 June 1936. He and Eileen were married by a non-resident vicar Eileen had known in the county of Rutland, according to the 'Rites and Ceremonies of the Church of England'. Orwell's profession was given as 'Author', and his father 'Retired I.C.S.' (Indian Civil Service). These details are public because, endearingly, St Mary's sells copies of them in polythene document wallets for the princely sum of £1.00.

St Mary's is a typically old English church, nearing its 1,000th year. Its first documented recording is AD 1190, when the land it was sitting on was gifted to the great abbey at St Albans. Like many churches in rural England it was never built to plan, so its structure evolved piecemeal. As resources became available – time, skills or a patron's money – the church would be improved. The porch, tower and side chapel were added in the 15th century, and further enhancements made in the 18th. The wealthy families who might have owned land in a parish became benefactors, paying for some stained glass or an impressive family vault or two. Being in pursuit of permanence they endowed many of England's 13,000 historic churches with tremendous artistic riches.

The church sits a stone's throw from Bury Farm, conveniently placed for participation in a harvest festival each September. Detached from the village via a short, tree-lined track which ends at the drive to the 'big' house, it is set in a large churchyard. The nave is long for such a small village, out of proportion to its squat bell tower. Suffice to say there is a lot of stone in its walls, and like many old churches, it is solidly built. Opposite the perimeter wall which sequesters the churchyard from the lane is a small pond. At this time of year, it appeared crestfallen: decaying remnants of green foliage, and a mud-grey, murky bottom. Little seems to have changed. Orwell once noted: 'The pond up by the church has become so stagnant that it no longer has duckweed, only the scummy green stuff.' It is a scummy pond still.

With a congregation at the time of my visit of 23, six of whom were non-resident, the church-going population of Wallington is not vast. Yet the church is well cared for and the parishioners eager enough to host a small display about Orwell's time at Wallington. Something is endearing about the sort of patch-and-make displays English churches and town halls put together, all sticky-backed-plastic and typewriter-made signage. Although it is better to see something than nothing, it is not a substitute for a proper visitor board or even – with an eye on a vision for Orwell tourism – a visitor centre. It would put the farm from *Animal Farm* on the map; school children could visit as part of their studies and tourists would arrive as part of a literary tour of England.

The church has that familiar musty smell, a permanent earth-like quality. As with a school, the odour of a church never changes. St Mary's has probably smelt the same since the 12th century. Sizeable circular metal rings, like the halos of angels, hang from the ceiling and dangle ominously over the solid, beige-coloured pews. The light from the large windows on every side streams onto whitewashed walls, framed by plain limestone arches which give the interior of an English church such character. There is a small wooden organ painted white, a com-promise on something bigger. It fails to conceal the bell-ropes dangling from the ceiling in the tower behind it and will struggle hard to fill the room with its chords. The hymns for the previous Sunday remained on the hymn board – always so imposing – in their thick gothic script: 130; 542; 313; 41.

Before I left I scanned the visitors' book, and spotted at least one Orwell fan making the rounds:

Visiting the church and village for the George Orwell connection, with my son George (Orwell influence) and Dad. Lovely church and bright and sunny morning.
6th November 2014

I smiled. After hastily jotting down a comment, I signed and left the church before darting down the path and into the car as quickly as I could. The light was fading fast, and having seen virtually no one since I had arrived in the village, I was eager not to hang around a desolate graveyard for long. The last gravestone before the way out of the church-yard is particularly gruesome – a profusion of carved skulls appearing to scream in agony and made even more fearful by their corrosion by rain. '1695' is just about visible through the lichen and moss burying the gravestone's browbeaten surface.

After a freezing, windswept and dull day of weather, an emotional and climatic contrast from the tropical thrills of India and Myanmar, I made my way back down the lane from the church. Joining the main thoroughfare again, I left the village and travelled along the sloping sunken road I had climbed when the sun was higher in the sky, and the marble of the chalk in the fields was visible in the bright light of our bleak midwinter's morning. Wallington is an archetypical English village surrounded by archetypical English countryside, and I can understand the attraction to Orwell of his middle-earth style retreat, in the maelstrom of his extraordinary life.

Wigan, Lancashire, England

Down and out (1936)

Until I visited the town, the image of Wigan Pier in my mind, courtesy of the title of George Orwell's famous book, was something along the lines of a seaside pleasure pier. The reality could not be further from the archetypal English seaside town, not least since Wigan is more than twenty miles inland. Its nearest seaside towns are Crosby and Formby, both affluent suburbs of Liverpool and culturally 'Scouse' rather than 'Mancunian'. What might be considered as one large conurbation in a larger country, in Britain is two proud cities, divided by a cherished eternity of tastes, accent and attitudes. Wigan has an identity of its own but culturally it is more Mancunian, and is administratively part of 'Greater' Manchester. It is however almost equidistant from both Liverpool and Manchester and could lay claim to being the 'capital' of Lancashire's coal fields, a swathe of towns and villages whose residents' primary activity for around 300 years was the mining of coal.

Aneurin Bevan, the Labour health minister in Clement Attlee's government, who became a close friend of Orwell as his editor at *Tribune* magazine, once described Britain as 'a lump of coal surrounded by fish'. Wigan and its surrounding hinterland have been so deeply mined that mining engineers over the centuries selectively sought to prevent sinkholes by retaining pillars of rock beneath important icons, including Wigan church. In a region mined so profusely, sinkholes are a common occurrence. A natural accommodation of the collapses in the landscape was the creation of a series of lakes south of the town, as the structural failure of one mine after another created a lunar-like post-industrial landscape.

Orwell's two objectives for visiting Wigan, and other towns and cities in the north of England in the spring of 1936, were first to explore the conditions of poverty and work, with a specific examination of conditions in the mines, and second to gain better insight into the culture of the English working class. He wrote: 'I went there partly because I wanted to see the most typical section of the English working class in close quarters.'

The Road to Wigan Pier is divided into two parts. Part one is a write-up of Orwell's diaries for the period, which runs from 31 January to 25 March 1936, and describes living conditions among the working class in the north of England. 'The Road' is important in the title, since en-route and after, he visited: Coventry, Birmingham, Stourbridge, Wolverhampton, Redbridge, Stafford, Stoke-on-Trent, Macclesfield, Manchester, Liverpool, Leeds, Barnsley and Sheffield. Part Two, often described by critics as the less successful, is a series of short essays on Orwell's transformation from conservative public schoolboy to democratic socialist, a restlessness which soon after led him to join the fight for socialism against fascism in civil war-torn Spain.

The book is one of the most powerful exposés of poverty in 20th-century Britain, not dimmed in the slightest by the passing of time. Prophesies in the book allude to the shape of his dystopic *Nineteen Eighty-Four*, with more optimistic predictions, such as automated machines that make the skills of labour redundant, standing the test of time. It is a book hard not to be moved by. At the time, criticism came from two quarters: those who challenged it by saying he only sought the worst in what he saw, and those who viewed certain passages in the book to be condescending to the poor, because they thought Orwell had written that they smelled. Kay Ekevall, his friend from Booklovers' Corner, bemoaned: 'I don't think he was a very objective person ... he only saw the side he wanted to see – you know, the really depressed, down-and-out workers. He didn't want to see anything positive about them.'

Criticism of Orwell seeing the worst is fair; there is not much to be positive about in *The Road to Wigan Pier*, despite the average standard of living being better in 1936 than it was in 1914, or 1870. But then that was the explicit purpose of Orwell's journalism in this book: to investigate and expose the worst because even if Britons' existence might be better elsewhere, in the town or the country, that in no way excused the continued existence of deprivation.

Orwell's commentary on the views of the middle and upper classes regarding the 'smell' of the working class was entirely prescient, i.e. they do not smell, or at least no more than everyone smells in some way, but the upper classes think they do. As with *Burmese Days*, the whole point was to expose a lie. The book sold four times as many copies as all of his other books combined, a total of 44,000 in the first year of publication alone. Two follow-ups have been penned in the period since Orwell's death: *Wigan Pier Revisited*, a 1981 polemic against the governments of Margaret Thatcher, and *The Road to Wigan Pier Revisited*, a 2012 polemic against the Conservative-led Coalition government. Neither seems to capture the simple, unbiased reporting of the original.

Orwell opens the book in the Brookers' Tripe Shop and lodging house, a 'two-up, two-down' terraced house on the Warrington Road in Wigan, demolished in 1977. These lodging houses, Orwell writes, were common in the period before the NHS and were typically home to the sick, old and destitute, who enjoyed low rents for minimal upkeep. The owners are described as a pecuniary pair, resentful of the sick who stay with them. They sold tripe – cow's stomach – which was once popular in Lancashire and is still more common to the diet there than elsewhere in the UK. He described the tripe being stored in a warm spot behind their sofa, and commented sardonically that, 'the Brookers never ate tripe themselves, I noticed.'

Evocative descriptions which characteristically force the reader to reflect on a simile they've probably never observed first hand, but can easily imagine, feature throughout Orwell's writing: 'in the morning the room stank like a ferret cage'. He also evocatively described the bed-bound Mrs Brooker, nagging 'in that peculiar watchful, loving way that invalids have'. What remains striking is the extent of absolute poverty before the war, but also an appreciation that Orwell was viewing those he observed through the eyes of – by any measure – a comfortable, upper-class prism. In various instances he reiterates the relativity of existence in these circumstances, such that even if the situation of the poor is considered horrifying by the visitor, it is all that those living that way have ever known and they make do in the best way they can. Even then, 'the best way' is not even a consideration. It is just how it is. And even the most charitable, well-meaning of the middle classes – then as now – should not force their standards on others.

The Road to Wigan Pier began the slow tide of resentment towards Orwell from those on the left. The vilification directed at him esca-lated, especially once Orwell turned once and for all against what he described as the 'crooks' running the USSR. *Animal Farm* and *Nineteen Eighty-Four* became very helpful cold war propaganda for the West, leading to further scorn from which his 'brand' among certain groups on the Left has still to recover. The process began in Wigan:

The truth is that to many people, calling themselves socialists, revolution does not mean a movement of the masses with which they hope to associate themselves; it means a set of reforms which 'we', the clever ones, are going to impose on 'them', the Lower

Orders ... it is strange how easily almost any socialist writer can lash himself into frenzies of rage against the class to which ... he invariably belongs.

Class is referenced either implicitly or explicitly throughout the book and is a theme featuring in much of Orwell's work. It is a consequence of his intrigue with the peculiarities of societal structures and those applied to England, especially. Speculation on the origins of this near-obsession is needless – his observations are powerful. For those in search of an answer I might suggest he was caught by a resentment created by his upbringing, and especially his education as a poorer scholarship boy in two schools filled with the moneyed old aristocracy or (more commonly) the nouveau riche.

Regardless, *The Road to Wigan Pier* is a book about class and its ramifications. He was attracted to Wigan partly for the reason that then (and as I was to find, now), working class culture remained intact and was not afflicted at all by middle England or 'southern' sensibilities. On choosing 'a Lancashire Cotton-town' he reflected: '[in them] you could probably go for months on end without once hearing an "educated" accent, whereas there can hardly be a town in the south of England where you could throw a brick without hitting the niece of a bishop'. He wrote: 'the essential point about the English class-system is that it is not entirely explicable in terms of money. Roughly speaking it is a money-stratification, but it is also interpenetrated by a sort of shadowy caste-system; rather like a jerry-built modern bungalow haunted by medieval ghosts.'

In his essay 'England Your England', which commanded Britons to contribute to the war effort irrespective of their political persuasion, he added:

England ... resembles a family, a rather stuffy Victorian family, with not many black sheep in it but with all its cupboards bursting with skeletons. It has rich relations who have to be kow-towed to and poor relations who are horribly sat upon, and there is a deep conspiracy of silence about the source of the family income ... It has its private language and its common memories, and at the approach of an enemy it closes its ranks. A family with the wrong members in control – that, perhaps, is as near as one can come to describing England in a phrase.

Class is as alive in Britain today as it ever was, in as much as, Orwell notes, class is defined as differing 'notions of good and evil, of pleasant and unpleasant, of funny and serious, of ugly and beautiful'. Wigan remains a distinctly working-class town and a proud one. I was struck by how little different, culturally, the town was from the 1930s. With my Home Counties upbringing, the town demonstrated to me clearly the customary difference between a northern former cotton town, and a southern market town, the latter replete with its prim Waitrose and farmers' markets. On first impression the gulf of difference seemed almost as wide as that between an English village and a French one.

Unusually Wigan remains very much a white British town with minuscule non-white immigration, in contrast to most other large British towns or cities where ethnic minority communities habitually account for between a fifth and a half of inhabitants. I concluded while I was there, however, observables that seem to be common to any English settlement. These cross-class boundaries exist wherever one might arrive – Banbury, Barnsley or Billericay. Wigan Market, rebuilt in 1987 and resembling, on the inside, something along the lines of Richard Rogers' Pompidou Centre – with neon-coloured piping smothering the roof – was where I noticed this first.

Markets such as Wigan's, with indoor stalls selling everything a supermarket does but for a fraction of the price, are common in northern towns. I recall an almost identical clone from the time I lived in

Sunderland, in England's north-east – the personalities operating the stalls, the shoppers and smells were almost the same. Just as the aristocrat or middle-class junky worships their dog, gardening, sausages and tea, so do the working class in both north and south. The breeds of dog, or the plants chosen, or the type of sausage are dissimilar, but the principles remain the same. Orwell was right to describe the English as a family with shared habits.

Visiting as I did in the approach to Remembrance Sunday, universal respect for recalling the sacrifice of those in war was evident – the emotion in every Briton is the same and directs a common seriousness. As cadet officers from the local regiment were selling poppies, the clink of silver teapots in a down-at-heel cafe could be heard; and grandmothers fussed over the winter annuals at the plant nursery; sausage sandwiches, dripping with brown sauce, were being devoured and outside the pet store, dog owners hauled away edible rewards for their beloved back home.

The journey from London to Wigan is an enticing one, with most of the route following valleys of ploughed fields, autumn-colour-turning woodland, spires of village churches and Georgian farmhouses set among large, forested gardens. As the Cheshire plains are passed the scenery changes, however, with row after row of back-to-back terraces racing off on either side of the track. Behind the chemical complexes and power stations, in the far distance, the cloud-shrouded ridges of the Pennines loom. As the railway passes through built-up Manchester and its surrounds, one derelict warehouse or factory after another can be seen backing on to the tracks, symptomatic of the decline of the manufacturing industries. On arrival at Wigan, the skyline across the town remains dominated by the clock towers of the cotton firms that once generated the town's wealth. Churches, in which the town's income from cotton was invested, are prominent too. Both varieties of building are a pale imitation of their former selves. Counting the structures from the arrivals platform in the glare of a chilly dawn sun, I set out to visit them.

It is hard not to be moved by the dereliction of factories which were once at the heart of their communities: close-knit societies where the sound of clogs on the cobbled streets heralded the arrival and departure of the next shift, a guarantor of wage work for one generation after another. Notwithstanding the context that the employment provided was more often than not for men, and that industrialisation on this scale was a relatively recent phenomenon, there can be no doubt of the human tragedy de-industrialisation has caused. In its wake is also dereliction, where buildings constructed for a purpose and with much more care than their modern warehouse equivalents, are gutted, roofless and haunted by the hive of activity once taking place within them.

Wigan Pier can be found a short distance from the main station and lies at the heart of the old industrial area. The towers of cotton mills extend far into the grey skies, as if the mill owners competed like the dynasties in that famous Tuscan town, San Gimignano, to see who could build higher. The silence of the area is strangely pervasive, with what was once one of the most bustling industrial centres of Britain, if not the world, now largely home to epiphyte plants growing from the crevices in derelict buildings, and pigeons fussing over their feathers on the remains of rusting machinery.

A few of the old mills have been restored and converted into flats, a road adjacent to one mill re-named – somewhat ominously – Heritage Way. The engineering firms that made cotton-processing machinery had complexes which have proved much less adaptable, and for the most part, are redundant or infrequently occupied by road hauliers or warehouse distributors. One of the sprawling sites, home to the former engineering firm – replete with the comfortingly earthy, northern name

'Eckersleys' Limited' – was once the largest manufacturer of ring spin-
ners in the world. Its sprawling home reminded me of the burnt and
hollowed-out remains of the British Residency at Lucknow, still a lov-
ingly preserved, pockmarked shell following its long siege during the
Indian Mutiny of 1856–7.

Following the course of a brook skirting the outside of Eckersleys'
site, I imagined the arrival of workers and thought of the wares they once
made being prepared and loaded for distribution or export. I thought of
L.S. Lowry's art illustrating the employment centres of the industrial
north, of beauty in industry. As my eyes diverted across the banks of
the river to small, corrugated-iron shacks housing rows of cooing birds,
a smile broke on my face on reflection that, despite the passing of all
these decades, pigeon racing, a pastime Orwell references in *The Road
to Wigan Pier*, still seems to flourish.

The pier itself is a short section of wooden decking attached to a
much larger early-Victorian warehouse built mainly of bright-red industrial brick. The 'pier' was a loading site on the Leeds and Liverpool
Canal, completed in 1816, and the channels today seem well-maintained
and operational. It is little used however, and all the narrow boats I saw
in the surrounds looked forlorn in the stagnant, litter-strewn water in
which they were resting. At one time this would have been the first
and foremost loading and off-loading port for Wigan's coal and manu-
factured wares, business which transferred to the railways once they
displaced the canals.

The building was renovated in the 1980s, and in 1984 (appropriately!) was converted into a pub, the Orwell at Wigan Pier. The
property had been repossessed and the pub closed at the time of my
visit. From peering through the grills erected to protect its windows from
vandalism and the town's squatters, the interior looked dated, as if it had
last been decorated in 1984. A filthy snooker table lay in the centre of
one room, with broken chairs and tables scattered around, resembling

the aftermath of some violent fight. Next door and part of the same complex, the even sadder 'Wigan Pier Experience' had 'CLOSED' signage on its doors. It transpired this Heritage Lottery Fund-style investment fell foul of cuts in local government grants, rendering its funding unsustainable.

Walking back towards the station in the direction of the town centre, making full pace underneath a railway bridge dripping with water filtering through from the track bed, I passed a once-attractive building to my left. The station hotel was in a sorry state and pathetically cared for. Its windows were universally forlorn, each flaking white paint, and filthy net curtains shielded what I expected was probably, in dim light, the remains of Miss Havisham. Many of the impressive, sturdy buildings in the town centre are in similar state of disrepair – a common sight across the very great number of deprived towns and cities in the UK.

The market square offered entertainment in the form of a small Ferris wheel and a merry-go-round. Despite the street being well-kept, the frequency of shops flaunting 'pound' in their branding was so numerous it was hard to look in any direction and not see a Pound Bakery, Pound Clothing or Pound World.

In the 1980s a number of people who could still remember Orwell's visit were interviewed to recall their memories. Sydney Smith ran a bookstall in Wigan Market, and he and Orwell became acquainted – a mutual interest in books being a litmus test of their friendship. Smith remembered: 'He was tall, six feet plus, a gentleman with a rather shabby raincoat and a dirty trilby hat. He was tall, thin, hollow-cheeked, with a sallow complexion and dark hair, but it was the fact that he spoke in a different accent to us, a more cultured voice, that impressed us most.'

It is easy to imagine Orwell wandering along the high street, among the stalls in the market and down the back-to-back terraces, a shabby raincoat, pencil and notebook to hand. At The Moon Under Water, one of the most popular pubs on the market square, he might have enjoyed fish and chips, or a pie, alongside a pint of the local ale. Orwell's 1946 essay, 'The Moon Under Water' detailed his idea of the perfect English pub, with its 'ornamental mirrors behind the bar, the cast iron fireplaces, the florid ceiling stained dark yellow by tobacco-smoke, the stuffed bull's head over the mantelpiece'. A chief executive of the Wetherspoon chain proposed exploiting the 'The Moon Under Water' name in a branding exercise in the 2000s, and a small number of its pubs took it on. Quite intentionally, its pub on Wigan marketplace was one of them. I am sure Orwell would smirk at the thought that pubs all over Britain have been renamed as a result of his essay.

⤚

The Brookers' house was a corner house and shop at a junction close to the centre of Wigan and on one of the main roads that lead towards the centre of town, the Darlington Road. The south-eastern part of Wigan is where much of Orwell's pacing of the streets took place, especially the suburb of Ince, which remains one of Wigan's poorest. The library, where he spent many hours researching living conditions in the town, would have been a short walk from his lodgings. Sleuths who have examined his diaries and *The Road to Wigan Pier* point out that the Brookers are referred to as the 'Forrests' in the diaries, and other inconsistencies have been discovered since it was published, too. It is more than likely aesthetic changes were made to the text given Victor Gollancz's disquiet about libel.

Triangular-shaped and jutting into the junction in the style of New York's Flat Iron building, photographs suggest the Brookers' house was a decrepit, two-storey mid-Victorian building, shielding what Orwell described as the 'labyrinthine slums and dark back kitchens with sickly, ageing people creeping round them like black beetles'. After demolition in 1977, the site became a traffic island. Traffic revolves listlessly around it, adjacent to a squat branch of the German supermarket chain Lidl, while an enormous, early 1990s post-modernist style magistrates' court dominates the view. In the near-distance, the thirteen towers of Wigan's largest estate, the Brook House, contain 500 dwellings, and the descendants of those who once lived in the old slums.

Fragments of the old architecture survive. Close to Lidl is a small back-to-back section of terraces which must have escaped the bulldozer: Brookhouse Street; Brookhouse Terrace; and Spring Street. An aluminium-shaded plaque, set on a moss- and lichen-covered block of stone, reads:

GEORGE ORWELL 1903–1950

THE WRITER GEORGE ORWELL, BORN ERIC
ARTHUR BLAIR IN 1903, RECEIVED NATIONAL
ACCLAIM FOR THE BOOKS HE WROTE BETWEEN
1920 AND 1950 DESCRIBING LIVING CONDITIONS
IN BRITAIN AND ABROAD. HE IS KNOWN TO HAVE
STAYED NEARBY IN DARLINGTON STREET AND
WARRINGTON LANE IN FEBRUARY, 1936, AND
AFTERWARDS PUBLISHED HIS WELL KNOWN BOOK,

'THE ROAD TO WIGAN PIER'

Wigan Library, location for so much of Orwell's secondary research, is an impressive, red-brick Victorian building: imposing, ornate, though not overbearingly so, and functional. Resembling a Jacobean country house, with chimneys built from limestone that soar into the sky, it was the first building in Wigan to have electricity after being completed in 1878. The local authority moved the public library in 1996, but the structure remains a civic asset. The downstairs now contains the Museum of Wigan Life, a small visitor attraction comprising a curious mix of mining artefacts and paraphernalia from Ancient Egypt, a collection donated to the town by a local magnate.

The upstairs contains the same local interest library and research centre in which Orwell spent many hours. This large room, with its black timber-framed and arched roof, resembling something like a village Sunday school hall, has changed little since. The shelves are lined with seldom-consulted texts, data books and age-old maps. I spent a very enjoyable afternoon wafting through Orwelliana, encountering several books I had not yet discovered such as *George Orwell: A personal memoir* by T.R. Fyvel, Orwell's successor as literary editor of *Tribune*, and *Chronicles of Conscience: A study of George Orwell and Arthur Koestler* by Jenni Calder.

Within these four walls, Orwell, hunched over periodicals and mining manuals, diligently researched conditions of life in the industrial regions. In the decades since his visit, the library has been assiduous in collecting newspaper articles mentioning the author. Several caught my eye: 'WIGAN looking for George Orwell lookalike', required for the opening of a new leisure centre in 1984, with a remit to be 'gaunt and gangling, about 6 feet 3 inches tall, [willing to] grow a certain style of moustache'. I can imagine the respondents being arranged in the style of a police line-up, candidates frozen and looking sternly ahead, with some literary type walking up and down to assess suitability.

Another headline, dated 1984, celebrated 'THE YEAR OF THE PIER'; an advert in the same paper declares Wigan's pier as 'the best-known pier in the world', which is not only probably true but no mean feat, given there is barely a pier to speak of. Using my smartphone to capture various articles and photographs for future reference, an officious library assistant corralled me by snapping: 'It is £5.00 for a photography licence, *they last half a day only.*' Carlton Melling, the present-day librarian's forebear who had fond memories of Orwell's visit, comes across as a much kinder type of librarian. He recalled in a 1983 interview: 'There was a kind of personal magnetism about him. I thought, eeh, we don't often see this kind of man here.'

Although often regarded as a reporter into social conditions, Orwell was preoccupied with coal mining in the north, and his diaries note in detail his visits to pits. Three mines were part of his itinerary. So typically, the observations are astute, comparing and contrasting the various mining conditions to which men were sent down. The mine at Wigan, 'Cribben's', was the most backward of the three – the other two, at Sheffield and Barnsley, though especially the latter, had undergone some modernisation. It is hard not to read Orwell's observations without some sense of bewilderment at the conditions of work, conditions which no doubt exist still in countries where deep mining is common. With coal seams of typically no more than a yard thick, 'We could at best kneel, and then not kneel upright, and I fancy the men must do most of their work lying on their bellies. The heat was also frightful – round about 100 degrees F. so far as I could judge.'

The three mines were analysed in terms of their engineering and facilities. At Cribben's neither was impressive, and Orwell's love of detail leads to fascinating accounts of safety and lighting procedures. For example, the mine maintained an elaborate, costly and time-consuming rotation of live canaries to test for gas, but had some electric lighting on its 'main streets', supplemented by mining safety lamps – a 'Davy' with gauzes which contained the flame (thus avoiding the risk of a deadly explosion deep below the surface) but still allowed oxygen to enter.

In Sheffield, a very old type of Davy lamp was used, with no electric lighting at all. Grimethorpe, in 1936 one of the most advanced in England, had: 'Electric lights ... – no Davy lamps used in the pit except for testing for gas'. He was also impressed by the engineering, where 'All the roads ... were high and well-built and even paved under-foot in places.' The baths were described as 'excellent' and numerous also, with there being 'no less than 1,000 hot and cold shower baths'. Soon after his visit, in 1942, all of the UK's coal reserves were nationalised, and the industry as a whole followed in 1947.

What is apparent is how inconsistent mining methodologies were across Britain's coal mines before nationalisation, at disastrous economic cost. The closure of mines was nothing new – a directory of mines in the Wigan area lists a hundred which opened and closed over the 18th and 19th centuries as reserves were exhausted – but the overwhelmingly small-scale nature of many mines meant the collapse of the industry was inevitable. Wigan's last mine closed in 1992; the last deep coal mine in Britain, Kellingley, closed in December 2015.

༄

The topic of food appears sparingly in Orwell's works, except for the seminal, thoughtfully conceived essay 'In Defence of English Cooking'. Tripe as an ingredient and the food consumed by miners is subject to passing analysis, but discussion of the Lancashire diet, or even some measure of respect for the county's tastes, is absent. The food consumed by the working classes in the region is typically referenced disparagingly, but then, as now, culinary traditions of any segment of an area's society offer insight into the class distinctions with which Orwell was obsessed. Nevertheless, my visit to the food stalls of Wigan Market, and outside in the windows of the town's bakeries and butchers, were a highlight of my time in the town. I left with a new vocabulary of foodstuffs, from Uncle Sam-style branded Joe's Mint Balls to the myriad names of the many forms of pie: 'butter and onion', and 'party meat'. I was similarly puzzled by the names for various types of offal snack, such as 'savoury ducks', and by the numerous terms applied to forms of tripe, assiduously regulated by the Tripe Marketing Board – an organisation of whose existence I am confident the vast majority of the British population is ignorant.

Large, rectangular trays of tripe coloured pale yellow, like the tar-smothered ceiling of a smoker's parlour, and with an unappealing appearance similar to the sour Ethiopian flatbread *injera*, can be seen in almost every butcher's in the town. Sales must remain buoyant, I concluded. Orwell refers in his diaries to the 'Lancashire method of eating [it] cold with vinegar', which he added was horrid. 'Tripe and onions', where it is heated in onion-infused milk and served with bread and butter, seems to be the more prevalent method today. The necessity of preserving food for consumption during a long day in the mines established other culinary curiosities, with feeding times coming to be known as 'going for your jack-bit'. No longer a concern for anyone living in Wigan, it was clear to Orwell that the miners' diets were composed mainly of cold tea and bread dipped in dripping.

Unlike other parts of the UK, where the variety and sophistication of the diet offer sharp contrast even compared with just twenty years ago, the range of food on offer in Wigan is limited. My abiding observation of the puddings available were garish trifles, smothered deep in bright-yellow custards, sprinkled with hundreds and thousands, *de rigueur* in the 1970s but now only likely to be found on the menus of restaurants which have not changed much in the decades since.

Before leaving I had one last visit to make. The stout tower of a church with a small bell tower can be seen very close to the railway station, and as ever when plants are growing from a roof, I was drawn towards it, wondering why the building had been allowed to fall into such a state. St Joseph's was a Roman Catholic church built in 1871, in the same industrial north red-brick style familiar to much of the town. Arriving at the boarded-up entrance, it became clear it was derelict and neglected.

Two pale-faced youths wearing hoodies passed by on the other side of the road as I approached, their side glances making their faces appear like the head of a monk in his habit. As they hocked up and spat into the gutter, I could detect a noise coming from inside the church. A groan was echoing through what must be the chancel, sounding as if a young person was experiencing some great form of psychotic trauma. The church sited now among half-a-dozen or so modern shop warehouses, I entered the nearest – a tiling retailer – to ask whether anybody knew about the history of the building and to discover how or why anybody had found themselves inside it.

Outside, in the car park adjacent to the church, a shop assistant told me not to go near because 'It's where "they" go.' The shop frequently finds needles scattered beside the church, she continued, and advised it is well known locally as a haunt for drug-addicted twenty-somethings thrown out of home. 'They' is one of those words in the English language universally used to sweepingly describe invisible minorities, not least in the pejorative tone reserved for those viewed as inferior in caste, class or economic status.

Reflecting on the train home, I concluded that *The Road to Wigan Pier* is, for me, as much analysing social hierarchy as it is poverty. One comment in part two, written more than ten years before *Nineteen Eighty-Four*, alludes to the nightmarish submission men and women might encounter in a cleaner, 'civilised' future: 'Bugs are bad, but a state of affairs in which men will allow themselves to be dipped like sheep is worse'; a world where all individual dignity is swept away to the benefit of some mysterious collective good. It is worth remembering that every 'they' is part of a family, England's family. They deserve equal recognition for being part of the striking, disjointed tapestry that constitutes English society.

Catalonia, Spain

Boat to Bilbao (1936–7)

M y boat to Bilbao, a Brittany Ferry from Portsmouth, was filled with late-middle-aged expats visiting their holiday homes: some 700,000 Britons live in Spain. I had decided, like most of those on board, to take my car and avoid not only another visit to an airport, but a long return drive down the western seaboard of France. The distances between the places Orwell visited in Spain are vast, so the journey is really only possible with a car – in hindsight this was not a decision I regretted. Northern Spain is blessed with some very fast and empty motorways, for long stretches the only other users seemed to be cars with their black-on-mango-coloured British number plates, almost always I noticed, lacking the European Union emblem cars usually have on the continent.

There are few more civilised ways to travel than by boat. The neat cabin with a towel and mini scented soaps, the narrow corridors and sense of fellowship with other passengers. Everyone on a ship is headed in the same direction and conversations between them are started with ease. Used to the usual constant hassle of distractions in London, I was quite happy to sit back and people-watch on the journey of just over a day. The weather turned quickly from a boiling June morning on land, into the swirling fogs of the Bay of Biscay.

George, accompanying me on my passage in the ship's humourless stainless-steel kennels, required regular exercise on their dedicated dog deck, which meant long stretches of time staring into the abyss of the Atlantic. George, so water-borne, would quite happily (and capably) have scaled the white railings to jump in were it not for my restraining. At other times he was passive, sitting upright gazing in amazement at the expanse of water passing before him.

The sight of land made his desire to jump in all the worse, the craggy, mist-shrouded and sinister skerries lining the coastline of Brittany the focus of his ambition. At dusk, rain sprinkling lightly over us, an enormous herring gull appeared from nowhere to swoop and swoon around the stern. We both, mesmerised by its movement out in the high sea, watched it intently – oblivious to us as it circumnavigated the vessel. No longer interested in the ship, the gull flew higher and started to make back for land, our eyes tracking it for well over a mile into the distant grey clouds.

Brittany Ferries is known for its fine dining, serving the sort of food one is likely to find in a high-end restaurant in London. I observed how quiet the dining room was, the silver cutlery and crystal moving in the silence between husbands and wives whose conversation died decades ago. The waiters wear bow ties and hold a starched white napkin over their forearms. I thought of Orwell as a waiter in Hotel X in Paris, wiping the sweat off his forehead and whipping carafes of red wine around.

In the morning I discovered the ferry had an open-air pool, a pleasant enough surprise, although less impressive when I dived in and realised it was cold sea water. Beside it was an elderly couple completing crosswords, as one is expected to do in retirement, and a lady in her fifties reading *Don Fernando* by W. Somerset Maugham. I reflected how fitting it was to find someone reading a Maugham on my passage across the Bay of Biscay, an experience and author of another era; the era in which Orwell would have sailed the same passage east to Burma.

I re-read *Homage to Catalonia* on board and was just on the final page when the call went out on the tannoy for dog owners to collect their pets and take them down to the car deck before it was to be sealed for arrival. One dog owner, whose accent placed her from Birmingham, accompanied me down. A regular on the service, she told me how outraged she was that the dogs are taken down first only to be left in the sealed hull until docking: 'If anything were to happen they'd all be killed, they're treating them like animals. It's disgusting.' I'm not quite sure she grasped the irony of what she said, but it spoke volumes to me of how greatly the English fuss about their dogs.

Orwell left for Spain just before Christmas Day in 1936, having spent weeks unsuccessfully attempting to find a means to participate in the fighting between the incumbent republican government and the fascists led by General Franco. John Strachey, a Labour Party politician, knew Orwell via Gollancz's Left Book Club, which he helped to establish, and assisted Orwell in finding a means to get to Spain. Strachey directed him towards the British Communist Party, who advised he travel via the Spanish Embassy in Paris, and then onto Barcelona. Orwell rang the Independent Labour Party (the ILP, affiliated to the Labour Party) who directed him to their secretary in Barcelona. He travelled by sleeper to, and onward from, Paris, staying with the American writer Henry Miller, who gifted him, of all things, a corduroy suit.

Before he went to Spain it seems he saw the battle between the two sides as simplistic, a 'good' (leftist) side versus a 'bad' (fascist) one. His experience of war led him to alter this impression, and not only helped him complete his journey to socialism but planted within him a scepticism of power set to dominate his thinking in the decade to come. Fenner Brockway, the General Secretary of the ILP, met Orwell after he left Spain, at Perpignan in French Catalonia and noted he had become 'far more mature as a socialist'.

Orwell wrote in *Homage to Catalonia*: 'I had come to Spain with some notion of writing newspaper articles, but I joined the militia almost immediately, because at that time and in that atmosphere it seemed the only conceivable thing to do.' His book has come to be seen as one of the most powerful and thoughtful works of war literature, renowned throughout Spain and the world as a fine first-hand account of the trauma of civil war. It also demonstrates Orwell's capacity to go beyond superficial reporting of something, to live war and write about it through the eyes of a soldier.

⌁

I was bound for the north-east corner of Spain, some 230 miles from Bilbao, and found myself on empty stretches of the A8 motorway that traverses the north of the country. The drive showed how empty northern Spain is, in contrast with densely populated England. There are huge spaces in between settlements: hilltop towns of cream-coloured houses clustered around a church, each with their square bell towers, and framed from behind by the craggy tops of hills coloured red, like the deserts of Arizona.

I find, living in London, that I need open space when I am able to leave my home city, and so I rented a house in a farming village just to the north of Huesca. This was the first destination on my Orwell trail around Spain. Although Orwell never visited Huesca, he was billeted just outside the city. It was besieged by anti-fascist forces for the entire duration of the war and never taken. Huesca is not large but big enough to be a centre for the sparsely populated plain surrounding it. Its vast hilltop cathedral dominates any perspective from which the city can be viewed.

Apies, a fifteen-minute drive north of Huesca and the location of my let, is accessed by a twisting and poorly maintained road, sections of which have begun to slump towards the plain below. The landscape levels out, perhaps after a climb of 500 or more feet, with a long, straight avenue leading to the centre of the village, distinguished by its smart, colonnaded square and a scattering of working farms. At my let, a converted barn on the edge of a farmyard, the open countryside was not more than a minute distant.

Behind the village rise the foothills of the Pyrenees, a row of what looks like a set of crooked teeth sealing the region along an entire length. The distance to the first cliffs is not great, perhaps a mile of very slightly undulating fields of dry, parched-yellow barley. The landscape was blotched by one or two derelict farmsteads, the sort which made effective hideouts during the civil war. The land is not rich, more scrub than anything, and the air was dry. The mountains suck moisture from the plains, harvest dust from the tractors making it drier. Everywhere seemed to have that hoppy smell of summer.

Huesca is a city around the same size as a larger market town in England. The old town is historic but small. The cathedral, at the highest point in the city and built on the site of a former mosque, dating from the time of Islamic rule over Spain, has been worn by centuries of attack by the elements. Miniature sandstone statues of the twelve apostles guard the main entrance, below which is an astonishingly large and worn step, the sort with grooves so large it is not impossible to think the Romans may have walked over them. Huesca was famous for its silver mines during the Roman period; the plain surrounding the city still pockmarked by spoil heaps. In contrast the modern and larger half of Huesca resembles something like an American new town of shopping malls and bowling alleys.

On my first day I visited the city's museum, a small octagon-shaped building enclosing a cool, palm-fringed courtyard, which was showing its penultimate day of an exhibition about Orwell. One forgets how Spain shuts down for most of the afternoon, and so before the museum re-opened at 4pm I spent half an hour meandering around the adjacent square. In one corner I noticed the cream pebble-dash lining one of the walls had been engraved. At eye-level height I could make out a scratchy '1 9 8 4'.

The exhibition was good, if only in Spanish, with an impressive display of posters and weaponry from the civil war, and of Orwell's movements around the region. He wrote in *Homage to Catalonia* that he should have liked to have visited Huesca in peacetime – an ambition he never fulfilled – and to have tasted the coffee there. 'Coffee in Huesca' was the title of the exhibition. I later learnt that a statue is planned to immortalise him forever, sitting sipping the coffee he never ordered.

No country I have visited in the course of my travels in Orwell-land does more justice to Orwell than Spain, which I thought curious. There are squares and roads named after him in every place he visited, exhibitions and pamphlets. He is respected in a way I have seen nowhere else. Spain became a democracy only in the late 1970s. Is there perhaps an attachment to a certain type of truth-seeker, buoyed on a sea of lies, that the Spanish find attractive? The civil war remains just about within living memory and is still controversial in a way most Britons would find hard to understand, with their centuries of stable government behind them. Unlike Nazi Germany, Vichy France or fascist Spain, young Britons have never needed to question in the same way what their grandparents did in their past. And, as a foreign journalist, perhaps Spaniards sense objectivity in Orwell's reporting, missing from Spanish accounts of the 1930s.

An interesting intellectual development took place for Orwell over the course of the war, which began his mistrust of political communication and the media. Developing an intimate first-hand experience of the civil war, he was aware of the relative influence of the various anti-fascist groups, especially his own POUM (*Partido Obrero de Unificación Marxista*, or the Workers' Party of Marxist Unification). They were scapegoated by other anti-fascist groups, creating something of a controversy, and one in which Orwell was well-versed to participate. This episode unquestionably set the logic in motion for *Nineteen Eighty-Four*, whose chief purpose was to explore the institutionalisation of untruth.

POUM, which was being ridiculed as a Trotskyist entryist organisation, was later banned by the faltering Republican government. Orwell and Eileen would experience the consequences of this first-hand as they fled from Spain across the border into France, away from Spanish government agents. The organisation was regrettably reported in the Western press in the way the Republic government wished it to be. Orwell, ever the reader of the British newspapers, noticed the difference between what he knew to be the facts on the front line, and the way the mass of journalists was reporting it; fake news before it became popular to talk about fake news.

Orwell wrote an article for the *New Statesman* to correct the narrative, but strangely, even having paid for it, they refused publication. Orwell wrote: 'One of the most horrible features of this war is that all the war-propaganda, all the screaming lies and hatred, comes invariably from people who are not fighting.' Even more eye-opening for him, as it is for all of us as we grow wiser, was that the manipulation of facts was not restricted to any one political viewpoint: 'One of the dreariest effects of this war has been to teach me that the Left-wing press is every bit as spurious and dishonest as that of the right.'*

On the second day of visiting Huesca I met Victor Lancino and his translator, Elana. Victor is the main man behind the planned statue of Orwell, and was also responsible for establishing a civil war museum at Robres, a village south-east of Huesca, located on one of the former

---

* *'With the exception of the* Manchester Guardian'.

fronts. He is the sort of person whose intelligence means they seem to have a thousand thoughts running through their head as one talks to them. Stout, and scruffily dressed, his beard and bulging eyes resembled the face of Edward VII – looking at you, but not into you.

They arranged to take me to *La Granja*, the large and nearby farmstead in which Orwell was billeted, and also Monflorite, *La Granja*'s nearest village, which was a hub for members of the anti-fascist coalition. *La Granja* is sited directly on a busy, straight national road and like Apies, is surrounded by fields of barley. The farm is now divided in two, with separate owners. Pedro, who owns the eastern half, greeted me on arrival but, like Victor, spoke no English.

Pedro's part of *La Granja* is surrounded by tall coniferous trees, almost dauntingly so, which were planted by him when he bought the farmstead several decades ago. The courtyard which Orwell describes in *Homage to Catalonia* is attached to his home and I noticed that, of all its paraphernalia, the vast stone cattle trough was one thing that possibly hasn't been moved since 1937. Exotic-coloured flowers spilled from window boxes, with *Amaryllis* the first to greet visitors by the expansive front door. Pedro motioned to me its common name – 'Mother-in-Law and Daughter' – so-called because each flower head ignores the other by flowering directly out from the stem.

Orwell slept on foul-smelling chaff in the church at *La Granja*, which is better kept today than it was in wartime. The small church adjacent to the farmhouse was, at the time of Orwell's stay, filled with manure, though having since been restored by Pedro is now passable as any presentable Catholic chapel. Mixed rows of lavender and rosemary line the path up to the church which, built on an incline, offers views stretching over the road and out towards the fields of barley beyond. A garishly tiled blue swimming pool, enclosed with military-style chicken-wire fencing, straddles the space between the attractive farmhouse and its church.

Wounded in the hand in or around *La Granja*, which was under regular shelling, Orwell was sent to a hospital in Monflorite, three miles away. Before we set off there, we peeked through the large, white, metal gates shielding the other half of the farmstead, opening straight out on to the national road. Victor pointed out bullet marks on the gates, which with their ricochet pattern, looked as if they were fired from a machine gun. To the left of the gate the wall was graffitied with *'Republica'*. The bullet marks and graffiti, extant over 70 years later, made one sense the civil war had yet to end.

There was more living history at Monflorite, where the town's small square is dominated by a church used as an arms dump during the civil war. It still appears dishevelled, almost 80 years after the war finished. It is in a bad state of repair, having lost one of its two squat bell towers from a shell, as incomplete and as unfortunate as the nipped ear of a cat. Victor pointed to a building next to the town hall, believed to be where Orwell was treated. As ever there is some confusion about which building on and around the square was actually where he was hospitalised, but a plaque has been attached to one of the most likely candidates:

In memory of the British writer George Orwell, who convalesced in the hospital of Monflorite in March of 1937, during the Spanish Civil War.

Orwell was treated here as winter was ending in April 1937. He wrote, while he was invalided, of how the coming scent of the spring reminded him of the Stores in Wallington, which had been sub-let to one of Orwell's aunties, Nellie Limouzin. By this time Eileen had joined Orwell in Spain too, appointed as a secretary for the ILP in Barcelona in February. Orwell wondered whether the wallflowers were coming out on their home, a longing for England joined by his contempt for Spain's 'milkless tea'.

Orwell's concern for the treatment of animals was also on his mind in Spain. Donkeys were trained to transport water independently over long distances, having been guided into the route. They were an essential supply line for fighters out in the arid scrub of Aragon and Catalonia. He noted: 'For some reason the Aragon peasants treated their mules well but their donkeys abominably', advising they would be kicked in their testicles if they did not move.

From Monflorite I left Victor and Elana, who directed me off into the emptiness of southern Aragon. The exhibition Victor helped to create in the small town of Robres was a half-an-hour drive away. Beyond that were the reconstructed trenches at Alcubierre. The road to Robres offered panoramic views across the landscape, which seemed to become ever drier and sparser. The villages I passed were small, but still of the standard Aragonese style with the bell towers and small marketplaces. They were all devoid of people in the heat of the afternoon, looking a little like stage sets. I imagined casts sitting, learning their lines, behind the pull-down stainless steel or plastic sunblinds shielding the windows on every building.

At Robres a restaurant was recommended to me, and so I sought this out as my first port of call. It was a lesson to me that recommendations of 'delicious food' are invariably subjective. The main course was not exactly memorable: poorly cooked pasta drowned in olive oil and garnished with tinned mushrooms. The entrée was more interesting, a local snack of roasted salmon wrapped in pastry, called *hojaldre salmon y queso*.

The stage-set town was strange, the silence and absence of activity creepy. I walked up to the church, which was locked, and could see what looked like a stork in the enormous nest of twigs it had made for itself on the top of the bell tower. Once I had spotted one of these there was no let-up – I came to find them on every tall, stand-out structure I passed in each town or village I drove through.

The civil war exhibition is housed in a civic building just down from the mound the church is built upon. It seems to have been lavishly funded and offers an impressive overview of the causes, fighting and legacy of the conflict. I was the sole visitor during my time at the exhibition, and would not be surprised if I was the sole visitor of the day or even the week. The curator seemed shocked when I opened the front door and entered into the small lobby, flustered as if her long-enjoyed peace had been disturbed.

Orwell inevitably features in the exhibition, and I enjoyed picking him out of the various black-and-white photos showing line-ups of troops, or of small town squares decked with revolutionary slogans and flags. He stands out like a sore thumb, of course. Bob Edwards, a member of the ILP and later Labour MP, who took a visceral dislike to Orwell – describing him as 'bloody middle-class little scribe' – paradoxically offers the best description of Orwell decked out for war: 'All six foot three of him was striding towards me and his clothing was grotesque to say the least. He wore corduroy riding breeches, khaki puttees and huge boots ... he had a yellow pigskin jerkin, a coffee coloured balaclava hat and he wore the largest scarf I've ever seen.'

The most powerful section of the exhibition shows the effects on civilians, which in a civil war fought between an atheist left and purportedly devout Catholic right, meant a substantial impact on the church as an institution. One photo showed a queue of nuns dressed in their habits leaving their bombed-out nunnery. Another included two priests clasping crucifixes, with two men each holding a revolver to their heads. I wondered whether this was a photo of an execution, and then remembered the rule of history to never trust photography.

From Robres I followed *Ruta Orwell* which leads to the restored trenches at Alcubierre. The road was empty for most of the journey, climbing away from the plains and towards a hillier terrain no doubt perfect for a stalemate in a civil war between the two opposing sides.

The trenches overlook a key position guarding the national road, but are accessed along a very stony, dusty track. I enjoyed taking my car off-road, although I'm not sure George enjoyed the experience very much. A cloud of dust engulfed the car, ripping through the terrain as a tornado terrorises the farms of Kansas.

On arrival, the site was devoid of visitors, the chirping of crickets the only sound. Of all the places I visited in Spain, this was by far the driest. I later understood why, as the area is adjacent to the Monegros Desert, receiving some of the lowest rainfall in all Europe. There was no soil, only rocky dust and little vegetation, save for wispy grasses and the greeny hue of the shrub *Santolina*. It cannot have been the most comfortable place to have been stuck in a trench and was in no way picturesque.

The trenches aren't large – 30 metres in circumference clinging to the knoll overlooking the national road – but they are deep. They may not of course have been the trenches Orwell manned for POUM, but they are, I am told, a faithful representation of what he would have experienced, except bereft now of the excrement and the rats which made conditions in the trenches hellish. In his essay 'Looking Back on the Spanish Civil War', he recalled 'the boredom and animal hunger of trench life'.

Orwell served in this area, and was shot through the neck somewhere in it. Conditions in the trenches were not only abominable, but scarcely worth the human misery, as Orwell quickly concluded when passed his first weapon – a German Mauser dated 1896. The twelve-member strong brigade he was put in charge of as a '*cabo*' (corporal) he described as 'a complete rabble ... an untrained mob of children, mostly in their teens'. Although nowhere does he mention it explicitly, his teaching experience in Middlesex may well have come in handy when it came to controlling them.

Orwell drew parallels with his time in the cadets at Eton, where his worries about the strength of his side were illustrated by his concern that 'our position could be stormed by twenty boy scouts armed with air guns, or twenty girl guides armed with battledores, for that matter'. Georges Kopp, Orwell's Russo-Belgian commander who became a close friend, described the conflict as: 'not a war … [but] a comic opera with an occasional death'. As for the pantomime theme, Orwell in his eccentric dress most definitely stood out from the crowd. As he walked through the trenches, his head stuck high above the parapet, so much so that comrades had to continually shout at him to get his head down. In *Homage to Catalonia*, he showed barely any fear of the risk of being killed but did wish to stay as far as possible away from rats. Despite almost entirely avoiding hand-to-hand fighting he managed to escape death twice; first when a shell landed near to him, and second (miraculously) surviving a bullet from sniper fire which passed clean through his neck.

Orwell thought that the bullet in the neck was the end for him. Fortunately for English literature, it was not. To think how different our world would be without the ease with which we can describe something as 'Orwellian'! The bullet got him at 5am on 20 May, missing his jugular vein by about a millimetre. It damaged a nerve governing a vocal cord, which meant he was unable to speak and only recovered full speech gradually. There are no known recordings of his voice – and only one film, that of him striding across a playing field at Eton – but there seems to be agreement from contemporaries that his voice was never quite the same after Spain. He wrote:

> *I felt a tremendous shock – no pain, only a violent shock, such as you get from an electric terminal … this ought to please my wife, I thought; she had always wanted me to be wounded, which would save me from being killed when the great battle came … My first thought, conventionally enough, was for my wife. My second was a violent resentment at having to leave this world which, when all is said and done, suits me so well.*

After the trenches, I drove all the way back to Apies, my temporary home in the foothills. I took George, who wasn't terribly taken by the heat and dust of Alcubierre, straight out into the fields behind my let. The air was so thick with humidity it felt as if it would blow into a thunderstorm at any minute. I quickly skimmed a flat stone into the ether and watched with amusement as George did his usual surfing across the thickly clad stalks of barley.

The most spectacular physical landform in the region is visible from these fields. The *Mallos de Riglos* are two gigantic pillars of sandstone appearing at the head of a canyon that splits this section of the Pyrenees' foothills in two. They look almost as if built from brick since the strata in the stone is visible from miles away. If they resemble anything I should say they appear as the gates to an underworld, and with their illumination by fork lightening later that evening, it was not beyond the imagination to think they were indeed an entrance to Hell.

⌒

The next morning, I left Apies to drive across northern Spain, bound for Lleida, via Barbastro. Both feature in *Homage to Catalonia* and were places which Orwell filed through between his arrival in Spain, at Barcelona, and his transfer to the 'front' of the war in Huesca. He typically travelled in filthy conditions by train, accompanied by a lot of alcohol. After he arrived back to Barcelona, on leave, to see Eileen for the first time since she had come to Spain to work, she wrote: 'He arrived completely ragged, almost barefoot, a little lousy [and] dark brown ... In the previous twelve hours he had been in trains consuming *anis*, muscatel out of *anis* bottles, brandies and chocolate.'

I took the non-motorway route for as long as I could, which was as far as midway between Huesca and Barbastro. From the steering wheel my peripheral vision seemed vast, screensaver-style skies stretching abreast a long, straight and empty road. The mountains which seemed always to follow the line of sight to my left became greener, a rocky sprawl of jade. Between intervals of half an hour the road would pass over canyons, with vertigo-inducing drops down into the luminous, emerald-coloured depths of the rivers that created them.

Barbastro lies about a third of the way between Huesca and the sizeable provincial centre of Lleida, a distance of about 70 miles. It was not somewhere Orwell took to kindly when he visited for the first time: 'Barbastro, though a long way from the front line, looked bleak and chipped', he wrote. Eighty years later I had a similar first impression. The main road through the town is straggly, with closed-down garages, former shop fronts with naked mannequins standing in them, and bars which look as if a fight is certain to break out.

As with every other place Orwell visited in Spain, somewhere has been named after him. In keeping with his first impressions of Barbastro, his name adorns a scrappy street of new developments, of mid-rise apartment blocks and charmless public parks. On one side of *Calle George Orwell* is the Spain of European Union-funded redevelopment – modern, ambitious and large-scale. On the other side is the Spain it is trying in vain to replace: dereliction, scrubland and stray cats. For a man with so much personality, this street seemed to have none at all.

I soon found the more authentic Barbastro, set back from the main through road. On his return visit some months later, Orwell recanted from his previous description: '... at the back of [Barbastro] there was a shallow jade-green river, and rising out of it a perpendicular cliff of rock, with houses built into the rock'. The cliff remains as spectacular as ever, but alas the river has been lined with concrete, and a large, supermarket-style car park covers the area from which the rock-hewn houses can be viewed. Somehow it didn't quite feel the same as Orwell described it.

From Barbastro I continued driving east, towards the city of Lleida. After Orwell was shot, he was hospitalised there, and a garden has been named after him. Another huge cathedral dominates the small hilltop of the city, but the surrounding area is fruit-growing country with vast plantations of oranges, apples, pears and grapes. Huge sprinklers sprayed water like cannons onto the fields, for future harvesting on an industrial scale.

The hospital Santa Maria still exists, a major regional hospital of a size I suspect to be different to when Orwell was treated there. It reminded me of Oxford's John Radcliffe Hospital, which is built as a series of connected white cubes. The memorial garden in Orwell's honour was opened only recently to celebrate the connection, which is a commendable celebration of his time in the city. An information board, cemented into the ground, reads:

> *Eric Arthur Blair (1909–1950), known as George Orwell, was an outstanding British writer and essayist. Antifascist militiaman during the Spanish Civil War (1936–9), wounded at the Aragon Front. Taken to Lleida, and cared for at the Santa Maria Hospital on May 1937, 80 years ago.*

I wondered whether '1909' was a typo in the English translation for '1903', but glanced up towards the Spanish, and it was there too. How annoying it must be for this to be pointed out to the plaque designer, long after the concrete cementing it in was dry!

From Lleida the next and final stop on the Orwell tour through Spain was Barcelona, Orwell's first destination in the country no less. After his sleeper from Paris, all the way through France, Barcelona was the first city he came to. It was also the base for the ILP's activity, and where Eileen would be based when she joined her husband in Spain in February 1937. Barcelona then was a long way from the tourist-friendly haven it is today. Orwell's description of his first impressions is dramatic, a city besieged by revolutionary fervour and all of the social and economic instability that comes with it: 'Practically every building of any size had been seized by the workers and was draped with red flags or with the red and black flag of the Anarchists; every wall was scrawled with the hammer and sickle and with the initials of the revolutionary parties; almost every church had been gutted and its images burnt.'

Orwell noted how the capitalist machine had been replaced by a system where 'human beings were trying to live as human beings' and that economic organisation had been 'collectivised' along Maoist or Stalinist lines, something which extended to the brothels as well as the bakeries, he observed. Orwell's initial enthusiasm seems to have been tempered, on a return visit to Barcelona when on leave, by a change in his understanding of the war. What comes across as incipient naivety evolved into a realisation that the circumstances of the war were not at all clear-cut. He wrote how the loss of Malaga: '... was the first talk I had heard of treachery or divided aims. It set up in my mind the first vague doubt about this war in which, hitherto, the rights and wrongs seemed so beautifully simple.'

⤺

The drive to Barcelona wasn't long – two hours – and started with the crossing of an arid plain, before rising to the cooler, pine- and fir-clad hills of the *Parc Natural de Sant Llorenc del Munt i l'Obac*, the national park enclosing Barcelona on its landward side. As I drove within 30 miles of the city, on the left from the motorway for most of the remaining journey could be seen the strange, contorted peaks of *Montserrat*. This is a famous mountain, the direct translation into English meaning 'serrated' from Catalan. I thought it to be a valid description: its terrifyingly spiky peaks, all closely packed together, resembled something out of the Emerald City – an apparition, almost.

I had been to Barcelona before, and long before my interest in Orwell and his work led to me beginning my tour, I had visited *Placa de Orwell*, the square named after him, in 2013. It had been at one time a place for down-and-outs, of drudgery and drug dealing. It is in the centre of the city and not far from the famous *Las Ramblas*. Increasingly said to be gentrified, there is not a great deal to see or do there. I suspect, as with the sad street which bears his name in Barbastro, somewhere had to be found to honour him and it was selected at random.

The first impressions of Orwell's arrival in Barcelona were recorded by Jennie Lee, wife of Aneurin Bevan and herself a Labour MP and minister in the 1960s. She was sitting in a hotel in Barcelona when Orwell walked in, and she remarked on his height and the bizarre size of his shoes, adding that he was a curious mix in being 'not only socialist but profoundly liberal'.

Orwell made several visits to Barcelona. His first was before being sent to the front, with further visits on leave to see Eileen, and another visit to recuperate from the bullet wound in his neck. As time went on, in the later spring, the situation became even more dramatic than what it had been when Orwell first arrived there. POUM had been banned, denounced by Communists as an organisation infiltrated by fascists, and conflict broke out on the streets. Ironically, not long after he arrived in Spain, Orwell gave serious consideration to leaving POUM for the International Brigade in Madrid, to 'see more action'. The more I read of his work, the more I find it peppered with amusing understatements.

Orwell was implicated for involvement in sedition as a consequence of his participation with POUM. He maintained a perpetual fear (not least when he and Eileen travelled through Spanish Morocco to spend the winter of 1938 in Marrakech) that he would pay for this one day by a visit from the Spanish secret police. Richard Rees, who saw Eileen in Barcelona, reflected in his memoirs published in 1960 that she seemed to be 'living under political terror' – something which does not sound overly dramatic when one learns that her hotel room was turned over by the secret police. She wrote: 'The police conducted the search in the recognised OGPU or Gestapo style. In the small hours of the morning there was a pounding on the door, and six men marched in, switched on the light and immediately took up various positions about the room, obviously agreed upon beforehand. They then searched both rooms with inconceivable thoroughness.'

Eileen's description of the inspection is not very different to the raiding of the room Winston and his partner Julia hire to make love in secretly in *Nineteen Eighty-Four*. I would be amazed if this were not the inspiration for it, given Orwell's description of the flood of the secret police in through the windows and the malaise that followed. Orwell's notes for *Homage to Catalonia* were saved because someone was quick-witted enough to hide them on the room's outside window ledge. His diaries from Spain remain, at the time of writing, in the NKVD (the secret police of the USSR) archives in Moscow.

In the late 1980s, documents were found in an archive in Madrid that showed that Orwell and Eileen were on a watch list, and had they been caught as they made a run for the French border, they would have been tried for 'espionage and high treason' in Valencia. Some members of POUM were caught, tried and hanged, a fate which may well have lain in store for Orwell. The inclination the Spaniards have for honouring Orwell is perhaps, I reflected, that it seems to be the only place in the world where he came close to losing his life not just once, but twice!

The headquarters of POUM, *Hotel Falcon* and *Café Moka*, a cafe next door where the Britons skating around the activities of the ILP and POUM in Spain often gathered, still stands today near Barcelona's *Plaza Catalonia*. The *Falcon* was housed in an ornate building with pretty cast-iron balconies and painted in stripes of magenta, to look as if, from a distance, it had been studded with pink wafers. It is not quite what one might call to mind when thinking of a Communist party headquarters, but then that was possibly the point: come the revolution, the handsome buildings of Mayfair's clubs might well find themselves smothered in the hammer and sickle.

I visited, in the north of the city, the site of *Sanatorium Maurin*, the hospital in which Orwell spent time recuperating following the wound to his neck. It is now the 'Benjamin Franklin International School', sitting in a complex of buildings which (as in the 1930s) enjoy a panoramic view of Barcelona. Far in the distance, the Mediterranean sparkled amid a plethora of warehouses and far-off cranes. The area is predominantly residential, with steep streets of colourful two-storey villas leading up towards *Tibidabo*; described by Orwell as the 'queer-shaped mountain that rises abruptly above Barcelona'.

The school, though it has 'international' in its title, is to all intents and purposes an American school. Like most American schools it is much smarter than its equivalents in England; taller on average, more solidly built. Just along the road from the school, at the start of a steep incline in the street, was a bright pink pig graffitied over the door of a stout, camouflage-green telephone exchange box. I thought it was fitting that something so close to a site with an association to Orwell could take visitors straight onto the pages of *Animal Farm*, or at least take me there.

During Orwell's final few days in Spain, he remarked on how normal parts of Spain seemed in contrast to the filth and risk-to-life he had experienced on the front. He and Eileen spent a few days at Tarragona, a city port south-west along the coast from Barcelona, where he noticed: 'The plump local bourgeoisie bathing and sunning themselves'; as if the fronts of the war were a universe away. The Duchess of Atholl, a Scottish Conservative MP nicknamed the 'Red Duchess' for her left-leaning opinions, was also in Spain around the same time and let it be known she wouldn't be compromising on culinary standards – she complained that her hotel had run out of butter. Orwell quipped: 'I hope they found some butter for the Duchess.'

Orwell's only souvenirs from Spain were a goatskin water bottle and 'one of those tiny iron lamps in which the Aragonese burn olive oil'. These must have accompanied him and Eileen as they made a quick dash out of Spain, assisted by the staff of the British Consulate. In Hitchcockian fashion they pretended to be English tourists, leaving Barcelona for Perpignan on 23 June and taking an anthology of Wordsworth's poetry to read on board. What a sight he must have been, all six foot and three inches, crammed into a railway seat and perusing *Composed Upon Westminster Bridge.*

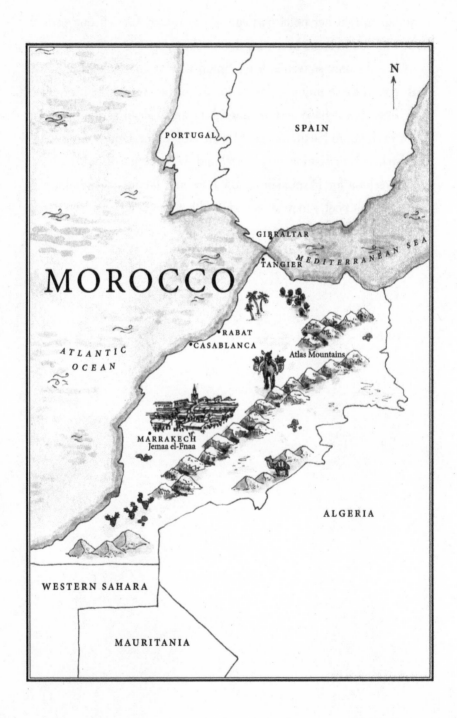

Marrakech, Morocco

Pink City (1938–9)

Marrakech is a sprawling city resting on an extensive plain. The view from the air must be the closest one can get to the sensation of landing on Mars: a dusty, red mountainous landscape. The city from above resembles a terracotta floor, squares of bright orange or red roofs, whose satellite dishes further encourage the sensation of arriving at a space station. The architecture is predominantly of cubes, all to the same design, as if cut and pasted. Where there is any contrast to this building style, as in the city centre, the same shades of pink plaster drape everything.

Like a variation on a theme, it is surely no coincidence that the taxis are also orange, like the cream that dribbles from a clementine-flavoured fondant. For all the blandness of architectural design, the inhabitants' dress does not disappoint. Men and women alike tailor their clothing to impress. I estimate that around a fifth of the residents were wearing Western dress. These, predominantly remnants of the French colonial population Orwell referred to in his essay 'Marrakech', ape the clothing of Marseilles or Nice. The remainder were wearing cloth of every bright colour, a distinctly memorable aspect of a trading city so famous in the history of North Africa.

Orwell's little-known jaunt to Marrakech comes as a surprise to many exploring his life for the first time. It was a necessary break as his health deteriorated badly in the spring of 1938; life in a cold, dank rural English cottage was not the best medicine for tuberculosis. Over that summer, Orwell resided at Preston Hall sanatorium near Maidstone in Kent. There was no question of returning to Wallington and so, after the job in India fell through, Orwell and Eileen considered a move south to Dorset. One of Orwell's uncles, a Limouzin, owned a golf course near Bournemouth.

But an offer was made, anonymously, for passage to Morocco and a six-month stay of recuperation in Marrakech. Although Orwell never knew who the donor was, it was L.H. Myers, a Marxist novelist and friend, who had provided the financial assistance. The total cost, eventually repaid with royalties from *Animal Farm*, came to £300. It is indicative of how low their incomes were that the break to escape the winter had to be paid for by someone else. The offer was gladly accepted. After arranging for the Stores to be sub-let, they left Britain on the SS *Stratheden* from the docks at Tilbury, on 2 September 1938.

Why Marrakech was chosen is not clear, not least since they would have to travel through Spanish Morocco to get there. Until 1954–5, when the country was decolonised, Morocco was divided into two: Spanish in the north, and French in the south. Like Bombay, which was gifted to England by Portugal as part of a dowry, Tangier was given to England and then passed first to the French, and then to the Spanish. The Agadir Crisis in 1911, a precursor conflict to the First World War, further demonstrated the region's strategic significance.

For Orwell, returning to Spanish territory so soon after his near-death in Spain, the prospect of travelling through Morocco was unsavoury. On the boat he happened to meet one of his old pupils, Tony Hyams, whom he had taught at Frays College in Hayes. Tony's father worked for the British administration in the Sudan and his family, like many on the boat, were colonials travelling east to start or resume government service. Hyams bounced up to his old teacher and later recalled how fearful Orwell seemed of going through Spanish Morocco, concerned he might end up arrested and back in Spain. He and Eileen had only narrowly escaped from Spain with their lives intact.

Although neither was harmed on the passage over, it was a distinctly unsettling journey. Orwell survived by consuming medication, whereas Eileen developed sea sickness and dysentery. She had mixed feelings about the trip to begin with and arrived in Morocco less than enthusiastic about their journey. They stopped at Gibraltar en-route, where Orwell picked up the latest English newspapers to devour developments simmering on the continent. From there they sailed to Tangiers, which Eileen described as a pretty city, and stayed in one of the European hotels. They then began their arduous train journey to Marrakech.

⌒

Not unusually for a visitor to a city so dependent on the tourist trade, the pleas of my taxi driver that the journey was 'long way' into the centre from the airport were disproved. The main airport, much smaller than I had expected, still quaintly ushers passengers on foot to and away from standing planes. It is close to the city centre, in fact not far short of a walking distance. As is usual for the first taxi journey in a foreign country, I left feeling my fare had not been well spent. But the driver knew his roads and, once the car entered the gates of the old city, which, as in most Islamic cities, is referred to as the *Medina*, mayhem descended on all sides.

It would be orientalist to think of Marrakech as a mysterious city full of spices, snake charmers and antiques. Almost everything in the centre is smartened up in some way for the tourist trade, often to the point where it appears artificial. Yet the city is still there to serve its primary purpose: a home for its million-or-so inhabitants. Most of these are indifferent to visitors, but a small minority can spoil the experience by chasing tourists' dollars.

The city has seen enormous demographic changes since 1938. For a start, it has increased its population by a factor of five, from 200,000 to over a million, and the once-large French and Jewish communities have gone. Unlike British India, where Britons lived for the most part temporarily, Moroccan cities developed large settler populations. Casablanca was majority settler European at the time of Orwell's visit, and Marrakech had a sufficiently large number of French settlers for them to dominate its cultural life and civic administration. As in Algeria, another French settler colony, these settlers were known as 'pieds-noirs' or 'black feet'. For the most part they returned to France after independence in 1956.

Marrakech's riads, its guest houses, must be some of the most enticing places to stay anywhere in the world. The Medina seems to be one enormous riad – almost every building doubles as a guest house. Each evokes the sensation of 1001 Arabian Nights; colonnaded walkways elevated around a courtyard. Some have a bathing pool at their centre, a welcoming method of cooling the febrile atmosphere outside their gates. I stayed separately at three, the most interesting of which was a good five-minute walk through a maze of passages which eventually led to a foot-thick wooden door. Behind this was a massive courtyard, with the bedrooms accessed via a narrow, enclosed staircase, carved from stone, as if in the turret of a castle.

In the morning guests typically ate their breakfast around a large table in the courtyard. The table had a surface of patterned blue tiling, like Spode ironed flat. With the open sky above the courtyard a hue of the bright, morning sun was reflected in its glaze. In sharp contrast to former British colonies, where stodgy sliced bread, and if one is lucky, Rich Tea-type Britannia biscuits are the culinary legacy, my experience in former French colonies is that the bread and the pastries are still a good match for anything one might find at a bakery in France. Breakfast at each *riad* was 'continental', crusty baguette accompanied with little bowls of unsalted butter and marmalade made from the city's groves of clementine trees.

Brushing the sharp-edged baguette crumbs off the pages of George Orwell's *Complete Essays*, I skimmed over 'Marrakech'. His geographically focussed essays are few and far between, still less essays written about somewhere without the intention of making a political or social point. 'A Hanging' and 'Shooting an Elephant' both fall into the latter category, critiques of the imperial system he felt no shame in damning. There are shades of this in 'Marrakech' too, but they are subtle, as if his political conscience had taken a back seat. 'Marrakech' reads as if he listed his immediate observations. He noted in one letter: 'This trip is something quite new to me, because for the first time I am in the position of being a tourist.'

The most memorable lines describe the plight of the city's donkeys. Just like the function of the goat and almost any other four-legged creature, the interest Orwell pursued around the purpose of domesticated animals in society flickers through. He wrote:

I had not been five minutes on Moroccan soil before I noticed the overloading of the donkeys and was infuriated by it. There is no question that the donkeys are damnably treated ... what is peculiarly pitiful is that it is the most willing creature on earth, it follows its master like a dog and does not need either bridle or halter. After a dozen years of devoted work it suddenly drops dead, whereupon its master tips it into the ditch and the village dogs have torn its guts out before it is cold.

The donkey is no longer a common sight in Marrakech. It is not as if, upon leaving the International Arrivals hall, a sea of crestfallen donkeys appears in view. It was not until my first full day that I walked into one. Steadily, I began spotting them in the quieter corners of the city. They still appear in more significant numbers in Marrakech than in Britain, where I imagine the last time most Britons will say they have seen one was as the costume in a Nativity play.

As for most of the city's inhabitants, life is more endurable today for the donkeys of Marrakech than it was in the late 1930s. Tourism has replaced subsistence agriculture as by far the most significant source of income, food is cheaper than ever before and cars are affordable for all but the poorest. Four-wheelers do most of the back-breaking work now. I noticed donkeys remain popular with hawkers; the first I saw was happily pulling a cart of strawberries.

Walking north into the centre I passed the Koutoubia mosque, the tallest structure around. It pierces the sky, an effect exaggerated by Marrakech being a predominantly low-lying city. Shaped like London's Elizabeth Tower, housing Big Ben, it is the city's largest mosque and dominates every perspective from the surrounding gardens. At an elevation of just over 250 feet it has stood the test of time: it was constructed some 800 years ago. Built from pink sandstone and its crest lined with hexagonal-patterned marine blue and green tiling, the tower's attractive golden globes perfect the design. It was the building in Marrakech I enjoyed photographing the most.

The *Jemaa el-Fnaa* is the centre of the city, a vast public square famous for its range of street entertainment which emerges over the course of the day. It should not be called a square at all, since it is really a misshapen public space of corners filled with makeshift restaurants and curio stalls. But it is lively, and with no building tall enough to cast shade, exposed to the full glare of the sun for the entire day. It is a dry and dusty place – Marrakech is a dry and dusty city – meaning there is no better place to be filled with stalls serving cool, sweet orange juice at a fraction of what the same would cost in a Western country.

This is tourist central, with coachloads of visitors of all nationalities, but mainly French and German, arriving to say they'd been there and to collect a trinket or two. The usual donkey or camel rides abound and, while many cafes and restaurants lining the perimeter are full, they are also, without exception, rather shabby. Various exits from the square lead to cavernous souks, with entrances surrounded by stalls selling multi-coloured rugs and pottery to match. I have visited enough tourist traps to know the score with bartering, but never cease to be amazed at the price reductions a stall holder will countenance. The biggest discounts of all are reserved for those who walk away; a small blue bowl I bid for falling from €40 to less than ten. It probably cost a euro to make.

In between the orange juice sellers in the centre of the square are smaller stalls selling a strange medley of collectables, seemingly drifted north from their natural habitats in sub-Saharan Africa. The traders on these stalls are predominantly black African, venturing beyond the Sahel to seek their fortune with whatever curiosities they can bring with them. The one I approached first had papyrus bowls filled with mummified rodents, while the trader quipped the 'most precious' objects for sale were hidden from view. He reached for a small copper tray, revealing to me the parched remains of lizards whose grey, ridged backs were juxtaposed by the spiral shapes made by their tails, preserved even in death, and the sinister voids of their eye sockets.

Another trader, sniffing the air for a sale, lurched towards me. I was ushered to view his wares, an eclectic jumble of flotsam. My eyes were attracted to two rows of ostrich eggs, carefully laid on a bed of feathers resembling the fluffy tread of a garish bathroom mat. Around them were arranged the pink, purple and green exoskeletons of sea urchins. Behind was a terrace of small glass bottles, each containing the lotion derived from one endangered animal or another, the trader assuring me what powerful aphrodisiacs they were. One, derived from a Rhino, I guessed from the blurred picture on the front, declared in large, bold text: '*Composé de Faiblesse Sexuelle*'. Or 'consists of sexual problems', from which I made the assumption it would provide the miracle cure for erectile dysfunction. I declined the €50 price tag.

Jemaa el-Fnaa's grand spectacle is its daily shows. Appropriately, since *Jemaa* translates as 'congregation', large crowds arrive over the course of a morning to see an orchestra of festivities: dancing, snake-charming and impassioned storytelling. It resembled some vast Speakers' Corner, middle-aged men spouting off on a curio-box to rapturous applause from crowds of onlookers. As is the case on that edge of London's Hyde Park, the crowding acts as a market in which the successful orator attracts a sprawling mass of sunglasses and filming smartphones, the unsuccessful leaving for the day and changing tack the next.

⤳

I soon found myself hailing a taxi and began the process of identifying Orwell's house. His and Eileen's first night in the city was at the Hotel Continental, which she soon realised was a brothel. This was followed by the Majestic Hotel, now no more but at that time one of the best in the city. Alas, it was a stretch too far for their finances, and they took a homestay on Rue Edmond Doutté. As in India, many of the colonial-era place names have been erased: Rue Edmond Doutté, named after a French writer with an interest in Islam, is now Rue Moulay Ismail. Letters from the pair were sent from *Chez Madame Vellat*, although there is little sign of either a guest house or Madame Vellat today amid the austere, orange-painted concrete colonnades of this busy side street.

I began by asking the driver, whose limited English guaranteed there would be many simply put, loud statements and finger-pointing to come, to drive to *Route Casa*. This is the main road leading to Casablanca and the road on which their villa stood, around five kilometres from the centre: 'entirely isolated except for a few Arabs who live in the outbuildings to tend the orange grove that surrounds it', Eileen wrote. This was a simple enough instruction, and after a taxi journey that would make skating on ice appear a model of calm, the driver declared: 'Here. Route Casa.'

The mayhem of the city's congested roads was over. *Route Casa* is not unquiet but seemed to see only the occasional truck or passing car, roving out of Marrakech towards the silent, distant desert. The Atlas Mountains loom closer here, their impressive silhouette much clearer on the edge of the city than at its centre. The area lining the road was, save for the red dust swirling in the air, much like any other on the edge of a large city. A football stadium could be seen in the near distance and the usual new car studios displayed their latest models. I was uneasy with this modern development, and the lump quick to form in my throat suggested that my hunt for their house would be a hopeless one.

Villa Simont had been owned by a butcher who did not live close-by but paid a group of Arabs to care for and pick the villa's orange crop. At the time the area was by all accounts much more accessible to the poorest people in the city than it is today. Palmeira, the nearest place name, is now *the* upmarket suburb in which to be seen and heard. Its large plots and high walls reminded me of Los Angeles, or the upmarket villas in the capital city of some banana republic or other. Faux Victorian street lighting, aping Dickensian London, and the country clubs and the golf courses are somehow so far removed from the simplicity Orwell desired in very nearly every year of his life. I cannot imagine he would want to live on this edge of Marrakech now. Wondering why it was so difficult to spot the villa, probably only a short driveway off the main road and made even more distinct by what Eileen described as 'a sort of observatory on its roof', I arrived at the reluctant conclusion it had been demolished.

Their life at the villa, brief as it was, resembled something similar to that which they enjoyed at the Stores. The villa had a large living area, two bedrooms, a bathroom and a kitchen which, while not enormous, came with a plot big enough for their newly acquired collection of animals to wander. It should come as no surprise that they considered buying a donkey but, after recognising it would be indulgent of them to provide only a temporary good home, decided against it. But a goat came, some hens – most of which died – and two doves. The latter Eileen described as hobbling, one after another, around the house. They no doubt had the unfortunate effect of infusing the sultry air with a pigeon-type stench, a smell familiar to the users of dank alleyways in London or New York.

As a welcome distraction from his writing, Orwell set to task creating a garden at the villa but became frustrated by the microclimate, describing it to a friend as 'like a huge allotment patch that's been let "go back", and practically no trees except olives and palms'. Seeds proved hard to germinate, and Orwell's mind wandered to recall the bounty to befall the forthcoming English Spring, the last before the outbreak of war. He wrote to Jack Common, then caretaker of the Stores: 'I wonder if anything is coming up in the garden. There ought to be a few snowdrops and crocuses soon.'

The uncertain future in the febrile years before war broke out in September 1939 is at the centre of *Coming up for Air*. Written in its entirety in Marrakech, Orwell wrote of a time before the spread of London, like paté onto toast, across Middlesex and into Berkshire. It is a unique description of irreversible change before the green belt was introduced, and England was yet to experience mass-car ownership. It is odd to think that the highways and byways around Henley were the topics of investigation amid the heat and dust of somewhere as different from Henley as Marrakech.

Orwell's views of appeasement towards Nazi Germany are not what one might expect. He was rampantly against the possibility of going to war with Germany and critical of the Labour Party, which, with Winston Churchill, opposed Neville Chamberlain's appeasement. Eileen wrote just after they arrived in Morocco that Eric 'retains an extraordinary political simplicity in spite of everything, wants to hear what he calls the voice of the people. He thinks this might stop a war, but I'm sure that the voice would only say that it didn't want a war but of course would have to fight if the government declared war.' He later scribbled to a friend: 'the bloody fools of the Labour Party infer that after all the English people do want another way to make the world safe for democracy and that their best line is to exploit the anti-fascist stuff'. But the war that everyone knew was coming and which would shape his writing so much, was still months off.

It is interesting to observe his reading habits during this period, seemingly unmet by the offerings of Marrakech's bookshops. In January 1939 he ordered from Frank Westrope, his old boss at Booklovers' Corner: Thackeray's *Pendennis*; Trollope's *The Eustace Diamonds*; Henry James' *The Turn of the Screw*; and John Stuart Mill's *Autobiography*. The selection of *The Turn of the Screw*, one of his favourite books as a pupil at Eton, is illustrative of the devotion he displayed for his preferred books and authors throughout life. Similarly, his request of John Stuart Mill's *Autobiography* is an insight into his progressive politics. As early as 1933, at the age of 30, he was defensive of Bertrand Russell in the slew of attacks the philosopher faced. He wrote from Marrakech to Herbert (later Sir Herbert) Read, that Russell might be a good person to pursue a movement against war. J.S. Mill was Russell's godfather, the trunk in the tree of wisdom of which the roots emerged from his father, the philosopher James Mill, and his best friend Jeremy Bentham.

~

My taxi driver was perplexed that I should want to visit *Route Casa* at all, and despite his best efforts, which included ringing around most of the contacts in his mobile phone, he was none the wiser about *Villa Simont*. On our way back to the centre I imagined him telling his friends what a madman he had driven today, asking to be taken to a motorway and then searching for a house for which the passenger had neither an address nor telephone number. Then, not a minute into the journey back, I yelled: 'STOP'. To our left, not a stone's throw from the lines of brand new cars seeking their gullible buyers and in front of a long wall guarding the large houses and swimming pools behind them, was a donkey chained to the ferrous stump of a broken water pump.

The donkey, advanced in age, was attached to a rein no longer than a yard. Around its hoof was an iron clasp so tight it had cut into the bone. There was not a drop of water to be seen, yet it stood upright and placid in the midst of its fateful home. It was standing in an area slightly smaller than a tennis court with broken bricks, putrid human waste and the corpses of two street dogs for company. Its owners presumably lived in the little shack on the edge of the open scrubland, next to which was an oval-shaped open hearth. Thick black smoke poured more than ten metres copiously into the sky, while two mothers and three infants peered in my direction. The children followed each of my steps meticulously, cat-like, as if observing the movements of prey. Leaving, I was amused to find Orwell's analysis valid for at least one sorry donkey in Marrakech, and so close to his old home.

The drive back passed through the broad avenues of Palmeira. I looked more closely at the perimeter walls of the oversized villas lining one street, noticing that they would be impossible to climb but still had their tops studded with broken glass. The redeeming feature of the area was its vegetation. In a climate where water is a luxury, bountiful gardens are a jealously guarded symbol of affluence. The city is famous for its Bougainvillea, a climber with deep-purple flowers which spills over walls and cascades down them like some mighty waterfall.

Having journeyed through the vast main square and into the large, nondescript part of the city that separates the *Jemaa el-Fnaa* from the old town and Marrakech's Jewish Quarter, I felt the mid-afternoon urge for a cup of tea. Bakeries doubling as cafes seemed to be common and looked invariably unappetising. Their facades are for the most part a dark, walnut brown. Plastered in a brittle plastic frontage, often broken around the edges to reveal the chipboard beneath, they splay plastic chairs out onto the pavement as their marker of territory. It was a relief to then find a bakery apparently clean enough and still full for the day with produce. I naively entered and ordered 'English tea', but as my eyes glanced down to choose my sweet, I sensed my pupils dilating. Each section of the cabinet was filled with flies, a rabble so thick it was difficult to see any of the items beneath them, to differentiate a pain aux raisin from a pain au chocolat. I was filled with so much repulsion that I left, and decided to settle on a reliably refreshing mint tea at the next authentic Moroccan cafe I could find.

Mint tea is treated as a delicacy. At the *riads*, the custom is for it to be provided for every returning guest, a welcome gesture for the parched tourist. Morocco is famous for its mint tea, served in small, solid-brass teapots and poured into thin, delicate glasses. The sound of pouring has a rippling effect, caused perhaps by the size of the spout, which soothes some of the fretting of a long day in the city's *souqs*. The scent of the tea is strong, even stronger if sugar is added, filling the courtyard with the sensation that one is rested.

Few residents seem to move around the city before noon. For the most part, however, Marrakech has a bustling evening economy, owing to the lower temperatures at night. I woke early and from my *riad* in the *Medina*, tried to find my way to the east of the city and into the Jewish quarter. Orwell paid particular attention to the city's Jewish community, which he noted lived in extreme poverty but survived through menial craftsmanship, mending shoes or metal bashing. He wrote in *Marrakech*: 'When you go through the Jewish quarters you gather some idea of what the medieval ghettoes were probably like,' and estimated the Jewish population at 13,000.

Finding it took some false starts. The *Medina*, which is surrounded by three-feet-thick and 30-foot-high walls, has just a few scattered exits in obscure corners. The signage is poor; where there is any, it is in Arabic. I tried my best to retrace the routes I had taken before to the correct exit, but kept leading myself up the wrong paths to dead ends with short, ancient-looking doors with perplexed locals putting their rubbish out. I met so many enclosed nooks I felt I was trapped in a life-size maze, the sort a child is fascinated by in a colouring-in book, and would not be able to escape until I determined myself to find the end of the puzzle.

The sensation that I was eight again was encouraged by figures sneaking around in the hooded *djellaba*, an all-enclosing Islamic style of dress I recalled from a Tintin comic. The *djellaba* is common in Morocco and offers the best means of disguise. The hem, which almost touches the ground, shuffles along so that the person within appears to be suspended above the ground. The dress is ghostly, as if to suggest an apparition is momentarily invading one's sightline, but thereafter removes itself hastily from view. The hood, which has a pointed end, shrouds the face and when the head is directed down, reminds one of a garment belonging to the legend of some sinister spectre; a medieval monk, or other.

The Jewish Quarter is just to the east of the *Medina*, but there are no obvious entrance or exit points, perhaps indicative of how that community was once treated. So it was a long walk around to it, and even then it is unclear where the area begins and where it ends. Even today, when there is barely any Jewish community at all, the people here are visibly poorer than those inhabiting the tourist-filled centre and *Medina* of Marrakech. The curio shops were suddenly curtailed, the streets became filthier and the passageways narrower. Wooden shutters seemed to dangle precariously from their hinges, unloved. The lower parts of the walls in the densely packed lanes appeared moth-eaten, pockmarked like the Blitz-era bomb damage one can still find in central London.

I was curious to discover whether there were any Jews left in what had been, in Orwell's time, a bustling ghetto of 13,000. Concluding the best place to reveal anything of their legacy would be the Quarter's sole remaining synagogue, I meandered through a myriad of passageways, dimly lit by the scale of the walls engulfing them. I asked one or two hovering locals, and they sent me off by a succession of left and right turns. Eventually, behind a scruffy, narrow set of twin inward-swinging doors, I found it. It was quiet and musty, with the atmosphere of a railway station that sees just a train or two a day pass through it. I learnt that there were around 40 Jews left in the city and only a handful who worship regularly.

Before long I found myself in another *souq* – they are hard to avoid in Marrakech. Orwell described the then-inhabitants, somewhat unfairly, to his old school friend Cyril Connolly, as people 'near a big town utterly debauched by the tourist racket and their poverty combined, which turn them into a race of beggars and curio-sellers'. It is hard not to share that impression in one of the *souqs*, where it would be difficult to swing a bat without hitting someone trying to sell you a hookah pipe. These warrens of passageways, only partially lit by the flicker of sunlight through the makeshift canopy covering them, abound.

The stalls I enjoyed most were those selling herbs or spices. The latter display mounds of cumin or paprika in broad-based steel drums. The stall holders shape the spices into spires, as if to ape the fine-tipped pyramidal hood of the *djellaba*. It is miraculous they remain intact. When they do collapse, presumably when no one is looking, the stall owners must surely act quickly to bundle the mountain back together again. The herb stall owners avoid this artistic licence, preferring large baskets filled to their brims. The names are appealing, dressed up in a mystique which quadruples the price of 100 grams' worth: 'Cummins Charm' or 'Pepper Menth'.

Along one alley, squeezed between two non-descript curio stalls, I spotted a whitewashed entrance to what one could imagine would be an artist's studio. With time on my hands, I wandered in and surprised myself by stumbling across a French-run cafe serving artisan salads and summer puddings. *La Famille* is an oasis of calm in the stressful desert of hassle and demands for *baksheesh* I had been familiar with since my first footsteps in India. Like the best restaurants, it had a limited menu, a choice of flatbreads and either of two salads. I enjoyed the atmosphere so much I spent the rest of my day there, smug in the comfort that this haven was not listed in my guidebook.

The seven months Orwell and Eileen spent in Morocco passed quickly. It was not long before they must have had to surrender the lease on *Villa Simont* and sell their menagerie of animals. Neither warmed terribly to life there, which in the same letter to Connolly, Orwell described as 'a beastly, dull country'. I think that is a little unfair on Morocco, which does have charm and plenty deserving of observation. Orwell's essay on the city is testimony to that and, of course, if it was such a dull place then he need not have picked up his pen and written about it. Nevertheless, the object of recuperation was not fulfilled. Eileen wrote scathingly of his health that: 'he has been worse here than I've ever seen him'.

They left Marrakech on 19 March 1939, with passage secured from Casablanca on 26 March on board a Japanese vessel, the SS *Yasukuni Maru*. During their time in Casablanca, he and Eileen spent a lot of time catching up on cinema, and they enjoyed casting their critical eyes over the propaganda films coming out from Mother France. Orwell described the 'good shots of the Maginot Line' in one film, scribbling in his diary that everyone now seemed to expect war. The *Yasukuni Maru* was empty; a consequence, he wrote, of a boycott by English colonists out east. Orwell and Eileen were impressed. With just twelve passengers in 2nd class on a boat built for 500, the food was 'slightly better than on the P&O and the service distinctly better'. The liner was torpedoed in the Pacific on 31 January 1944 by the USS *Trigger*, with the loss of 1,188 men.

The relaxed days of liners crossing the Bay of Biscay in six days are long gone. I made do with a delayed British Airways flight to Gatwick, returning to a chilly, wet, blustery March evening in London. Catching the (also delayed) train from Gatwick back into the capital the neat but sprawling terraces of south London flashed by. When Orwell and Eileen returned to London, the spectre of war was looming for Britain. The next six years of their lives would be shaped by the Second World War.

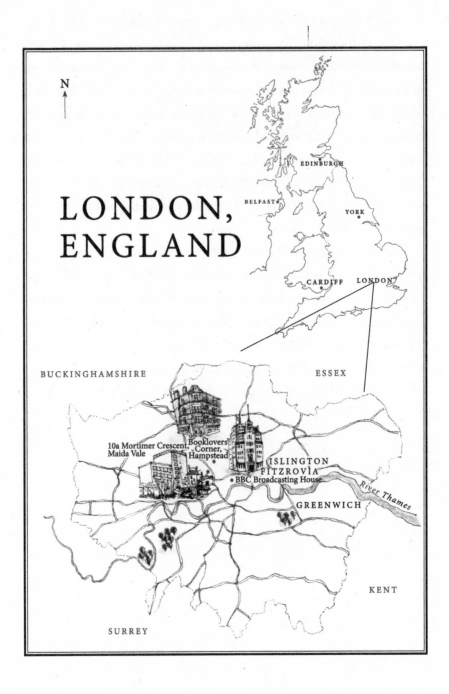

N

LONDON,
ENGLAND

EDINBURGH

BELFAST

YORK

CARDIFF   LONDON

BUCKINGHAMSHIRE   ESSEX

10a Mortimer Crescent,   Booklovers'
Maida Vale   Corner,
                          Hampstead

                    ISLINGTON
                    FITZROVIA
                    BBC Broadcasting House

                    GREENWICH   River Thames

                                          KENT

SURREY

Fitzrovia, London, England

Bombs, and the BBC (1939–45)

Among the more unusual destinations for theatregoers in London are the city's 'theatre pubs' – old-fashioned locals replete with a fully functioning theatre tucked away at their rear. It was in one of these in Islington, on a humid evening in August, that my research into Orwell's wartime experience of London began with a visit to a performance of Tony Cox's play, *Mrs Orwell*. With an actor playing Orwell straining his lungs to splutter in the disrupted tones of an English gentleman beset with tuberculosis, and the commands of his nurse echoing between the four walls of the tiny stage and auditorium, I re-imagined the London of the 1940s from the comfort of our times.

During his last decade Orwell at last achieved widespread fame, his intellect and personality shaped by the war that ravished Western civilisation for the six years from 1939. But by the end of 1948 he would be bedridden, and just 21 days into 1950, he would be dead. Against the background of an extraordinary life, the 1940s for Orwell were his most active, his writing now paying enough to ensure he did not need to work. His output, and the quality of it, is dizzying.

Cox's *Mrs Orwell* is a compelling and sad introduction to the demise of a great man, performed for the first time in the Red Lion Pub in

Islington. My student halls were a stone's throw away from here, on Rosebery Avenue. I must have walked past the pub a thousand times and never had it occurred to me that it was a theatre, as well as a pub. Appropriately, with its deeply engraved floral wallpaper and Victoriana, it is the sort of pub Orwell admired: a London of old which seems to be ever threatened by the sea of change engulfing it.

Islington was the last part of London Orwell called home, where he had a flat in one of the handsome terraces that make up this well-preserved part of Georgian London. On the top floor of one of the townhouses, Orwell, his adopted son Richard and a nanny would live after the war in between visits to Jura. Visitors recalled Orwell's presentation of afternoon tea – there was always a spread of sand-wiches and cakes – and his obsession with ensuring that the tea was sufficiently brewed. He was so dedicated to making good tea that he devoted time to writing about it, his essay, 'A Nice Cup of Tea' published in 1946.

The first apartment he and Eileen occupied, one of a total of four permanent residences during and after the war, was a top-floor flat in a building on Chagford Street, a mews in Marylebone neither far from the station of the same name, nor Baker Street. It is said that, during a war in which the Germans were bombing the city so intensively, the rent for top-floor flats was cheaper than those on storeys lower down. This sort of economy I now see to be typically Orwellian, and could easily have delivered the quick death he so desired.

Having lived in London for ten years, I am possibly a weak candi-date for being an objective observer of what is now my home city. And yet for the first time, distancing myself in researcher mode for the day, I realised how utterly absurd life in London can be. On the streets and the tube and buses, the thronging mass of people is at best selfish, at worst rude. I am inclined as a Londoner to exhibit these traits myself – it is as if Londoners are so bound up in their existence that they lose an appreciation for the greater whole. Perhaps this is why the city's architectural cohesion is next to non-existent, the pursuit of selfishness.

As Orwell lived in so many places, it proved to be a tiring day for a dog to spend traipsing up and down tube escalators. I've never seen George so exhausted after a day out, which is saying a lot for a springer spaniel. Doing the rounds, we often found ourselves surrounded by a rush of sad faces, pacing directly with not a thought for anything other than their objective in mind; a city of sprinting automatons who are unwilling or unable to engage with those around them. When strangers do talk in London, on the tube or elsewhere, it is unusual; almost high-risk.

As in Hayes, which is a community of communities, London is a victim of its success. The pull of people here, which is primarily economic, leads to a transient society in which very few people lay down anything more than superficial roots. Unlike in a village or small town, where, by and large, everyone knows one another and is thus accountable for their actions, London is incapable of forging the bonds of trust upon which civilisation is meant to be built. People can act as they wish because they are able to lurk in the city's anonymity.

To some extent, this is the case in any large city. London responds to any attack on its sense of self-worth by stressing its inclusivity and sense of solidarity. And yet, as any visitor who walks more than 500 metres across a residential area can see, the city is starkly divided into relatively small enclaves of mostly white British or foreign affluence, and vast estates or areas of low-rise, quasi-slum housing in which those on lower incomes struggle to exist in one of the most expensive cities on earth. London is essentially a plutocracy supported by a vast workforce paid to service its needs.

The way in which people drift in and out of the city, as foreign residents or British nationals abroad, as well as the swell of tourists, likewise leads to circumstances in which its residents care less about their surroundings. Rubbish can be thrown because the city is not 'theirs'; home is somewhere else. I have a love-hate relationship with London – one I share with Orwell, who escaped it at any opportunity he could get – and cannot, as some do, argue that it is a model of success for social cohesion, or of living in general. In *Keep the Aspidistra Flying* he made his feelings clear:

> *London! Mile after mile of mean lonely houses, let off in flats and single rooms; not homes, not communities, just clusters of meaningless lives drifting in a sort of drowsy chaos to the grave!*

> *There is something horrible about London at night; the coldness, the anonymity, the aloofness. Seven million people, sliding to and fro, avoiding contact, barely aware of one another's existence, like fish in an aquarium tank.*

꒰꒱

One admirable quality about the capital is that a visitor can always discover something new. The vicinity of Baker Street station I thought I knew like the back of my hand, but as so often when one is a zombie stomping apace to catch a bus, I had never taken the leisure of looking up. I left for Baker Street mid-morning, arriving in time for my morning latte, and entered one of the umpteen trendy coffee shops which now seem to be taking over London. Everyone knows the sort – a blackboard outside with diary-writing script advertising the latest import of Ethiopian bean, perfectly formed croissants and pain aux raisins; bare wood and 1950s furniture.

After spending £3.75 on a small latte, I sat outside the cafe with George. We were sandwiched between London Underground's Lost Property Office and tourist shops selling mini British postboxes and other trinkets, luxuries available to the hordes of tourists visiting Sherlock Holmes' house at 221B Baker Street. My eyes flicked up to the large Art Deco frontage opposite, and to my surprise I saw high up, at the length of the height of a man, a mesmerisingly impressive engraving of a lighthouse, the stone carved to reveal its torches of light shining out in each direction. I thought of stormy islands and the shipping forecast, of seafaring and seaside smells.

Baker Street and surrounds is one of the worst-polluted corners of central London, so the thought of some Hebridean breeze blasting us over a beach was welcome. It was this environment that lured Orwell to Jura perhaps because, like many writers, he required geographical as much as intellectual space in which to write. Chagford Street, the birthplace of the 'BENTLEY MOTOR CAR' a blue plaque on the row of mews told me, at the centre of overpopulated and, at that time, metal-bashing London, can never have provided this.

The building he and Eileen lived in for just over a year is now called Chagford House, a large, four-storey residential building of stone and London brick, resembling a Victorian presbytery. It reminded me of the pseudo-Georgian buildings forming parts of Eton College; a stately building with carved eaves and prim Georgian four-by-three pane windows. I suspect it once belonged to the Anglican church across the road named St Cyprian's – coincidentally the name-saint of Orwell's preparatory school. I stared at his flat number – eighteen – wondering who would answer if I pressed the bell.

During Orwell's lease, the building was called Dorset Chambers. As I walked out of the street, I thought of how the English love of its countryside is reflected in so many of the place names of its capital. Chagford is a small market town on Dartmoor, the National Park in Devon, and Dorset the inspiration for so many of Thomas Hardy's novels about life in rural Victorian England, a world Hardy perceived to be under threat from the forces of industrial change.

This tendency of the English to make every attempt to recall country living, which was shared by Orwell, lies deep in their psyche. In J.B. Priestley's *English Journey*, which I was reading the week of my visit, Priestley observed: 'The English ... do not willingly let go of the country once they have settled in a town; they are all gardeners, perhaps country gentlemen, at heart.' Priestley's journey, between the rich and industrial regions of England, influenced Orwell's decision to write *The Road to Wigan Pier*. They reached the same conclusions on social justice.

From Chagford Street, we walked along the western edge of Regent's Park towards Abbey Road, home to Orwell's second wartime flat. It is hard not to miss the Islamic influence on this area of Marylebone, which contains the enormous Regent's Park Mosque. This change since the 1940s – as for the transformation of Hayes, and of London in general – is noticeable, and comparatively recent, but Orwell is likely to have seen the beginnings of it. The mosque was preceded by an Islamic Cultural Centre, opened in 1944, so this part of London would have experienced some cultural diversity even in Orwell's time, though it may have been barely noticeable. Regent's Park Mosque was, I learnt, built on land exchanged by King George VI for a plot in Cairo, on which an Anglican Cathedral had been built. The government of Egypt demolished the cathedral, which stood close to the famous Egyptian Museum, for a new road in 1978.

Abbey Road and this part of London is cluttered with pre-war apartment blocks, mostly built with wealthy residents in mind. They line Regent's Park – 'Viceroy's Court'; 'Stockley House' – and are in general solidly built, constructed to last. St John's Wood has always attracted an affluent demographic; today it is popular with expatriate Indians and Americans, for whom the range of expensive eateries and shops inevitably cater. I should imagine Orwell would not have been a regular visitor to these; he was observed more than once eating a tin of cold baked beans.

Langford Court, to which he and Eileen moved in 1941, is an imposing building some seven storeys high, a rabbit warren of one-, two- and three-bedroom apartments. In the 1940s it would have been considered modern and high-quality housing, in contrast with the ubiquitous slums of the era. Today it feels as if very little has changed since the decade in which it was built. The windows, steel-framed and single glazed, do not seem to have been replaced in the 80 years that have passed. I considered that the flats' interiors probably remain Art Deco and that neither the expensive lifts nor the equipment will have been replaced over the period.

The entrance to the block is a little below street level, accessed via a sloping drive partially filled on the street side with a border of colourful annuals, the sort typically found in municipal gardens. I could quite imagine that the floral display greeting residents has not changed a jot since the days when Orwell would have been rushing in and out of the entrance – nothing much else seems to have altered. The porter spotted me and asked me who I was after. Around once a month, he said, people come. 'He didn't live here very long', he said. I stared at the '111' on the buzzer and wondered once more who would answer.

Unlike in Chagford Street, they would not escape the Blitz here. Orwell recalled seeing the bombing of East India Docks from the front door of Eileen's family house in Greenwich, on 26 August 1940, which he regarded as his 'first' raid. A few days later he and Eileen were woken by a bomb exploding in nearby Maida Vale, which he noted placed him 'mentally back in the Spanish Civil War, on one of those nights when you had good straw to sleep on'. On the night of 11 July 1941 London was bombed heavily and a garage close to Langford Court set on fire. Smoke filled the building, and they were evacuated after a warden observed: 'There's still someone in number 111!'

In terms of the effects of the war generally, Orwell recorded a crisis in London on a scale that is hard to comprehend today. He observed how all over south London there were destitute people 'wandering about with suitcases and bundles'. On one occasion while walking along Oxford Street, which was unusually quiet, he saw pedestrians walking over shattered glass and 'Outside John Lewis, a pile of plaster dress models, very pink and realistic, looking ... like a pile of fresh corpses.'

Orwell resented that he was not immediately offered any formal role in the war effort, suspecting his political activities in Spain had put paid to that. He applied for war service, but at 36 was too old for active duties and in any case was ruled unfit as a result of his weak lungs. By the outbreak of war Orwell had, it should be recalled, already spent long periods in sanatoria and also a six-month break for his health in Morocco. He did, however, join the Home Guard, the St John's Wood Company, being appointed Sergeant, and took his responsibilities seriously. In his diary for 16 June 1940 he noted: 'there is nothing for it but to die fighting, but one must above all die fighting and have the satisfaction of killing somebody else first'.

Shortly after he and Eileen moved to Langford Court in April 1941, Orwell was recommended for employment at the BBC, in the Indian Department of the Empire Service (today's BBC World Service). Despite having been opposed to war, Orwell had committed himself to the war effort as soon as it began. He explained his commitment in the essay 'My Country, Right or Left', which sought to persuade Britons that, regardless of their politics, now was the time to put aside differences and work together for the common goal of victory over Germany.

I think that, as in so many other ways, the world was worse off for Orwell having been taken from the 20th century aged only 46. He would never live to see the BBC comedy series *Dad's Army*, where he could I am certain self-identify with aspects of its various characters. I can imagine he would have analysed the series for an essay, comparing his real memories of the Home Guard with how they were portrayed in it. He would have enjoyed the English love for mocking one's own, a sort of self-deprecating modesty.

And what would Orwell have made of Margaret Thatcher; of Ronald Reagan and Mikhail Gorbachev? Or Nelson Mandela, or Robert Mugabe? For a man raised to be a great imperialist, serving one of its police forces for five years and wondering when the whole sham might end, he could have glanced back from the safety of 1980 to the past three decades of the dismantling of Greater Britain, and observed what a different world had been created over the course of his lifetime: from empire into a European community of nations.

~

Orwell was considered for employment at the BBC because of his writing ability and Indian experience, both in Burma and being from a long-established Anglo-Indian family. He was recommended by the Director of Empire Services, R.A. Rendall, with his reference provided by the reputable surgeon Arthur Keith stating: 'Mr E.A. Blair is one of the most vigorous thinkers and effective writers in the younger generation. He has a wide knowledge of countries, of peoples and of their ways of thinking ... he is loyal and very sincere in his thoughts, speech and acts.'

As with *Dad's Army*, Orwell would no doubt have a view on the contemporary BBC, which is different, and yet perhaps not so different, from the organisation he knew in the 1940s. It is apparent that he did not wholly enjoy his employment there, describing the BBC as 'something halfway between a girls' school and a lunatic asylum'. (More rudely, he also described it in a letter to Alex Comfort, author of *The Joy of Sex*, as 'a mixture of whoreshop and lunatic asylum'.)

Room 101 in *Nineteen Eighty-Four* was a place of torture, psychological and physical, for those the State in Orwell's dystopia considered to be worthy of re-indoctrination. The concept was inspired by his experience of the BBC – 'Room 101' being a room in a now-demolished part of the BBC's Broadcasting House that he regularly visited for meetings. In general, it seems he found the BBC's atmosphere stifling. I am not convinced that a large bureaucracy like a national broadcaster was the right environment to allow so liberal and original a thinker to flourish, as if Orwell's literary genius was being shoehorned into too-tight-fitting shoes. He was as insulated as he could be, tucked away in the Indian department of the World Service, and his contributions were, as might be expected, thoughtful and imaginative. It has been suggested that the rigour provided by daily broadcast improved his writing. He toiled for long hours, working harder than in any previous job.

Orwell resigned in September 1943, but not because he felt, as in Spain, a process of editing resulted in the filtering of information by the authorities. In his resignation letter he explained that: 'On no occasion have I been compelled to say on the air anything that I would not have said as a private individual.' Though, in the next paragraph, he complains that the promotion of 'British propaganda' to India was not having any effect. Orwell's description of his broadcasting as 'propaganda' goes some way to suggesting that he thought the BBC's efforts were not entirely directed at 'truth'. But in short, he seems to have realised their efforts were wasted, little-listened to. India had its own successful broadcaster in All India Radio, and he decided that his energies could be better invested elsewhere. He joined the magazine *Tribune* as its Literary Editor, based at their offices on the Strand, in November 1943. There, he began his famous 'As I please' column. *Tribune* remains in print today, although seems to have had a chequered history of dancing between the 'soft' and 'hard' left of British politics.

It was typical false modesty on Orwell's part to claim that his time at the BBC was wasted. His output was the greatest it ever reached, with the production of over 200 newsletters for broadcast either in English or the Indian languages, in something like 24 months. The diversity was impressively Orwellian too – he deliberately slanted the output of the department towards literature and culture. A collection of essays he edited for broadcast was published as *Talking to India: A Selection of English Language Broadcasts to India edited with an introduction by George Orwell* in 1943.

Impossible to find and with no copies for sale in the world so far as I could tell, I chanced – on the bookshelves of the London Library – to discover a well-worn copy tucked away in a seldom-visited corner described as 'Literary Anthology'. It is a very interesting little book, filled with broadcasts on eclectic topics. In its introduction, Orwell described the talks as 'predominantly cultural ... with a literary bias', and the titles range from 'Edward Gibbon' by E.M. Forster, to 'Prison Literature' by Reginald Reynolds. Included in the volume are speeches given by Indian nationalists allied to Hitler, such as Chandra Bose. He ended the book's introduction in his characteristically clear prose with a warning: 'There is a difference between honest and dishonest propaganda, and Bose's speech, with its enormous suppressions, obviously comes under the latter heading. We are not afraid to let these samples of our own and Axis broadcasts stand side by side.'

In the period since Orwell left its employment the BBC has found it difficult to acknowledge its relationship with him. The absence of any statue of Orwell was a seven decades-long national disgrace, only rectified by the BBC in November 2017. What is even more discomfiting is that the BBC rejected the suggestion that a statue of him be erected for years because it might compromise the perception that the BBC is politically neutral. Such an odd justification, given Orwell is admired by both left and right. A confidential personnel report on Orwell found in the BBC Archive and written by the Director of Indian Services, L.F. Rushbrook Williams, concluded: 'I have the highest opinion of his moral, as well as intellectual capacity. He is transparently honest, incapable of subterfuge, and, in early days, would have either been canonised – or burnt at the stake! An unusual colleague – but a mind, and a spirit, of real and distinguished worth.'

Not everyone was pleased with his contributions, however, with one BBC executive having questioned whether he should remain on air owing to the quality of his voice. It is strange to think that for a writer who worked for a radio station for two years, there is no known recording of his voice. A memo sent by J.B. Clark, controller of Overseas Services, in January 1943 queried 'the basic unsuitability of Orwell's voice', which he described as 'unattractive and unsuitable for the microphone'. We may never be able to assess its suitability for ourselves, sadly.

Room 101 was not the only aspect of *Nineteen Eighty-Four* inspired by Orwell's experience of the BBC. He worked long hours to achieve the output he did at the Corporation, often starting early or working late into the night. As always intrigued by the working classes, he observed how at 6am 'a huge army [of charwomen] arrives ... they have wonderful choruses, all singing together as they sweep the passages'. Throughout *Nineteen Eighty-Four* the nursery rhyme 'Oranges and Lemons' is used as a means of remembering pre-totalitarian London, more often than not sung by a washerwoman.

The Orwell statue was a long time in planning. It is the result of a noble and lengthy campaign by a man who did not live to see his vision come to fruition, the one-time Labour MP and then peer, Ben Whitaker. His widow, Baroness Whitaker of Beeston, also a member of the House of Lords, took on the campaign and can rightfully be proud to have seen it erected finally. It is said that, when her late husband asked the author John le Carré for his opinion on an Orwell statue, he answered: 'All the statues of generals in London should be melted down for it!'

One early proposal was that the statue should be placed on Jura – where no one bar the Scottish island's inhabitants and the small number of tourists who visit would see it – but eventually, it was agreed that the most appropriate location would be within the confines of the recently extended BBC at Portland Place. Martin Jennings, who also made the statue of John Betjeman at the St Pancras Eurostar terminal, was commissioned to create it: life-size, bearing forward with a cigarette in hand, and erected on a plinth to make it loom over any passer-by. The following is inscribed on the wall to the left of the statue:

> *If liberty means anything at all, it means the right*
> *to tell people what they do not want to hear.*

Orwell would possibly have raised an eyebrow to think of statues being put up of him, let alone on the doorstep of his old employer the BBC. There can be no better place for it; erected at a well-known smoking spot for stressed BBC employees.

⌒

Eileen went into the war effort more successfully than her husband, joining the Censorship Department of the Ministry of Information shortly after its outbreak. For Eileen the cost of the war would soon be devastating. Her brother Laurence, working as a surgeon in the British Expeditionary Force, was killed by a bomb during the evacuation of Dunkirk. She was very close to him, maintaining a regular exchange of letters, and it is said she never recovered from the loss.

In between the return of Eileen and Orwell from Morocco and the outbreak of the war, Richard Blair died at the age of 82. Southwold had remained his home until the last weeks of his life. Orwell wrote to Leonard Moore, his literary agent: 'I was with the poor old man for the last week ... he had a good life and I am very glad that latterly he had not been so disappointed in me as before.' His relationship with his father was never easy, 'The English Rebel' versus the retired Anglo-Indian. But there was reconciliation in the end. Orwell's mother, Ida, died from a heart attack in London in March 1943.

In 1942 Eileen moved to the Ministry of Food, working with the novelist Lettice Cooper to produce economical recipes for the nation's housewives. The Home Service, today's BBC Radio Four, broadcast a programme called 'The Kitchen Front', and part of her work involved guiding its producers. After her and Orwell's efforts to become self-sufficient at Wallington – they kept the lease on the Stores throughout the war, it being a welcome refuge from Blitz-affected London – she must have been well-positioned to advise on how to utilise spare egg whites or day-old potato peelings.

From Langford Court Orwell and Eileen moved slightly further north, although still within walking distance of Abbey Road. I had a clear idea of what 10a Mortimer Crescent, Maida Vale should look like, my mind poisoned by the idea that any flat in Maida Vale is generally to be found in those vast red-brick apartment blocks built in the late Victorian and Edwardian eras. They line most roads in Maida Vale, as if Mount Etna had erupted and showered every building in sight with red-glowing volcanic ash. I respect the architectural uniformity and the aspiration to combine function with beauty.

Imagine, then, my disappointment to arrive at Mortimer Crescent not only to find that the original street plan was a series of largish Victorian semi-detached villas, of the usual north-London type, but that the 'revised' design was a 1950s housing estate built on the embers of a street which had been almost entirely destroyed by war-time bombing. I had known Orwell and Eileen's flat here was bombed, they having moved into temporary accommodation in 1944, but for some reason allowed my prejudices of 'what architecture in each London village looks like' to cloud my imagination.

The most tragic aspect of the bombing of Mortimer Crescent is not so much the multiple-storey council estate that supplanted the Victorian crescent, which is decent enough, but the fact that half of one of the old semi-detached villas escaped the bombing. Together with a cobbled-together extension replacing the destroyed other half, which detracts even further from the building's former grace, it looks like a sad warrior of yesteryear: engulfed by change, like a dog caught in a strong wave. As with so many parts of London left pockmarked by the Luftwaffe, the crescent is a sorry spectacle.

A bright-red Royal Mail postbox stands just outside the 'survivor'. I thought of Orwell, the prolific man of letters, dashing for the last collection and posting, stamp encrusted and all, the envelopes containing what anyone can now read among the pages of the published collections of his letters. It is curious to think of him writing letters and his diaries, noting down the number of eggs his hens hatched or how many potatoes he had planted that morning, not knowing that generations hence would be poring over their contents.

A block of flats surrounded by smart lawns now stands on the site of the house containing their flat, replacing all that was destroyed by a flying V1 bomb in June 1944. Neither Orwell nor Eileen was home at the time, but his beloved library was – and the manuscript for *Animal Farm*. He spent several days trying to find it, clambering over the remains of his flat and possessions as a gangly lobster might potter on the seabed. He recovered most of his books and transported them daily to his office at *Tribune*.

Orwell told T.S. Eliot, the poet who rejected *Animal Farm* on behalf of Faber and Faber: '[The] manuscript has been blitzed which accounts for my delay in delivering it and its slightly crumpled condition, but it is not damaged in any way.' To think that this slim novella, one of the bestselling novels of all time and among the best novels of all time, should so nearly have been obliterated.

As a result of their desire to start a family, Orwell and Eileen had decided to adopt, and in 1944 took care of Richard (Horatio Blair), who was born in the Newcastle Area in May 1944. They both seem to have been ecstatic about having a baby, although after Eileen's abrupt death in 1945 Orwell was forced largely to outsource care for him, primarily on the basis of his own progressively failing health. In one letter Eileen referred to baby Richard as 'a very thoughtful little boy as well as very beautiful'.

In early March 1945, Orwell travelled to the recently liberated territories of Western Europe, with the intention of reporting on conditions. Basing himself in Paris, he wrote for the *Observer*, for which he had been writing since 1942. Along with many other reporters, he stayed at the Hotel Scribe, on Rue Scribe close to the *Galeries Lafayette* department store, and told friends how he had taken to wearing a beret.

In the long term, it is clear Eileen was intent on escaping London too and was as excited about a Hebridean project as was Orwell. 'From my point of view I would infinitely rather live in the country on £200 than in London on any money at all. I don't think you understand what a nightmare the London life is to me,' she wrote to him shortly before her death. She handled much of the negotiations for securing the lease on their home, Barnhill, at the northern end of the Isle of Jura, and developed a good relationship with its owners, the Fletchers.

The letters Eileen sent her husband in the run-up to her unexpected death seem to become increasingly searching, as if somewhere deep in the subconscious she was uncertain as to whether she had much time left. The loss of her brother still affected her profoundly, but she also had concerns about money. She needed to have an operation to remove a growth on her ovaries, and was ineligible for the cheaper surgical rate, so opted for less expensive treatment. 'I really don't think I'm worth the money', she wrote to Orwell from Greystone, her family house in Carlton, County Durham in mid-March.

Eileen took the possibility of her death seriously. In the approach to the operation, she wrote 'should I die on the table on Thursday...', in reference to her preparation of a will, and feared for the financial arrangements she could make to secure Richard's future and of who might care for him. She examined the options, rejecting the idea that Orwell's sister Avril might take him (it was actually she who would raise Richard after Orwell's death) and instead suggested her sister-in-law Gwen, who would have 'a proper house in the country' for her children and Richard, who she 'adores'.

The last letter she drafted to Orwell, but which she did not send, was written as she lay in bed as her anaesthetic was provided. Even as she lay there, she did not know the details of the operation she was going to have, content to leave her fate in the hands of her surgeon. Her letter ended: 'This is a nice room – ground floor so one can see the garden. Not much in it except daffodils and I think *Arabis* but a nice little lawn. My bed isn't next [to] the window but it faces the right way. I also see the fire and the clock.'

The cause of death on 29 March 1945 was a heart attack, apparently as a result of the anaesthetic. She was 39. Orwell returned directly from Paris to stay at Greystone and soon after she was buried in Jesmond cemetery in Newcastle. Orwell took Richard down to the flat in Islington, where he was looked after by his close friend and former Russo-Belgian commander Georges Kopp and his wife, and then returned to Paris alone.

⌐⌐

From Maida Vale I travelled back into central London, with the aim of having supper at the Wheatsheaf, one of Orwell's favourite pubs, a short walk from the Tottenham Court Road end of Oxford Street. I was reminded of his guidance on what makes a fine pub and looked forward to an authentically British fish and chips supper and some real ale.

Fitzrovia and its drinking holes have always had a reputation for attracting creative types. Today, tech start-ups and architectural practices abound. In the 1940s the literary set mixed and mingled in the Wheatsheaf, among others. Orwell was attracted by its Victoriana: mock Tudor in appearance, with lots of dark wood and stained glass inside. Today its offerings seem reasonably unpretentious. I ordered my fish and chips, re-read Orwell's essay on the perfect pub – The Moon Under Water – and settled into some people-watching.

Eileen and Orwell had mixed happily in literary circles throughout the war. While they still made frequent weekend visits to Wallington, Orwell had also befriended T.R. Fyvel, the writer and Orwell's successor as literary editor of *Tribune*, via an introduction made by their joint publisher, Fredric Warburg. Warburg and his wife, and Fyvel and his wife decided to set up a joint home on a farmstead near Twyford in Berkshire, 'Scarlett's Farm', to which Eileen and Orwell became frequent visitors. Fyvel later recalled endless days of walking through Berkshire downland with Orwell, immersed in sophisticated conversation.

Orwell also met his literary hero from childhood, H.G. Wells, by then elderly, and Graham Greene. On one occasion, in 1941, Wells was invited to Langford Court for supper with a mutual acquaintance, Inez Holden. The meal was followed by an almighty row between the two writers. Holden recalled Orwell looking like an 'embarrassed prefect' in the company of Wells, to whom he remained deferential. He met Greene through another mutual friend in June 1944, when they met for lunch at a restaurant on Dean Street. It is said their literary interests had much in common and Orwell agreed to write a preface to a book that Greene was assisting through to publication.

After leaving the Wheatsheaf, I decided to walk all the way to the old offices of *Tribune* on the Strand. I walked through Soho Square with its acid-rain damaged statue of Charles II, and the strange half-timbered hut at its centre. Along Charing Cross Road, once lined with book-shops but now home to only a handful, I glanced through the windows to see what was on display. As usual, the same threads of Orwell's life appeared as if by magic. In the same way *Agapanthus Africanus* seems to pop up everywhere along the Orwell trail in England, in the window lay *Picturesque Nepal* by Percy Brown, and *The Ghost Stories of M.R. James.* Then I spotted a beautiful leather-bound antiquar-ian copy of Johnson's *A Journey to the Western Islands of Scotland* and recalled a note Orwell left in his diary as early as August 1941: 'Thinking always of my island in the Hebrides, which I suppose I shall never possess or even see.'

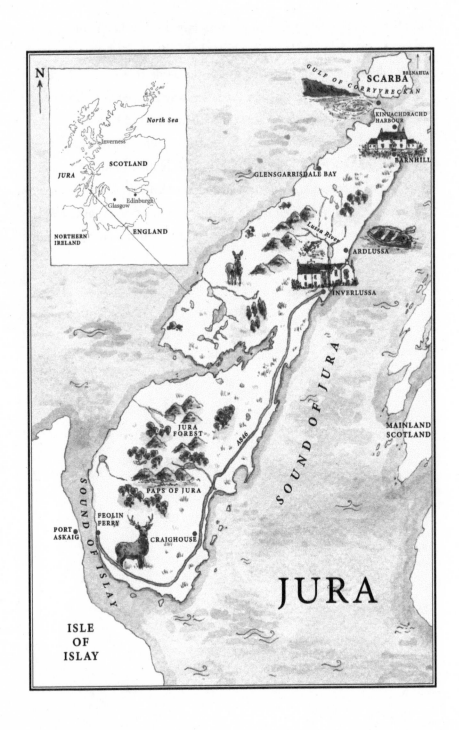

Jura, Argyllshire, Scotland

An extremely un-getatable place (1945–9)

E ven by the standards of the highlands and islands of Scotland, Jura remains, as described by Orwell, an 'extremely un-getatable place'. He had first heard of Jura – as the crow flies, 65 miles west of Glasgow – from David Astor, editor of the *Observer* between 1948 and 1975, whose family owned an estate there. Orwell had been writing for the paper and became acquainted with Astor in 1942, although they had common ties to Eton, and many mutual friends.

The island's association with Orwell emerged by chance rather than anything else. Astor and Orwell became great friends, and his editor suggested he use Jura as a base for recuperation. But the significance of this 'un-getatable' place looms larger than perhaps anywhere else in the writer's legacy. It was here, between 1946 and 1948, that Orwell developed and wrote the concept for *Nineteen Eighty-Four*, a dystopia of a form he had, since his earliest years, been set on writing.

〜

The first perspective one sees of Jura is its lengthy eastern coastline, along which most of its population lives. The island's only road, officially the A846, stretches along this coast. Along it, largely, live the island's 200-or-so inhabitants. This number is significant since, by means of comparison, the Isle of Wight is of approximately similar size but with 700 times the population; 144,000 versus 200. And the Isle of Wight is by no means an endless sprawl of settlements – for many, it represents an idyll of country lanes and listless English rurality.

Jura is a desolate place with an interior seldom visited and even more rarely explored. The entire west coast is entirely uninhabited with no roads at all, not even footpaths. In fact, like the Vikings that controlled this part of Scotland until 1266, the last inhabitants of one of the small crofting communities on the west coast made water their primary means of transport, and survived using their own boats, dependent on the tides and currents that enclose Jura on all fronts. The last of these communities, mostly single-family crofting units, moved away in the 1940s.

It is no exaggeration to say that the west coast of Jura is one of the loneliest places in Britain. It certainly felt like that exploring its northern extremities where, in every direction, there is scant evidence for human habitation of the world at all. As a consequence, people are in short supply on the island, outnumbered twenty-to-one by the island's 4,000 deer, perhaps serving as the origins of its name in Norse, *Dy Oer*, pronounced 'Joora' and translated as Deer Island.

There is no direct permanent ferry link to the mainland from Jura, but in the summer a passenger ferry operates from the small village of Tayvallich, a remote port whose approach through fine, ancient woodland virtually obscures the quaint jetty that comes into sight as the end of the single-track road approaches. As in most of the region, the legacy of the last ice age is apparent in the remnants of a dried sea loch that can be seen as cars meander in and out of passing places for oncoming traffic.

Now meadow, the beds of these lochs became raised as the immense pressure on the bedrock exerted by glaciers was lifted. Jura's coast is lined with raised beaches, cliffs and caves, which were of curiosity to Orwell. (With the right imagination, former islands, now part of dry land, can be worked out by the eye too.) They remain a source of intrigue for residents on the island; they add to the sense of mystery that surrounds its landscape and the people who live there.

The ferry runs to a timetable of sorts, but is really an informal service provided for the benefit of the broader community, one in which isolated settlements are united in a camaraderie that is by nature distrusting of outsiders. In the case of my journey across the Sound of Jura, the stretch of deep water separating Jura from the mainland, I was the sole passenger. It was more convenient to deposit me closer to where I was staying, at Ardlussa, to the far north of the main settlement at Craighouse, which shaved half an hour off my passage.

The word Jurassic came to mind as I walked for the first time through an ancient oak woodland that skirts the eastern coastline, forming part of the Ardlussa Estate. The woodland is drenched in a permanent mist that penetrates the lung like no other (one islander I mentioned this to agreed, replying: 'There's an industry there if we bottled it'), and being on a steep aspect, the woodland climbs quickly up what are the sides of a mountain poking through from the Atlantic below.

Vegetation overhangs everywhere, a mix of native species and the curious presence of the non-native *Rhododendron Ponticum*, whose garishly pink flowers provide a taste of the exotic on an otherwise bleak Hebridean island. To add to the prehistoric theme, the jetty at which the passenger ferry arrived was evidently one that is used sparingly, with large clumps of long grass growing through blocks of smooth, rounded granite, like something found at Stonehenge.

The waiting car, arranged by the ferry since my journey was cut short by docking further north than usual, belonged to a villager who had been delivering supplies to the settlements that dot the single-track road. Orwell's diaries for 1946–9, written in the isolation of one of the

most remote houses on the north-east coast of the island, refer often to
the implicit framework of neighbourly support required in a community
spread so thinly: exchanging fruit and vegetables with each other, lending scarce technical equipment or anything else in short supply. In this
respect life on the island has changed little. Without it, it would not be
able to continue.

From there a short journey followed along the A846. This 'road'
is barely worthy of the name. In England, it would be described as a
bridleway for the most part. It is 30 miles or so in length, allocated
just one day of maintenance a year by Argyll and Bute Council, the
local authority of which Jura and the other surrounding islands form
a part. But it is a lifeline – today, as in Orwell's time – for most of
the inhabitants of the island. Rivers flow under the road at numerous
points, meandering quietly out to sea or gushing in the way only a lively
Scottish river seems to.

Four of Jura's rivers bear wild salmon, the Lussa being closest to
Orwell's house at Barnhill and on which he would occasionally fish. It
was so enjoyable an activity for the author that, as he lay dying in 1950,
his fishing rods stood in the corner of his hospital room, in anticipation
of their use during his hoped-for recovery in Switzerland. The Lussa
is a peaty river, flowing rapidly where the road dips down before its
arrival at the Ardlussa Estate, the centre of one of the seven estates the
island is divided into. Orwell's own home at Barnhill further north is
one of the seven, containing hill lochs in which he would also fish, this
time for trout.

Ardlussa is a hamlet composed of a scattering of houses all owned
by the big house. Beyond the turn-off to the estate marked by a cattle grid, the road remains public for another five miles, after which it
becomes private – this forming most of the remaining way to Barnhill.
The big house's entrance on the road, capped with the head of a stag
as an ode to the stalking industry that generates much of the estate's

income, is the lesser of its aspects. On a walk back from the north of the island this majestic building can be appreciated fully: a fine lodge standing some distance back from the sea, on a gentle incline that reaches towards a shallow bay.

Subject to the clashing of clans for most of the modern period, until relatively recently the whole of Jura was owned entirely by one family. This family, Clan Campbell, was eventually triumphant in a succession of spats between warring tribes. They consolidated their control over the island between the 16th and 18th centuries but progressively sold it off piecemeal over the first half of the 20th century. The number of estates has gradually risen to seven in the time since, but only one of them is permanently inhabited by its owners: the 18,000-acre Ardlussa Estate.

Thus descendants of the same Fletchers that leased Orwell his home in the 1940s, becoming close friends and confidantes of the author, greet visitors. Claire and Andrew Fletcher stand outside their house, their company a mayhem of free-range dogs and children in much the same way their forebears must have greeted Orwell on his first visit. His arrival in May 1946 followed correspondence between him and the present Laird's late grandmother, Margaret. Her brother had been introduced to Orwell by the Astors, but following his death during the war, the burden fell to Margaret and her husband Robin (at that time isolated as a translator in a Japanese Prisoner of War camp in Burma).

Orwell's description of the island as an 'extremely un-getatable place' suggests he was intent on finding somewhere without the bother of others. All the evidence indicates however that his nearest neighbours – the Fletchers at Ardlussa, and beyond Barnhill, the Darrouchs at Kinuachdrachd – became good friends and exchanged far more than polite greetings. Friendship speedily developed into affection and, as Orwell's son, his nanny and his sister moved to Barnhill, these were relationships that only grew. Orwell's entry in the Fletchers' visitor book is marked simply on 22 May 1946, as 'Eric Blair, Barnhill' and later, when he stayed en-route to hospital for treatment on his lungs, as 'Eric'.

My first glance at Orwell's entry in the Ardlussa Estate visitors' book, only recently entering its second volume, demonstrated to me how little-followed this mysterious man is. Dickens, Hardy, du Maurier; the places they lived are monuments to the myths that have been constructed around them. Orwell is one of the world's bestselling authors; his books are still at the centre of the British school curriculum. His writing even created its own adjective, a place in the English Language alongside Dickensian or Hardyesque. But his entry in the visitors' book is not behind glass. I'm holding it. And as I would later find there was certainly no wooden National Trust oak leaf, or cream tea, to greet me at Barnhill; only wind and a silence broken by the sound of the tide and my own authoritarian demands in search of George, the dog, as he chased a seagull or two across some rocks.

The big house at Ardlussa is vast and divided between smaller private accommodation for the Fletchers, and a much larger public area reserved for bed and breakfast. Along with the few following in Orwell's footsteps, the main audience for the stags' heads that line the wall takes the form of those who arrive on Jura to create more of them, the deer stalkers. Large parties arrive and are catered for before a long day of stalking to manage the deer population on the estate. I've never tasted better venison.

Couples in pursuit of romantic weekends away and those seeking solitude are others who visit. But on a weekend at the end of June, I was the sole visitor, occupying a room with a sun-filled, east-facing window on the corner of the house, favoured with the same view looking towards the sea as the bay enjoys back to the house. The bay window in this bedroom became my favoured corner of the house, it being so light at the height of midsummer that I was able to read late into the evening one of the many Orwell-related books to be found scattered around.

Walking to and fro along the corridors, it was easy to imagine Orwell's lanky, awkward frame retiring upstairs to bed, following one of the many long evenings he would spend talking with the then laird, recently returned from the Far East. Margaret Fletcher, reflecting later, had little to say about the conversations she'd heard between her husband and Orwell, only that it was 'Man's chat', in which she had little interest.

The atmosphere of the drawing room, home to these discussions, can have changed little in the intervening 70 years. Surely, over their whisky, they would reminisce about their days at Eton and of the Far East. Contemporary politics too must have featured, with independence soon to be granted to India. Musing over the planning for the long walks to come I enjoyed reimagining these scenes by the warmth of an unseasonal open fire, pondering whether they ever conversed in the Burmese language familiar to both.

Several references in Orwell's diaries and letters underplay the effort of the walk to Barnhill, such as this, from a letter to Richard Rees dated 5 July 1946: 'It really isn't very formidable, except that you have to walk the last eight miles.' The round trip can be done in a morning, but the journey is not complete without the onward walk to the Gulf of Corryvreckan, home to the famous whirlpool which almost resulted in Orwell's death in a boating accident in August 1947. Orwell misread the tides, having intended, for some bizarre reason, to attempt anchoring in the whirlpool, resulting in the boat overturning and the small party managing to swim to a nearby islet. They were rescued by a passing lobster-catching vessel. The Gulf of Corryvreckan, lying between Jura and the vast lump of rock that is Scarba (an uninhabited island to the north, possessing on most days its own hat of cloud) is so treacherous that it was considered unnavigable by the Royal Navy until the 19th century.

Even for a twenty-something, the walk is an arduous one. The first section within woodland and mainly 'worked' land can be driven through. The final four miles, past the end of the 'public road', must be walked, unless consent has been provided by the landowner. I'm not entirely sure why anyone would want to take a shortcut and drive, however, since the first glimpse of Barnhill far down below the road – sheltered by its inlet rather than commanding it – and framed by the Atlantic and Knapdale coast, is undoubtedly improved by the suspense of the walk that precedes it.

Rarely have the views provided by a country walk been so incredibly beautiful that I've scarcely been able to believe my eyes. Being in the company of herds of deer and birds of prey every step of the walk to Barnhill (and back again) is memorable to the point that, once it is over, walkers only ever want to put their boots on and repeat it all over again. That Orwell enjoyed this walk, or ride (since he was apparently notoriously dangerous driving his motorbike along the single-track road), is unsurprising.

~

The contrast between the house at Barnhill and the famous novel written there could not be greater. A substantial, imperfectly whitewashed homestead with two large barns attached to its rear looks down over a wild garden and, below that, an even wilder meadow. Presumably, it is another raised former beach, home to a sea of wildflowers, including orchids so prevalent they might almost be considered a weed. The house is approached gable-end through an old and battered steel holding fence. Although it can be leased, Barnhill goes for weeks without residents. Being off-grid and only a little less primitive than it was when the Blairs lived there, the queue is not as large as one might imagine – but then, this is the 'un-followed' Orwell.

During interviews later in life, Margaret Fletcher would comment on the spartan existence the Blairs experienced at Barnhill. Orwell pursued complete self-sufficiency, and the furniture and interiors were basic. Recalling the first time she met him, at the roadside entrance to the big house at Ardlussa, she remembered 'the impression he was content as long as he had a roof over his head, and a loaf of bread to eat'. Eggs, butter and milk could be bought from a house further north at Kinuachdrachd, but other than this – then, as today – it would be every man for himself. Significant amounts of his time were devoted to keeping Barnhill functioning, from the boat's engine to the orchard he was trying to establish. The orchard (and his allotments) did not survive his first winter away from Jura over 1946–7. I longed to find some surviving fruit tree, clinging on after all these decades, but there was none.

The small bay below the house has no beach per se, and it is hard to see where a boat could be moored safely. Seaweed abounds, however, which Orwell began to cook selectively. It was from this small bay that much of their food – especially lobsters from their traps, and small crabs – would be caught. Intriguing commentary in his diaries ranges from instructions for skinning a rabbit to the importance of treating lobsters with care: 'When putting a lobster in the box after it has been in the water for some time, one should be careful not to drown it. The way to avoid this is to dip it in water a number of times before finally dropping it in. A lobster needs a cubic foot of fresh sea water every 24 hours, so that the box must be well aerated.'

Another entry reflecting his admiration for obscure details and powers of observation noted: 'the lobster's claw is not always on the same side: is as though some lobsters were right-handed and some are left-handed'. His recording of goings-on also seems to have inspired episodes in *Nineteen Eighty-Four*, with several attacks by rats on children being reported on the island. He noted in his diary for 13 June 1947: 'Two children at Ardlussa were bitten by rats (in the face, as usual).'

Many people, I am sure, imagine Orwell to have been bookish, deeply philosophical; political in a defiant sense. I think this obscures a much more practical mind, evidently one that sought activities that could only be completed with hands to exercise the body, while the brain could (for one or two hours a day) apply its magic.

This is demonstrated by his genuine appreciation of the natural world. His diary records in meticulous detail the flowering of plants; even in *Nineteen Eighty-Four*, the emergence of a crocus from the ground was undeniable evidence that even totalitarianism couldn't stop spring. A typical entry, from May 1946, describes: 'Bluebells in profusion everywhere. Primroses still full out, also thrift (on rocks almost in the sea.) Wild iris just coming into flower. These grow within a few yards of the high tide mark. In spite of the drought, grass very green where it is not overwhelmed by rushes, which are the worst weed here, worse even than bracken.' This could have been written the day of my visit. Yellow-headed wild iris was profuse and the bluebells were still out, despite my visit being timed for the very end of June; the delayed days of spring.

Although his study was downstairs, most of *Nineteen Eighty-Four* was written in the room above the kitchen, a room with a view directly out over the bay and to the east coastline of Jura beyond. He preferred to write in absolute isolation, to ensure his illness could not spread – to his young son above all – and was so ill for much of his time there that even completion and the typing of the manuscript, which he did himself, would have proved challenging.

Margaret Fletcher observed that she believed he thought that he had little time left to live, noting he often repeated that he was determined to finish a book that 'contained an important message'. I couldn't look up to the window of the room where he wrote *Nineteen Eighty-Four* without imagining the shattering of its glass and a herd of Thought Police abseiling through the ensuing chaos. Enjoying their brief times together in an equally unloved room above the junk shop that would end their time, both as lovers and individuals with the capacity to think above the terror that surrounded them, Winston and Julia saw their peace invaded with something quite the reverse of what one would expect in a farmhouse on a distant part of a remote Scottish island.

The interior of the house has changed hardly at all since the 1940s, containing much of the flotsam a home so near a beach is likely to accumulate over decades of casual habitation: driftwood, crab shells, colourful stones collected by children; Thermos flasks; old tablecloths. An old-fashioned cast-iron typewriter sits on the windowsill in the hall. In the sitting room, a small 8×6 framed photograph of 'Eric' nestles on a mantelpiece.

The stove and a 1940s-style kitchen remain, quite possibly the same that the Blairs would have used. The community consisted of (at various times) Orwell himself; his sister Avril; Richard and nanny Susan Watson; Bill Dunn (an injured serviceman, who would later marry Avril); and Richard Rees (Orwell's former editor on the *Adelphi*, one of the papers for which he had written). Damaris and Jamie Fletcher, present owners of Barnhill and a branch of the Fletcher family that owns Ardlussa, are dedicated to preserving the property in the spirit in which Orwell and his coterie lived: 'We have worked hard over more than twenty years to keep not only a roof over it but the interior as close to what it would have been like in Orwell's day.' They share the anecdote of enjoying Sunday lunch in the kitchen one afternoon. Two uninvited visitors to the house walked in and began wandering from room to room before being confronted with something along the lines of 'And what on earth do you think you are doing?' Their response: 'But this is George Orwell's house', was met with: 'It isn't George Orwell's house, it's actually mine!' They then proceeded happily to give them a tour of the house.

The only life in the house on my visit was a trapped bird, fighting to escape through a window in the kitchen, which startled me as I crept around Barnhill's exterior. Momentarily thinking of my own George,

I occasionally had to remind myself to call him loudly to heel, as Avril or Susan would have to the real George, with lunch on the table or a visitor to greet.

⤸

Orwell mused long and hard over the title for what eventually became *Nineteen Eighty-Four*, which was chosen as an inversion of the last two digits of the year in which he completed the novel. '*The Last Man in Europe*' was given serious consideration as a working title, something one imagines he may have felt, undertaking so many barren walks in search of sustenance. The wilds of Jura extend beyond Landseer-quality, oil-canvas landscapes; it is an island of pests which are not easy to avoid.

Much like the rat from Winston Smith's nightmares in Room 101, the snake is one of those creatures for which many human beings harbour an innate fear. Orwell was no exception. Reading page after page of Orwell's diaries on Jura, the repeated references to snakes he had seen or killed fuelled my imagination with visions of my spaniel emerging from an adder pit, tail between legs and ears drooping, with venom from a bite which could see him off to an early grave. (I was cautious at first but reasoned the chance of his being bitten was still low.) The walk to Barnhill itself was reptile-free, but strangely, beyond it, up to the Corryvreckan viewpoint, they appeared with virtually every other step, lying, curled-up, in the short grasses either side of the road. I immediately hauled George onto his lead and wrapped it tightly around my wrist. None of the adders I saw, warming up under the sun, moved at all as we thudded through. Neither George nor I were inclined to disturb them.

The track to the viewpoint bends down towards a bay, the closest functioning jetty to Barnhill, which by the end of Orwell's time would provide a home for a boat he could use to sail to Ardlussa or Craighouse, before rising again to the harbour at Kinuachdrachd and onwards to views down over the Gulf of Corryvreckan. A serviceable track turns into a path, and the way eventually peters out into deer trails that pass through moorland, heather and bog. This part of the island is least travelled: if the track is followed around this peninsula, walkers will arrive on the desolate west coast. Even Andrew Fletcher, the owner of vast tracts of it, chooses not to visit for long.

Various legends surround these parts of the island. The gulf is named after a Norse king, Breacan, who was guaranteed to marry the beautiful bride of his choosing if he was able to prove his worth by surviving passage across the whirlpool. Drowning, his dog retrieved the body to one of the near-by skerries (a 'small sea isle', in Scots), maybe the one which also saved Orwell during his rendezvous with death. Another strange tale I wasn't able to verify fully involves a human skull: the famed 'Skull of Maclean'. Victim of the Campbells who came to dominate Jura, Maclean's clan deposited his body in the open air at a cave in Glengarrisdale Bay. It lay there intact for more than 300 years and may well have been the same skull that Orwell came across during one of his walks to the west coast and which was noted in his diary for 7 June 1946: 'Fine (weather) all day. Walked to Glengarrisdale & back ... Old human skull, with some other bones, lying on the beach. Two teeth (black) still in it. Quite un-decayed.'

The skull and bones have long since disappeared, and accounts vary between those I tried to clarify the story with. One claim goes the skull was stolen in the 1970s and never seen since; another that a man of questionable sanity borrowed the skull and was found talking to it one evening by the island's special constable, with the voyeur being sent away and the skull ending up in a glass case in a Glasgow museum. Whichever is true, the fact it was able to remain in situ for more than 300 years, barely disturbed, is a testimony to the infrequency of visitors

– man or animal. Staring down at the eddies that fill the stretch of water separating Scarba from Jura, it isn't hard to imagine Viking longboats appearing from east or west. From the place names to the ghosts that linger along the coast and in its caves, the waves of historical influence over the island are evocative.

⌁

Wearily beginning my walk back to Ardlussa, mostly under cloud but with the occasional flash of sunshine, crickets began to croak and the sea, now to my left, was silent and flat. Orwell would describe the sea as 'like glass' in these conditions; a simile I wasn't able to appreciate until gazing out across that stretch of open water, by then with these millpond-like qualities.

With my departure from Jura back on the passenger ferry (on this occasion I had the company of two other passengers, day trippers to the distillery at Craighouse), my thoughts went 2,000 years further back, to see the island in its geological context, it being easier to appreciate the full scale of the island and its smooth, rounded mountain tops from the water.

Buoys bobbing in the Sound, appearing like giant orange footballs, were especially distracting for George who, not much distance from his days as a puppy, still stares at curiosities with intensive awe. Mist enveloped the island's 'paps', the peaks of the mountains that dominate the interior of the island and rise sharply above its coastline. The sea was rougher, the boat producing a continuous spray.

Jura is composed mainly of Quartzite, a hard rock metamorphosed when a mountain range as high as the present-day Himalayas was created just over 400 million years ago. In the time since, this mountain range has been denuded almost to its base to reveal these rocks and, in the process, amid other tectonic shifts, placed them on their side. Jura is a very old man, eroded virtually to his ankles, and then turned on his side to bare the soles of his feet.

Containing some of the oldest geology to be found anywhere in the world, there is no better place for Orwell to have written the timeless novel that is *Nineteen Eighty-Four*, endowing humanity with the 'important message' he felt he had to leave behind. Returning to dry land, I could think only of Orwell spending the seasons there foraging for food and taking his humanity to the brink with the creation of Newspeak, Thoughtcrime and Room 101. 25 October 1947:

Beautiful, clear, windless day. Sea somewhat calmer. Pruned gooseberry bushes (old ones). Applied sulphate of potash to fruit bushes and strawberries, and the two espalier apple trees ... saw a piece of honeysuckle in bloom yesterday, in a bush that had ripe berries. One or two flowers on the thrift, must be second blooming. Forgot to mention, saw some starlings about a week ago.

Sutton Courtenay, Oxfordshire, England

Standing alone in every sense (1950)

I t was not yet fully light as I drove out of London in the direction of Oxfordshire. Of all the counties of England, Oxfordshire is perhaps one which people most associate with timeless Englishness, close to London but also a landscape of undulating hills and church towers. Oxford and its surrounding towns and villages produce, it has been suggested, the closest accent there is to 'received pronunciation', otherwise known as the Queen's English. It is affluent, strikingly so in parts, and a county associated with power.

It was this power which brought George Orwell to be buried in the county, at the church of All Saints in the village of Sutton Courtenay, close to the market town of Abingdon, just south of Oxford. Orwell had no personal association with this church – indeed, for long stretches of his life he seems to have rejected faith altogether – but he wished to be buried in the traditional rites of the Church of England and in a parish churchyard rather than a municipal cemetery. The English churchyard is, of course, one of those easy-to-come-by bastions of Englishness. It is the image that comes to mind for many when they are asked to define it.

Sutton Courtenay became Orwell's final resting place because his close friend David Astor had a house there and knew the rector of the church. Since Orwell was not a practising Anglican, at any rate not to the extent he was a member, a picturesque and quintessentially English churchyard needed to be found. All Saints fulfilled the bill, as enduring a representation of Orwell's conservatism as there could be. Astor's grave, the tombstone made of dark slate and his name engraved in a large, italic font, lies directly behind Orwell's, where he was buried in 2001.

Orwell's last home in London, or indeed anywhere, was 27b Canonbury Square in Islington, close to the busy junction adjacent to Highbury tube station. This was the flat he would reside in during his return visits to London from Jura, and which had been, for a very short time before her death, Eileen's home too. 'Home' for Orwell, and the base for his library, remained Barnhill. It seems he maintained the belief throughout 1949 – the penultimate year of his life and in which he was almost entirely hospitalised – that he would be returning to Jura, for the summers at least.

This, like other aspects of his last year alive, seems to have been fantastical thinking. His health during the months on Jura in 1948 had deteriorated so much that a lengthy bout of recuperation would be necessary. A series of hospitals and specialists were introduced to assess his condition, most of which seem to agree that his tuberculosis would kill him sooner rather than later. The recommendation from all quarters was that rest and recuperation would represent the best treatment, alongside (unsuccessful) attempts to treat him with some of the new antibiotics being trialled.

Orwell was never a 'well' man – something of an impending doom features throughout his fiction, if not so much in his non-fiction – and he can never have expected to live a long life. He had become used to coughing up blood regularly, a phenomenon which must not have been helped by his smoking, and the drug trials he pursued seem only to have made him worse. In one instance they turned his skin yellow. Astor, who would be best man for Orwell's second wedding, described him as 'looking like Gandhi, all skin and bone' when he saw him for the first time at University College Hospital (UCH).

Professor James Williamson treated Orwell's tuberculosis after his last departure from Jura, at Hairmyres Hospital in Glasgow. He later explained: 'His disease was of a very chronic nature. It was confined to the upper part of both lungs, mostly his left lung, and he had positive sputum ... his lungs would have been tough, like leather.' It is hard to imagine how debilitating this now-curable disease was for so many sufferers.

When TB was a major cause of death, sanatoria existed all over Britain, where patients would be able to recuperate away from the unhealthy urban centres. After his stay at Hairmyres, it was to one of these that he was moved, at Cranham in Gloucestershire. He was no stranger to sanatoria, having spent bouts of time in them previously, and seems to have believed that his visit there was another stay of respite before recovery. No such improvement was forthcoming; over 1949 his physical health drained away. Harold Nicolson, the writer, politician and diplomat who co-created the gardens at Sissinghurst in Kent, recalled: 'My memory of him is of rather a poor little man, sitting in a chair in the corner. He was shrunken and seemed miserable and obviously very ill.'

It was thought that TB was best treated with lots of clean, cold air. Cranham was a series of huts located on the top of a hill, near to Stroud in the Cotswolds. It was one of these huts that Orwell made his home from January to September 1949. He read avidly and still wrote, but also continued his interest in those pursuits of the English countryside he adored so much. He wrote for instance that he had found a stream with trout in close to Cranham, and suggested his sister Avril might send his fishing bits to him.

The abiding feature of Orwell's stay in Gloucestershire, he explained, was the birdsong, leaving one with the impression that this period of his life provided Orwell with one final prolonged exposure to the eternal qualities of rural England. His reading was widespread, and he took to regularly completing crosswords. He used to sit in a deck chair at the front of his hut, a tower of books resting next to him, with regular intervals to take tea. In spite of his treatment, he kept drinking. Orwell requested Richard Rees send him two bottles of rum.

Orwell re-read old favourites – Hardy's *Jude the Obscure* and *Tess of the d'Urbervilles*; Dickens' *Little Dorrit* (commenting that his favourite character, William Dorrit, is 'quite unlike most of Dickens' people') – and many writers' works which have since fallen into obscurity: Israel Zangwill's *Children of the Ghetto*; Marie Bashkirtseff's *Journal* and May Sinclair's *The Combined Maze*. As ever his reading interests remained varied and his letters invariably critiqued what he had been reading this week or that.

Likewise, he became concerned for his library back on Jura. The damp climate seems to have been as harmful to his books as it was to his health. He instructed Richard Rees to light fires at Barnhill to keep his books dry, later thanking him by letter for looking after his library in his absence. As an indicator of Orwell's long-term plans, he also commissioned new bookcases for Barnhill, as if he intended his home on Jura to be a bibliophilic haven for when he was recovered.

Visitors were frequent, with the usual roll call of illustrious friends making their way to Cranham's obscure corner of Gloucestershire. R.H. Tawney, the famous economic historian at the London School of Economics, had a weekend home nearby and he and his wife would visit from time to time. Paul Potts, the Canadian poet, and Margaret Adams, the wife of Britain's leading historian of the mid-20th century, A.J.P. Taylor, also came. Thus a steady stream of intellectually stimulating company was maintained.

In February he received a letter from Jacintha Buddicom, who had discovered from an aunt that the famous George Orwell was her lost childhood friend, Eric Blair. This reconciliation forms part of an unfortunate – and heartbreaking – tryst between Orwell and his child-hood sweetheart. After becoming estranged from Orwell, Jacintha began an affair which resulted in an illegitimate child, who was sent abroad for adoption to Canada, and thereafter she spent a lifetime of regret and remorse concerned by the wrong dealing life seems to have played her.

Several letters were exchanged, each puzzled by how they had fallen foul of each other and updating each other about their lives since they last met in the early 1920s. They discussed their past, Orwell noting what a kind nature Buddicom had towards animals, but how she was less kind towards Orwell after his departure for Burma. She did not respond to his last letter, having read *Nineteen Eighty-Four* and thinking it a horrifying book, but was devastated when she learnt of his death.

In spite of Orwell's requests for them to meet, Buddicom did not go to the lengths required as he lay dying in London's UCH. In her memoir, she is unable to explain why she did not go. She learnt of his death and attended his funeral, sitting in the back row, an unknown entity among the audience composed of London's literati. Her memoir reads as one long testament of remorse and she seems to have had an unhappy life. She died in 1993, leaving it to her cousin, Dione Venables, the founder of the Orwell Society, to explore their lives with the hindsight made possible by death. Her illegitimate daughter died in a car crash in Canada in 1997.

Featuring throughout Orwell's correspondence for 1949, which admittedly ends more or less entirely after he entered UCH in September, is a longing to recover and live, either to watch his son grow up and to provide for him or to continue writing. He wrote to his publisher Fredric Warburg: 'I have the strongest reasons for wanting to stay alive', and spoke of the writing ideas budding in his head. There was *A Smoking Room Story*, a novel about his experiences travelling by boat to and from Burma; an essay on Evelyn Waugh; and a concept for a book about the war. In April he told his friend T.R. Fyvel: 'I have a novel dealing with 1945 in my head now.' Other than returning to Jura he imagined raising Richard in Edinburgh, or relocating to Brighton and spending winters in Sicily.

Those around him and his doctors must have understood that these ideas were optimistic, and to watch this precious friend deteriorate physically must have been painful, a loss which many of them – not least those closest to him – spent the rest of their lives regretting. The double tragedy is that he lived just shy of the widespread adoption of the use of antibiotics for the treatment of TB, which is now a curable disease in developed countries. A request for him to participate in the trial of antibiotics went all the way to the Minister of Health, Aneurin Bevan, but the unfortunate side effects meant they were not effective.

Some constants in his life – a love of England and country pursuits; the tea-drinker; the avid reader – remained until the end. Others did not. I have concluded that by the end of his life Orwell came back circuitously to the conservative philosophy of his youth, a belief in gradual change and the importance of patriotism in building a cohesive society leading to a rejection of the radical socialism he is so often (perhaps wrongly?) associated with. He did not hide much of this logic, which I believe began after his experience of fighting for 'the Left' in the Spanish Civil War. In other respects, the war radicalised his sense of economic and political injustice, but it seems equally to have encouraged a questioning of the sentiment and objectives of leftist politics.

No part of the canon of his work makes this more evident than *Animal Farm*. It is a work of such creative genius it is a wonder whether it will ever be surpassed; not a single sentence resists Orwell's exploration of a society of 'equals', which ends inevitably in a failure of the animals' hope with the replacement of one form of tyranny for another. Elsewhere, his essay 'England Your England' directs Orwell's opprobrium to the radical left of which he is so frequently considered to be an integral part:

> *England is perhaps the only great country whose intellectuals are ashamed of their own nationality. In left-wing circles it is always felt that there is something slightly disgraceful in being an Englishman and that it is a duty to snigger at every English institution, from horse racing to suet puddings.*

> *There is little in them except the irresponsible carping of people who have never been and never expect to be in a position of power.*

It seems that by the end of his life Orwell came to believe the future lay in a patriotism which could unite the peoples of Britain, almost in a way which would mean the upper echelons of society would see the errors of their ways and act benevolently towards those less fortunate. He did not live to see the Conservatives concede to the opposition Labour Party the permanence of a welfare state, nor the progressive, paternalistic conservatism of prime ministers Harold Macmillan or Alec Douglas-Home. I can see him admiring both – each were also Old Etonians, like himself – but disliking the rhetoric and bearing of Margaret Thatcher as somehow 'un-English'.

Some on the left felt betrayed by Orwell, not only because of his social conservatism but by his involvement with an official government agency advocating Western propaganda against the Soviet Bloc in the early days of the Cold War. He became acquainted with Celia Kirwan, who worked for a new Foreign Office agency charged with propagandising for the West by Clement Attlee, for the first time during the war in Paris. Kirwan was tasked with drawing up a list of writers to prepare copy critical of the Soviets and worked closely with Orwell to assess the relative merit and dependability of certain writers.

This list courted much controversy in the decades after his death with parts of the files remaining, at the time of writing, still withheld by the National Archives. Many on the radical left viewed it as contemptible, Orwell working with the UK government against the interests of the Communist Bloc. Of course, to feature in the list would have had some impact on the prospects of the writers included. It is viewed by some, including one of Orwell's leading biographers, D.J. Taylor, to have not been as useful as many on the left might have feared: 'Not very sensational is a fair enough description both of the roster sent to the IRD and the exercise on which Orwell and Rees were engaged.'

⌣

The drive to Sutton Courtenay during the morning rush hour, zig-zagging across the back roads of Oxfordshire, was crowded. Oxfordshire is so desirable a place to live that homes are crammed into any feasible space, but the roads are the same size as they always were. For most of the journey, cars were in slow single-file procession: stressed-out parents taking their children to school and commuters headed for work in the larger settlements of Reading and Oxford.

Today Sutton Courtenay is a sprawling village, half historical – predominantly Georgian, so far as I could tell – and the other half modern development mostly dating from the 1960s, 70s and 80s. It seemed to me that neither had much to do with one another, which is often the way where the historical parts of a town or village are monopolised by the middle and upper classes, and a newer area is home to newcomers from outside. The historical part contains the church and most of the village's amenities: it still has a village shop and several upmarket pubs. One pub, the George and the Dragon, is ideally situated adjacent to the graveyard in which Orwell is buried.

What is puzzling is why Orwell chose not to be buried with Eileen, at Jesmond in Newcastle, nor with his parents. I have been unable to confirm what grounds he gave against being buried at either location, although it is understood he wished to be buried in a proper English, Anglican churchyard, and this was the task put into the hands of Astor. That he chose not to be buried with Eileen may be in part because of his remarriage, in his hospital room, to Sonia Brownell, on 13 October 1949. The marriage came as a surprise to literary circles in London; it was Orwell's parting gift to his already complex character. It added to the sense of mystery surrounding his life, not least because Sonia was herself a complex character, and spent the rest of her life working to protect his legacy. Astor, who was a witness at the marriage, reflected long after: 'I can't help saying it was an embarrassing occasion. I don't think she thought he was dying ... I think both of them were acting in some sort of fantasy way.'

Sonia Orwell's background offers, in my view, further grounds for understanding George Orwell, his social background and the circumstances that informed his political and social views. Like Orwell, she was born in India, at Ranchi in 1918, and spent a lot of time in Calcutta where her father was a shipping broker. He was secretary of the Tollygunge Jockey Club, still one of the most exclusive clubs in Calcutta, at Tollygunge in the south of the city. He died in circumstances which were never made clear, when his daughter was four. Suicide is thought to be a likely cause of his death; if it was, then this mixed parental psychosis may account for Sonia's plethora of painful emotions as an adult.

When her family returned from India, she was sent to a Catholic girls' school in Roehampton. For most of the rest of her life, it seems she rebelled against this strict education. She went to secretarial college and soon found herself a part of London's literati. She started work at *Tribune*, as an assistant to Orwell's childhood friend Cyril Connolly.

She and Orwell were first introduced by Connolly over dinner at some point over winter 1941–2, but they do not seem to have become closer until Orwell based himself back in Islington, after his return from war reporting on the continent.

I had instinctively warmed more to Eileen than Sonia. Sonia has been described as a 'gold digger' by some of her critics, but I realised the more I researched her life and her time with Orwell that she offered him something he needed in his last years. He also gave her something she craved, much commented on by their contemporaries. The artist Francis Bacon, for instance, explained: 'She lives in terms of others' creativity ... she has no illusions about being creative herself.'

It was, of course, something of an achievement for a dying man in his 47th year to marry such a popular and vivacious young woman. The age gap, some fifteen years, surprised as many people then as it might now. I conclude that their relationship was primarily intellectual, and served this purpose rather than any other. Orwell told Astor by letter in July 1949: 'I intend getting married again. I suppose everyone will be horrified, but it seems to me a good idea.' Arthur Koestler, when he heard of the news from Orwell, advised: 'I have been saying for years that she is the nicest, most intelligent and decent girl that I have met during my whole stay in England.'

Orwell moved to UCH from Cranham on 3 September 1949, into Room 65 in the private wing of the (by then) nationalised NHS hospital. Pamela Warburg, the wife of Orwell's publisher Fredric Warburg, knew a chest specialist at UCH, Dr Andrew Moreland, and arranged for the transfer (Moreland had also treated D.H. Lawrence, another Warburg author, which was how Mrs Warburg came to know of him). Upon arrival, Astor had arranged for a welcoming present, for which Orwell was characteristically grateful. He wrote to his friend: 'Thanks ever so for sending those beautiful chrysanths and box of peaches that actually met me on arrival here'.

The room was small, but large by the standards of a public hospital – and of course not simply a bed on a ward, being private. There were a chair, table and books to keep him company. Visits from an illustrious roster of friends continued right up until his death. Lucian Freud, for instance, would visit regularly, as did Evelyn Waugh and Francis Bacon. His old tutor at Eton, Andrew Gow, also made an appearance. For most of his last stay in the hospital, he would have been lonely, outside visiting hours. Audrey Dawson, head nurse for Orwell's treatment, remembered: 'He was always, as I recall, sitting up in bed in a rather old camel-coloured woollen cardigan. He was always courteous, but not very communicative. He didn't complain a great deal.'

Plans to take him to Switzerland were made in December 1949. Dr Moreland, when interviewed in the 1980s, advised that prospects for his recovery were minuscule and that patients were often transferred to Switzerland to allow them to die in comfort. Sonia took charge of organising the flights, with assistance from Orwell's close friend T.R. Fyvel, who had contacts in the Swiss Embassy. Orwell may have had expectations that he would return in good health – he had his fishing rods sent to UCH to accompany him. At or around this time the then-prime minister Clement Attlee sent him a get well letter in light of the news of a deterioration in his health. Sadly, so far as I could discover, the letter has been lost, but the Orwell Archive does contain an envelope from Downing Street dated January 1950.*

The last person likely to have seen Orwell alive, in The Rosenheim Wing of a building that was demolished as part of a redevelopment scheme in 2015, was the poet Paul Potts. Potts, who later wrote an essay entitled 'Don Quixote on a Bicycle' reflecting on their friendship, went to visit him on the evening of 20 January 1950. He observed that Orwell

---

* Professor John Bew, Attlee's biographer, did not recall coming across anything while he researched his book *Citizen Clem*.

was sleeping, and so left his gift, a casket of strong tea, his favourite, at the door. He wryly noted later that he wondered what had happened to it. At some time in the earliest hours of 21 January 1950, Orwell had an enormous haemorrhage of the lungs and died in his sleep.

Orwell left an estate valued at just under £10,000.00, or about a third of a million pounds in 2022 prices. The figure is fairly meaningless – £10,000.00 in 1950 put him well into the comfortable classes, although it is believed much of this came only very late, in royalties from the first (and vast) sales of *Nineteen Eighty-Four*. Three days before his death he wrote a new will, transferring his literary estate to Sonia, with provisions laid on for Richard's future. Orwell had put him down to attend Westminster School, which would not have been cheap. In the event, his son attended the Loretto Convent in Edinburgh.

The funeral was arranged for 26 January at Christ Church, overlooking Regent's Park, a peculiarly imposing venue and in one of the grandest corners of London, if not the Earth. Deconsecrated by the Church of England, rather appropriately it has now been renamed St George's Cathedral, as the mother church in London of the Greek Orthodox Church of Antioch.

The service was arranged by two of Orwell's friends – Anthony Powell, the novelist, and Malcolm Muggeridge, the journalist. It included the funeral lectionary from Ecclesiastes and three hymns: 'All people that on earth do dwell', 'Guide me, o thou great Redeemer' and 'Ten thousand times ten thousand'. Powell later, oddly since he had planned the service, described it as 'one of the most harrowing' he had ever attended. Orwell's niece Jane Morgan recalled: 'It struck me as being rather an odd sort of funeral for Eric. It was all rather large and pompous and dark.' The coffin was driven from London to Sutton Courtenay, where he was interned on the same day in a simple service using the traditional Anglican funeral rites from *The Book of Common Prayer*. Sonia and Astor were the only people present.

Sonia was devastated by her husband's death and seems to have spent the rest of her life remorseful for not having served him better in his last few months. She instead threw herself into defending his legacy, collating and editing his letters and diaries, and founding the Orwell Archive in 1960. The poet Stephen Spender, who knew Sonia until her death in 1980, believed she never recovered from the shock of losing him. Hilary Spurling, her biographer, concluded she was 'driven by demons she could not really control'. Her emotional history seemed to be one long roller coaster ride: she regretted the drowning of a friend when sailing as a young adult, whose death had enabled her survival; had an abortion shortly after the war, with the father believed to be Arthur Koestler; and in 1959 overdosed in an attempted suicide.

She seems to me to have been a perfect match for Orwell, an interesting and complicated person. When Spurling first met Sonia Orwell at her London flat, adorned with art and the walls lined with books, she was 'taken aback by her unexpectedly demure appearance in what I soon realised was her standard uniform of dark skirt, woolly cardigan and plain, high-necked white blouse'. In her later years, she and friends would make Celtic tours of Brittany, Cornwall and Scotland. Reading became, in the end, Sonia's sole joy, Spurling concluded. An intensely loyal friend, she sat with Ivy Compton-Burnett, the novelist, W.H. Auden, the poet, and Joe Ackerley, the writer, as they died.

Sonia's decline seems to have accelerated after some sort of existentialist crisis in 1977. She sold her flat, put her belongings into storage and moved to Paris. She became immersed in a legal battle for the rights to Orwell's literary estate, which seems to have been monopolised by unscrupulous solicitors and accountants. She also reluctantly agreed that Bernard Crick, the political scientist, be invited to write the biography Orwell himself had willed should never be written. She fell out with him, just living to see the publication of the biography at the end of 1980. She wrote: 'I now feel I've just been sucked into some gigantic machine which pays no attention to the fact that I am existing and suffering: I don't count anymore, nor does George.'

In 1979 her close friend, the Booker Prize winner J.G. Farrell, died by drowning. This was another blow to someone who admired her friends, and their talents, so profoundly. She strove to live to finish the legal battle for the rights and the publication of Crick's biography, surviving long enough to witness both. An allowance was provided for Richard and a house bought for him; she also passed him the rights to Orwell's literary estate once they had been secured through the courts. She died in Paris in December 1980 – Francis Bacon paid for her last hotel bill. There was barely enough money in her estate to pay for the funeral.

⌇

The church, pub and a scattering of beautiful houses in large plots with front gardens filled with hollyhock and withered fruit trees surround a small green, crossed by a path running parallel to the busy road passing through Sutton Courtenay. The scene could easily appear on the covering wrapper of a box of chocolates. There was a sign attached to the squeaking gate of one cottage advertising 'organic windfall apples', and a racing-green coloured sign that looked like it dated from the 1950s, erected by Sutton Courtenay Parish Council, advising against parking unless motorists would be happy to be presented with a fine of £20.00.

The tower of the church faces onto the village green, and the churchyard can be entered through one of two gates, both of which are at either end of a path that circumnavigates the churchyard. The rear of the church and churchyard cannot be entered without passing through a grove of yew trees which enclose the church tower on both sides, and which, once traversed, open up the vista of a sizeable grave-speckled churchyard interspersed with mature trees. As English churchyards go, it seemed fairly unremarkable, although notices on boards at both the entrance to the churchyard and the church itself indicate where the graves of George Orwell, and also former Liberal prime minister Herbert Asquith, are to be found.

Before I approached the grave, I walked around the outside of the church trying in vain to understand how to gain access to the inside. Sadly, in the past decade or so, gangs of thieves have toured the countryside, tearing from the roofs of England's churches their lead, or stealing other valuables from inside if they can enter. These crimes are an unfortunate violation of Britain's priceless architectural heritage, but one the police seem powerless, and in any case not sufficiently interested in, to stop. The result is that churches are now usually locked other than when open for services or for some other purpose.

Fortunately, having met the curate on her arrival, I was allowed in to survey the church's interior. All Church of England buildings seem to smell the same – a stale air combining the smell of mould with that of decaying hymn-sheet paper. It is a wonder to think that generations stretching over a thousand years have walked in and around this building, its worn terracotta tiles and stone denuded by centuries of sole-treading. The floor is so uneven I imagine it is a hard building to navigate for anyone unsteady on their toes, the tombstones laid beneath one's feet adorned with worn gothic script depicting the lives of the inhabitants' tombs below them.

There is a small exhibition detailing Orwell's life, complete with old Penguin paperbacks of several of his books. A vase made by a school pupil from a nearby secondary school for an art project rests on the nearest window, gourd-shaped and covered in the very many famous names of his books. Beside a large pillar is a wooden sideboard, upon which the church's visitor book is rested. I enjoyed flicking through the comments, many of which were moving tributes written after a visit by adoring fans to the grave of their favourite author:

'In memory of George ORWELL'

'A visit to see Eric Arthur Blair, whose
work changed my life forever.'

'Our second visit to pay respects to Eric Blair. He would have
written a diary entry about the weather (sunny),
perhaps his garden (tomatoes doing well) with a separate entry
about the nature of humans to take away freedoms,
hard fought. A remarkable legacy often abused – but one
which will be read anew by each generation.
[In Chinese characters and English] – Long live the truth.'

The curate, by now engaged in a detailed conversation about church finances with a member of the congregation, glanced at me before I left. I thanked her for opening the church, to which she replied: 'And what will you place on the grave? Many leave a coin.' I inevitably hadn't considered this eventuality and had no prior reason to bring something. It annoyed me that I probably should have foreseen something like this, my mind racing through a list of trinkets dotted around my nearby parked car.

I went back outside to fumble inside the car, opening glove compartments and skimming my hands around the inside of the side pockets. There was nothing either appropriate or appropriately sized. Then I remembered, in the ashtray, there was a stash of euros left from my tour of northern Spain. I extracted them one by one, scanning my eyes over their reverse. Amid a flurry of Brandenburg Gates and Irish harps, I found a single Spanish 50-cent piece, replete with a portrait of Cervantes and inscribed 'Espana, 2000'.

I walked in the direction of the bottom of the churchyard, where I knew Orwell's tomb lay. George, spotting a squirrel, shot off and danced in and among the yew trees. As I teetered gradually towards the grave, expecting the tombstone to come within my line of sight, a surge of emotion passed through me. The dew squelched beneath my feet as I passed fresh flowers on a grave, their strange beauty frozen in silence, and the dark green of an ancient yew tree contrasting with the yellows and oranges of a perfect autumnal morning.

For three years I had followed this man's life. Along this journey I had absorbed so much of the places associated with him; re-learning the lessons instructed by his works. At times it brought me to the brink of exhaustion; bewildered by the multitude of written sources and the havoc of disappearing on a flight or off in a car down some lonely country lane. He had become some part of me, my mind composing a story of him defined by place, and uncontrollably igniting connections between one fact or observation and another.

At the back of my mind, I knew it would end here at Sutton Courtenay. A visit I had purposefully left as my last, providing contrast between the beginning of Orwell's life on the steamy plains of India and its permanent future in a cold Oxfordshire grave. I arrived laden with trepidation, to stand before his grave:

Here Lies Eric Arthur Blair

Born June 25th 1903

Died January 21st 1950

I put my hand in my pocket to find the Spanish coin and rested it on the crest of the gravestone alongside 26 English pence, an American dime and a copper euro piece. A small round stone ball of what I thought to be slate, painted with a Spanish flag and scribbled with 'Espana 1936–7' lay amid the coinage. I winced, imagining it would have been preferable to have left an Indian rupee, recalling it was in India where Orwell's journey to Sutton Courtenay began.

Next time, I thought, as I walked back in the direction I had come, the Tudor appendage of the Church porch and its ancient door passing me on my right. I walked through the procession of yew trees before me, their spiders' webs sparkling in the early morning sun.

⌣

He was someone for whom I had, and I think most of his friends had, a very big affection. He was loveable. And he was loveable in the deep sincerity of his disposition, which was a very beautiful thing. If he took a position and then the position was challenged in some way, and he felt it was faulty, then he would abandon it ... He had this strange blend, you see, of extreme conservatism plus sympathy with revolutionary causes. He stands alone in every sense.

Malcolm Muggeridge

Further Reading

There is an array of books about Orwell. Towards the end of my writing, I realised one should read everything with some degree of scepticism since I noticed recollections of the same 'facts' about Orwell's life more often than not contradict each another. I found most of the principal biographies, some more than others, too speculative. Those interested in reading more might wish to judge for themselves. Inevitably more is understood about Orwell with the passing of time, so the later biographies are likely to offer better insight than those written some years ago. The biographies I recommend, in order of date of publication, are Bernard Crick's *Orwell: A Life*; Gordon Bowker's *George Orwell*; and D.J. Taylor's *Orwell: The Life*. If I should be asked to choose one, I would opt for *Orwell: The Life*.

I found Orwell's collected diaries and letters, both edited by Peter Davison, of immense value in understanding the man and his life, historical evidence which has not been sifted or filtered. They are both in print and published by Penguin.

The many more detailed analyses of his life, often exploring a specific tangent of his life and times, seemed too subjective or speculative. They will be of limited interest to the general reader. Jacintha Buddicom's *Eric & Us* and Hilary Spurling's *The Girl from the Fiction Department* are both short, interesting reads which offer sound analysis on Orwell through the prism of two of the leading women in his life:

his childhood sweetheart and second wife, Sonia Orwell. *The World of George Orwell* is an enjoyable exploration of Orwell's life and times, written as a collection of essays in the main by contemporaries or close friends. Finally, Stephen Wadhams' *Remembering Orwell* is a superb transcript of interviews undertaken in the early 1980s, at a time when so many of those who formed Orwell's world were still alive. It was republished in 2017 under the title *The Orwell Tapes*.

Armstrong, Stephen. *The Road to Wigan Pier Revisited* (London, Constable, 2012)

Bowker, Gordon. *George Orwell* (London, Little Brown, 2003)

Brennan, Michael. *George Orwell and Religion* (London, Bloomsbury Academic, 2016)

Buddicom, Jacintha. *Eric & Us* (London, Finlay Publisher, 1974; 2006)

Calder, Jenni, *Chronicles of Conscience: A Study of George Orwell and Arthur Koestler* (London, Martin Secker & Warburg Ltd, 1968)

Crick, Bernard. *George Orwell: A Life* (London, Penguin Books, 1982)

Colls, Robert. *George Orwell: English Rebel* (Oxford, Oxford University Press, 2013)

Connolly, Cyril. *Previous Convictions: Selected Writings of a Decade* (London, Hamish Hamilton, 1963)

Cox, Tony. *Mrs. Orwell* (London, Oberon Press, 2017)

Davison, Peter. *George Orwell: A Life in Letters* (London, Penguin Books, 2010)

Davison, Peter. *George Orwell: Diaries* (London, Penguin Books, 2009)

Fyvel, T.R. *George Orwell: A Personal Memoir* (London, Weidenfeld & Nicolson, 1982)

Gross, Miriam (Ed.). *The World of George Orwell* (London, Weidenfeld & Nicolson, 1971)

Hitchens, Christopher. *Why Orwell Matters* (New York, Basic Books, 2002)

Larkin, Emma. *Finding George Orwell in Burma* (London, Granta Books, 2011)

Observer Books. *Orwell: The Observer Years* (London, Atlantic Books, 2003)

Orwell, George (Ed.). *Talking to India* (London, George Allen & Unwin, 1943)

Rees, Richard. *George Orwell: Fugitive from the Camp of Victory* (London, Secker & Warburg, 1961)

Shelden, Michael. *Orwell: The Authorised Biography* (London, Minerva, 1991)

Slater, Ian. *Orwell: The Road to Airstrip One* (New York, W.W. Norton & Company, 1985)

Spurling, Hilary. *The Girl from the Fiction Department* (London, Penguin Books, 2003)

Stansky, Peter and Abrahams, William. *Orwell: The Transformation* (London, Granada, 1981)

Sutherland, John. *Orwell's Nose* (London, Reaktion Books, 2016)

Taylor, David J. *Orwell: The Life* (London, Vintage Random House, 2004)

Venables, Dione. *George Orwell: The Complete Poetry* (London, Finlay Publisher, 2015)

Wadhams, Stephen. *Remembering Orwell* (London, Penguin Books, 1984).

West, W.J. (Ed.). *Orwell: The War Commentaries* (London, British Broadcasting Corporation and Gerald Duckworth & Co. Ltd., 1985)

Permissions

Acknowledgements

I will never read a book again without sparing some thought for the writer and those around them. As Orwell wrote:

> 'Writing a book is a horrible, exhausting struggle, like a long bout with some painful illness. One would never undertake such a thing if one were not driven on by some demon whom one can neither resist nor understand.'

In each location I am grateful to the assistance of at least one thoughtful supporter of my research and writing – in some locales, such as Eton College or India, many more. I found, the longer I spent writing and researching, how solitary writing can be, reflecting it is a good job I enjoy my own company. I expect this is because writing a book is so personal a project, and one's motivation and understanding of a topic can ultimately only be understood by the writer and them alone. I must start by thanking my immediate family for their support, critical reading of the text and encouragement – Dr Peter Lewis; Shelagh Hampton; Dr Patrick Lewis and Dr Kate Gordon; David and Laure Lewis; Fiona Lewis and Christoff Gurney. In addition, I think often of my grandfather, Rhys Lewis, and my great aunt Catherine Redmond for imbuing me with an intellectual curiosity I appreciate long after they have passed.

A number of people along the way provided factual information, anecdotes or signposted me towards fountains of knowledge unknown to me. These include both branches of the Fletcher family on Jura – Mimsie and Jamie Fletcher, the owners of Barnhill, and Andrew and Claire Fletcher at Ardlussa; Eleanor Hoare and Michael Meredith at Eton College; Victor Lancina and Elena Colombraro in Spain; Nyo Ko Naing in Burma; Mark Walsh in India; and more generally, Richard Blair, Quentin Kopp, Dione Venables, Masha Karp; and Neil Smith in the Orwell Society. Separate to this were people who assisted on logistical aspects of planning travel and accommodation – Anne and the late Brian Hammond at Framlingham in Suffolk; Jane and Paul Carling whose Hebridean island, Belnahua, provided respite for me following my exploration of Jura; and Jane Manson and family for lending me their house in French Catalonia, at Ville-Franche-de-Conflent, to write the chapter on Spain. I am grateful also to my immediate neighbours in London, June and Ashley Mehmet, who looked after George for those trips he was unable to accompany me on. He adores them both.

Separately, a number of people accompanied me on certain trips, or through their friendship and support know I am grateful for their encouragement – Ski and the late Anthony Harrison; Martin and Rachel Pick; the late Baroness (Shirley) Williams of Crosby; Dr Timothy Leunig; Anthony, Harriet and Theo Mould; Hon. Malcolm and Clare Orr-Ewing; John and Mary Braybrook; Mark and Hilary Stanley; the late Gillian and Alan Clube; Margaret and Ian Burch; Chris and Sarah Shaw; Hon. Ivo and Hon. Xanthe Mosley; Julia Rowntree; Ben and Charlie Willbond; Clare Cowen; Nick Hammond; Robert Langford; Shreena Patel; Katie Wolicki and Emile Figueiras; Jessica and Alexander Halban; Marcus and Kirsty Garvey; Julia Maude and Mike Campbell; Meng Lu and David Salant; Dr Victoria Tuke; James Bull; James Allgrove; Jameisha Majevadia; Daisy O'Brien; Gemma Ralph; Eugenia Fafalios; James Lester; Leo Ringer; Maud Sampson;

Val Glover; Deborah Simmonds; Jane and Andrew Fenwick and family; Alexandra Pisar-Pinto; David Pinto; Max Odey; my brilliant agent Clare Grist-Taylor and Ellen Conlon, my editor at Icon. Many of the above also read and commented on the manuscript. Thanks also to my typesetter Marie Doherty and my illustrator Brittany Davies, who I met by chance at her stall at a Christmas market in Oxford, read the manuscript and produced maps of the highest order for each chapter.

Jane and Paul Carling, whose wisdom and love of life never ceases to command my respect, deserve special recognition in keeping me going. I also wish to recognise the founders of the Old Hall Bookshop, Brackley – Mr John and the late Lady Juliet Townsend – as well as staff former and present, for inspiring my love of books and of reading from my teens and up. It is the best bookshop in Britain.

Finally, my thanks for the writing time and research facilities provided by Coutts & Co; Eton College; The London Library; Gladstone's Library; The Savile Club; and the branch and staff of Le Pain Quotidien at Palermo, Buenos Aires, Argentina.